P9-CRE-864

The Closer We Are to Dying

Copyright © 1999 by Joe Fiorito

All rights reserved. The use of any part of this publication reproduced, transmitted by any form or by any means, electronic, mechanical, photocopying, recording, or otherwise, or stored in a retrieval system, without the prior written consent of the publisher – or, in case of photocopying or other reprographic copying, a licence from the Canadian Copyright Licensing Agency – is an infringement of the copyright law.

Canadian Cataloguing in Publication Data

Fiorito, Joe, 1948 -
    The closer we are to dying

ISBN 0-7710-3119-X

1. Fiorito, Joe, 1948 -   . 2. Fiorito, Joe, 1948 -   – Family.
3. Journalists – Canada – Biography.   I. Title.

PN4913.F56A3   1999   070'.92   C99-931280-4

We acknowledge the financial support of the Government of Canada through the Book Publishing Industry Development Program for our publishing activities. Canadä

We further acknowledge the support of the Canada Council for the Arts and the Ontario Arts Council for our publishing program.

Typeset in Bembo by M&S, Toronto
Printed and bound in Canada

Page 322 is a continuation of the copyright page.

McClelland & Stewart Inc.
The Canadian Publishers
481 University Avenue
Toronto, Ontario
M5G 2E9

1 2 3 4 5   03 02 01 00 99

In memory of Dusty Fiorito
20 November 1917 – 2 June 1996

This book could not have been written without the help of my mother, who has stories of her own to tell. Thanks to my brothers, who heard and saw it all. I am indebted to my cousins Matt Fiorito, Jerry Courtney, Jim Fiorito, Dave Fiorito, and Bob Fiorito. And I will be forever grateful to Mary Cryer, Carmel Lumley, Vic Fiorito, and especially Peter Silvaggio. If there are any errors of memory here, they are mine alone. Thanks to Dinah Forbes, for her faith and patience. And to Susan Mahoney, as always.

This rain that blinds the windows with its mists
Will gladden in suburbs no more to be found
The black grapes on a vine there overhead
In a certain patio that no longer exists.
And the drenched afternoon brings back the sound
How longed for, of my father's voice, not dead.

– Jorge Luis Borges, "The Rain"

The more one remembers, the closer perhaps one is to dying.

– Joseph Brodsky, "Less Than One"

Home

North of Fort William, the cold black highway cuts across the hills, disappears in the trees, and appears again on the far edge of the lake, leading itself away, away, until it is lost in the horizon. South of town, a slow brown river draws itself past the grey scree at the foot of Mount Mackay. The river underlines a row of scrapyards and paper mills and the long docks of the grain elevators where rusty ships from Russia, China, and Poland lie at anchor.

The wind from the east is thick with the smell of creosote and malt; the wind from the west smells of grain dust, topsoil, and sulphur. On rare bright days, the air is clean and tastes of fresh water and wet wood.

The mountain is a small flat blade of stone.

In summer it is blue; not as blue as the lake, but a deeper blue than the sky. In winter it is streaked with ice, and there are evenings when the great flat weight of it is lost behind a curtain of snow, or under the wet, white clouds that drift in from the mill.

Summer blue, winter white: water, sky, and stone.

Late at night, the freight trains rock along the tracks behind our house: chains of hopper cars piled high with reddish ore, tank cars dripping oils and acids, boxcars stacked with rolls of newsprint for the cities to the east, the south, away. . . .

In the darkness our small house trembles in the earth.

I lie in bed and listen to the bells at the level crossing. I can almost hear the low voices of my parents. My father tells a story; his voice is sweet, my mother leads him on. I can hear dance tunes on the radio. The news is from elsewhere, not here.

The train disappears in the distance.

I rock myself to sleep.

The phone rings in the middle of the afternoon.

My mother sounds tired, empty, a little sadder than usual. We haven't spoken in some weeks. I know what she's going to say. I've always been able to decipher her tone of voice. There are times when I find it annoying; no surprises. But knowing what the other is about to say has been our habit for years, hard-won.

When I was not yet old enough for school, my father came home from his mail route late one afternoon. He'd been drinking. It was payday. There were bills due at the B&B Grocery. But he'd been buying rounds at the Victoria Hotel because he was thirsty and he'd earned the right to a drink, and the Vic was close to the post office where he worked. Now he was home, he was broke, he was lightly drunk and chipper.

My mother lost her patience. They began to squabble.

"You have no right to drink beer when there isn't enough money to put food on the table! *I'll have a drink when I want a drink, god damn it. You can't tell me what to do.* I'll tell you what to do when it comes to this house and these kids. *Ah to hell with it, and to hell with you, I'm getting out of here.* That's right, you coward, run away."

Dusty made for the door. And when his back was turned my mother slapped at him, she pounded his shoulders, she reached for the hair on the back of his head. He turned to fend her off. She tried to claw his cheek. He slapped her in return.

I was sitting on the couch with my arm around my brother; he was too afraid to cry. We watched. And then something seemed to snap in Dusty. "Jesus wept!" My father tore off his belt and began to whip her. He hit her arms, he hit her shoulders, the thin belt raised red welts.

Grace fought back. And then he dropped his belt and his hands were at her throat and he was choking her now. She was a fish out of water in his hands, wriggling, gasping for air. He squeezed her neck, and she made a choking sound, and then she weakened and her legs began to buckle.

And I knew he was killing her.

I jumped from the couch and ran across the room and leapt on his back. *Don't hurt my mother, don't hurt my mother, don't you hurt her.* I clung to his shoulders. He tried to shake me off. I wasn't sure if he'd turn on me but I didn't care if he did. She might be able to break free.

And then he let her go.

He reached behind and grabbed me; he lifted me up and looked me in the eye. I didn't care what he might do. I looked back. As if he remembered something, he set me down on the floor and picked up his belt. My mother staggered to her feet.

She couldn't sob, she couldn't make a noise. He threaded his belt through the loops of his pants. She held her hands to her bruised throat. He stalked into their bedroom. I could hear him swear as he rifled through a couple of pairs of pants in his closet, looking for pocket change, nickels and dimes, anything, enough for one more beer. And then he left the house. He did not slam the door. I flinched anyway.

I returned to the couch and put my arms around my brother. My mother looked at me. There was a sort of calculation in her eyes, an appraisal of her pup. She went to wash her face. Years later, she said I'd saved her life. I probably had. The rest is blank.

No, that's not entirely true.

From that moment on, I knew how to read her. And I knew there was something in my father that was easily, and unpredictably, unleashed. He was capable of anything, at any time, for any reason.

The next day, he behaved as if nothing had happened.

And I began to study him. If I sensed a certain brooding, if the air around him was charged, if there was a scent of alcohol in his sweat, I hushed my brother and plotted the route of my own escape. I glanced at my mother every time he came home.

We shared the intuition of prisoners.

Not long after my father had tried to strangle my mother, my smallest brother became ill with whooping cough. It seemed to me, as I lay in bed and listened, that he was not going to get better. At night he fought for breath with elastic and horribly liquid gasps; every time he got a lungful of air, he coughed raggedly out of control.

I tried not to listen. When the night train went by, the rhythm of it lulled me briefly to sleep, even through his coughing. But I woke this night when my mother opened the door to our bedroom and plucked him from his crib. A shaft of light from the hall lay in pieces on my bed. I heard the voices of my parents. I'd heard them fight before. My brother coughed, as if to interrupt them with his helplessness. I thought he must be dying.

I got out of bed. My mother was in the kitchen drinking a cup of tea. She looked exhausted.

"Where are they? Where's Dad?"

"On the front porch."

"What for?"

"The air is cooler; it's easier to breathe out there."

My father was sitting in the darkness on the top step, cradling my brother in his arms. My brother was bundled in a blanket. It was unusual to see my father hold him like that, unusual because, although he held us and kissed us often, he also beat us. Daily solace was my mother's job.

I sat beside them, holding my arms around my knees for warmth. The stars seemed to be made of glass needles. The night air was thinner, but my brother's coughing continued.

Finally my father placed my brother in my lap. He rose and went into the house. For cigarettes, I thought. I was glad to help, but unsure of what to do if my brother began to cough again.

Dusty returned with a mug of whisky cut with hot water, lemon, and sugar, a feather of its warmth rising in the air. It smelled good, but it frightened me. I'd thought whisky was bad; it changed my father. When he drank, he couldn't stop until it was all gone. It made him wild, it made him weep. He spooned some into my brother's mouth.

"Why are you giving him that?"

"It will help him relax. If he relaxes, he'll be able to breathe, and if he breathes easily, maybe he'll fall asleep. He needs to rest if he's going to get better." I said nothing. My father must have sensed childish disapproval. "I did the same for you, when you were small."

I nodded, as if I remembered.

Between gasps, my brother managed to swallow some of the sweetened alcohol. He coughed, he swallowed, he coughed again, but after a time the whisky did its job. Dusty had succeeded where my mother had failed, somehow.

I imagined myself, a child his arms. I considered what I couldn't understand. He'd tried to kill her; I'd saved her life.

She and I were complicit. But when he held my brother, he won my heart. I knew he loved me. I didn't doubt it. I didn't trust it. But I knew it.

I asked for a taste of the whisky, heady, tart with the lemon, and still warm. He gave me a drink.

I came inside, and looked at my mother.

She knew.

When the phone rang in the middle of that afternoon, my mother merely said hello; it was all she had to say. I understood at once that my father was about to die. There had been no warning; none was needed. He'd been ill for some time.

"How bad is he?"

"You'd better get here right away."

I had read the tone of her voice correctly, but intuition is not a reliable way to learn details. I pressed her for information.

She sighed, relieved to recount the specifics. Dusty had been taken to the hospital a few hours earlier. He was delirious. He couldn't speak. He'd collapsed and shit himself. The ambulance had come. And the neighbours had peered out their windows. The doctor said he would not live long.

Yes, he was in pain. Yes, he could talk. No, he wasn't making sense. Yes, he was getting plenty of medication; that was why he was delirious. No, there was nothing more to do. He was dying now.

You'd better get here and see for yourself.

I very nearly said, "He's getting what he's always wanted."

I said no such thing. I kept my mouth shut. Each of us makes a different set of calculations, and pays a different price, in order to make a life and endure the love of the one with whom we've chosen to live. She'd suffered her own losses and had made her own deals with him, the details of which had long since ceased to be my business. She said he had a few weeks to live, perhaps only a few days.

It's always been difficult for me to go back. I feel as if I am entering the half-light of remembered deaths.

My aunt Jo spent her last months tied to an oxygen tank. The last time I saw her, she lay in her bed; there were tubes in her nose, her thin hair was sweaty and plastered to her forehead. The visit was an awkward intimacy in a small house. She did not want to be seen in her nightie. She did not want to be seen dying. I reached for her hand; she turned her head away.

When my uncle Dave was diagnosed with cancer, he scraped up some money and went to Mexico for laetrile treatments. He came home pretending to have hope. He ate vitamins by the fistful, he changed his diet, and his hair turned from grey to coal black. He died gaunt, but radiant. Dave's wife, Millie – they'd split up years before – returned to his side, sat by his bed, and read to him from the Rubaiyat. She died a few years later.

My aunt Tree spent her last years in a nursing home. Her room was eight feet wide by twelve feet long. She was unable to speak or walk or use her left hand after her stroke. But she could purse her lips; "Mmm. Mm-mm." It seemed she lived like that forever. Dusty would visit her from time to time. He'd tell her stories, and he'd sing the old songs: "*Ay compa're, i voi sonare, i chi sona u mandolina. E coma chi sona u mandolina, a-plink, a-plink, u mandolin', a-tippity, tippity, ta.*" Tree couldn't speak, but – a small miracle common among some of those who've had a stroke – she could sing along. It was as if she needed the music of another voice to find her own. And then she died.

My uncle Frank eroded slowly, the way a mountain loses the form of its shoulders to the weather and is blown away. He raged, he lost his eyesight, he imagined himself surrounded by schemes and plots and betrayals. He had ninety years of dying.

For a time, it seemed that I only returned home for funerals.

Each one diminished my father. He grew quieter. He'd been the baby, and the others had now gone where he would have to go. With each death, he was a little more alone.

At the funerals, I wanted to ask if he heard what I heard, gazing at the gentle wreckage of those who remained, a kind of ticking: *not much time, not much time, not much time.*

I lived far away in the Arctic, on the prairies, in Quebec. The life of an exile. When the phone rang at an odd hour, it always struck me like an alarm clock: *time's up.*

His time was up.

While there was no unfinished business between my father and me – we'd come to terms with each other long ago – there was now this one thing left to do. I would go home. I would sit by his side and take his hand. If he had things to say, I'd listen. If he gave up hope, I'd reassure him. If he lost his faith, I'd tell him faith didn't matter. And if he wanted a drink, and could keep it down, I'd pour it for him. There was no need to grieve; he was about to die. I wanted to watch. I wouldn't have saved him if I could. I wouldn't have missed it for the world.

I swept my work away and bought a plane ticket.

Row 17, Seat A. I know the flight path by heart. I've made the trip often enough.

The airplane makes a beeline as it skims across the water, aiming for the town. It comes in low over the tops of the mills, passes across the face of Mount Mackay and makes a wide, sweeping turn as it approaches the runway. I look out the window as we descend. Below is the graveyard where my grandparents are buried. There are new rows of headstones every year, and they are like the stones the frost lifts from a farmer's field.

The old house is filled with the invisible embers of memory. I know where the bed was when my youngest brother leapt up and fell on a forgotten kitchen knife. I can see the corner of the basement where my oldest brother curled into a ball after Dusty beat him senseless. With my eyes closed, I can find the hole in the bedroom door made by the rasp my next-youngest brother threw at my head; had I not slammed the door, the hole would have been between my eyes. I can show you where Dusty's piano stood. And there, just inside the front door, is where Grace fell when he was choking her.

My son is flying in from Vancouver. I haven't seen him in a year. He is lean and handsome, and he was exceptionally close to my father. He has no idea of what is about to happen; no idea of what to expect of me, of his grandmother, or of Dusty.

My son is full of sap; death is new to him.

But he is here and, along with my mother and my brothers, we make plans to divide the day into a twenty-four-hour death watch at the hospital. I take the graveyard shift. I don't call it that in front of the rest of the family, nerves are too frayed. But I insist on sitting up nights. My brothers work during the day, they need to sleep at night. I've taken time away from my job, and besides I'm used to late duty, odd hours.

I have another reason.

My father was always the last one to go to bed. He came home late, he stayed up late. He dozed, he woke, he smoked. If he had company, he wanted to talk. He told the family stories, fragments from the time of his parents, the adventures of my uncles.

As a child, I'd listened eagerly.

Later, when I was in my teens, I shut my ears because I was full of resentments and I thought he was full of shit, with his endless ribbon of myth about our origins, the whisper of old murders, and the tales of those who had died before I was born.

He spoke of his mother and father, his brother Tony, the things he'd been told about the old country, his tales of the Depression. When I moved away from home, I found myself going over these old stories in my head. I knew now I'd never hear them again. He was dying.

This was my last chance.

The First Night

*H*e is unconscious, fitful. He is lying on his back under a single sheet; his hips are sharp as the corners of a box. He is in a semi-private room; there is one other bed facing his. I'd sleep on it, but I am afraid to close my eyes. It is obvious that others have died lying there.

It is quiet; the drugs they administer to the old men on the cancer ward work all too well at night. The dying need their rest. And all the old men on this floor are dying.

I do not want to sleep, in case my father speaks and I am not awake to hear his last words. If he dies tonight, his death will not be unobserved.

I read *Heart of Darkness* in the half-light. In a way, my old man is Mister Kurtz. Bullshit. I have come home, the equivalent of going upriver to see Kurtz. Also bullshit. I'm the one who is delirious.

And then it is suddenly morning, and in the new light I see how bad he really is. His skin is yellow and slack. His flesh is spare, there is a sore on his scalp, there are bruises from needles on his arms. He is collapsing into himself. He is as good as dead.

The night nurses hand over their charts to the day nurses; their whispers are a way to measure which old men have crept an inch closer to the end while everyone else was sleeping.

A fresh crew of orderlies whistles off-key, carrying their cups of sweet and milky coffee, their cardboard boxes of yeasty doughnuts. The nurses' aides push trolleys of breakfast.

My father is awake now.

He is tired from the weight of his illness. His eyes are dull. A nurse props him up against a bank of pillows. He weighs so little, she is able to cradle his upper body and shift him with one arm. She draws a syringe full of his dark and oily-looking blood. A nurses' aide washes his face with a cloth and sets a tray of food before him. He looks at me.

I'm not sure he knows who I am.

He is unable to speak. He stares at his hard-boiled egg as if it might be a riddle. I tie a bib around his neck. He purses his lips; his chin juts forward like a child's.

Before I can get my bearings, another old man is brought in and laid on the second bed. He is little more than long bones in a nightshirt. He is blind, his cheeks are sunken, his eyes are empty in their sockets. He has climbed down to the bottom rung of the ladder of the dying. He stinks of death.

And his misfortune is my comfort. My father is not quite as skinny, not quite as bad off as this.

Not yet, not yet . . .

No one officially acknowledges the presence of the blind old man, because not everyone has seen his chart; without a chart, he doesn't yet exist, and so he can be safely ignored. But the old man is on full, if feeble, alert. He listens for the squeak of rubber-soled shoes on the floor. His nostrils twitch. He smells toast and hard-boiled egg, antiseptics and perfume, weak coffee and baby powder. Although he can't see and is about to die, he says in a high and chipper voice, "I'd very much like a cup of tea with my breakfast. Oh, nurse? Do you think I might have some breakfast? Might I have a cup of tea?"

The only nurse within earshot is silently drawing a second vial of my father's blood; the nylons under her uniform are more eloquent than she knows. From across the room, the old man hears her, smells her, senses her.

"Oh, dear. I'm really quite hungry. I haven't had my tea yet. I love my toast and tea in the morning. Can anyone hear me? Is anyone there? I'd love a cup of tea."

My father is sitting up now. He is limp, his chin is resting on his chest. His eyes are closed, his hands are lifeless in his lap. But I can tell he is listening. He recognizes the old man's accent. My father has a fondness for the English.

He'd speak up on behalf of the old man if he could; his knee always jerked for the weak, and for any species of under-dog, purebred or mongrel. But he is too heavily sedated, and if he does happen to open his mouth, he will not get a chance to speak. I am poised to strike with a bit of egg in a spoon.

Eventually, a nurses' aide comes by, takes the blind man's pulse, and asks if he'd like breakfast. The old man is unable to detect her rank. "Oh, yes please, nurse!" She fusses with a tray of medicines. And she lectures him.

"You should have been here last night. That's when the breakfast cards are filled in. If you want to have breakfast in the morning, you have to fill out your card at night."

"But I wasn't here last night."

There is a shred of vigour underneath the whine; I despise him for it. The nurses' aide returns in half an hour and leaves a cold tray on a table by the blind man's bed. He hears her leave, he smells the food on the tray, he waves his hand limply.

"I do so wish I had a cup of tea. I love my tea in the morning."

He is helpless. I can't help him, I won't.

The squeak of shoes is his cue. "Good morning, nurse. Will you help me have my breakfast? I can't see, or I'd do it myself. Nurse, may I have a cup of tea?"

"There isn't any tea, there's coffee."

"Oh, dear. Oh, my. Oh, well, I'd love some toast."

"There's no toast, there's cereal."

"Oh, dear. Oh, my. Nurse, do you think you could put some milk in my coffee, please?"

"I've already put your milk in your cereal."

He whimpers. "But I don't eat cereal!"

At last, my father musters a rueful smile. And then, moments later, he wrinkles his nose. He caught the scent of it before I did. The blind old man has shit himself.

Death, here is thy dominion.

It's hard not to stare at my father, now. I don't know what I see, exactly. He is dying. Perhaps I see that there is nothing to be done.

The frail old man is also dying, but he makes an infant's sounds of pleasure as the nurses' aide wipes his bottom with a warm wet washcloth. And it occurs to me that he has soiled himself for pleasure.

If Dusty opens his mouth, I will spoon-feed him egg. "Come on, Poppy. You've got to eat." But he purses his lips tightly, I'm sure because of the smell in the room, and takes nothing. Not egg, not juice. He shakes his head.

It has been a long night. The old man is taken to another room. My brother arrives for the start of the morning shift. He nods, I shrug. He says nothing, neither do I. There's nothing to be said; it's all too obvious.

I go home to sleep.

My father was a bushtown bandstand idol.

Everybody knew his name. For fifty years he played the trombone, the banjo, and the stand-up bass in bars and meeting halls and little dance joints: self-taught swing and blues and Dixieland tunes in trios, quartets, quintets. He strutted

in the city marching band, he blew comic trombone rasp-
berries at the elephants when the circus came to town. He
was not ours.

He belonged to the crowd.

He was handsome. His skin was olive, his hair was dark
and wavy. He was trim, neatly formed, and agile the way
some smaller men are. He had high cheekbones, small feet,
and strong hands. His upper lip was flattened slightly, from
years of being pressed against the mouthpiece of his trombone; the imperfection made him look slightly dangerous.

His weekends followed a pattern. He'd come home from
the post office Fridays after a few glasses of beer, drop his
mailbag in the front closet, grab a bite of supper, and take a
nap. He'd wake an hour later and sing to himself while he sat
in the bath. He'd whistle while he stropped his razor, and he'd
hum snatches of tunes while he shaved.

And then he'd get dressed.

He was a star. We were broke. He was a musician, a per-
former. We made sacrifices for him; he worked for us. We
wore hand-me-downs. My mother's dresses were shabby. Her
best clothes were the crisp white uniforms she wore when
she waited tables or tended bar. Together, they made barely
enough to get by.

But Dusty had his Tip Top Tailors suits, a maroon blazer
with black lapels, and three tweed sports jackets with flannel
pants to match. He sent his white shirts to the laundry.

When he was ready to leave the house – his cheeks
smelling of bay rum, a scarf thrown around his neck just so,

and the belt of his trenchcoat knotted loosely – he'd load his car and drive to a spaghetti job, musicians' slang in the Lakehead for a dinner dance at the Finn Hall, the Polish Legion, the Moose Hall, or the Ortona.

He was an indifferent musician, as I came to learn, but he had flair. He played with a stylish yearning, and he was in demand because there always came a moment, late at night, when he'd had enough to drink and it was time for him to sing. He'd park his cigarette in an ashtray and set his whisky and water on the piano. He'd loosen his tie, and sidle up to the microphone. He sang the usual undemanding pop tunes of the day. But his signature song was "Georgia."

And there were nights when couples on the floor stopped dancing when he sang. They held each other and swayed, they wanted to listen, to bask in the warmth of his yearning, to feel the way he felt when he sang. He could bring the house down with his voice. Men lit his cigarettes, told him jokes, sent him doubles. Women sighed and thought he sang for them; sometimes he did.

He took what he could get. And came home late.

Saturday nights were the same. He always drank when he played. Whisky freed his voice. But there were also nights when the crowds were small and the men who ran the halls sent drinks to the musicians; it was easier to get away with paying less than union scale if the band was drunk.

Sundays, hungover or not, Dusty put on his city band uniform, the scarlet jacket with its brass buttons and gold frogging, the cap with its shiny black patent peak, and the navy-blue trousers with a red stripe up the leg. I shined his shoes.

When he grinned, I couldn't help but love him. He might have been quick to cuff my ear, or to strap me with his belt if I misbehaved, but he was just as quick to pick me up and kiss my cheek. When he was ready to play a dance, he looked so happy and took such pleasure in the moment that I smiled at the sight of him, even if he'd laid hands on my mother, even if he'd beaten me or my brothers before he left the house.

My mother worked as a hostess in the supper clubs. She worked three nights a week and came home late herself. After a time, especially during the years when their marriage was an uneasy truce, she was unwilling to wait up for him.

My brothers and I were often left to look after ourselves at night. We squabbled and ate popcorn and watched the fights on television. After I rounded them up for bed, my younger brothers slept hard, or pretended to. My older brother ran with a rough crowd. He had reasons of his own to stay out late; he looked after himself.

Dusty went out happy and came home drunk. Apart from rage, drink was his defining weakness. I was afraid of him when he was sober; but I feared for him when he was drunk, and I thought it was up to me to lie awake, as if staying awake would bring him home. And so he played late, and I stayed up late.

Listening, waiting, wishing him safe.

I could tell how much he'd had to drink by the noise he made when he returned. How long did he sit in the car with the engine running? Was he careful as he unloaded his instruments? If he made cautious noises, he was sober, but if I heard clumsiness it meant he was drunk, and I'd get up and give him a hand.

One night, later than usual, I heard the crunch of car tires in the snow. I waited to hear the trunk slam shut, and then the bump of his foot on the steps, and a series of thumps, and a *sotto voce* "Jesus wept!" as he came through the door.

I heard nothing. I got up. The car was angled, idling half in and half out of the drive. The windshield was iced over, and the lowbeams cut through the clouds of soft white exhaust which enveloped the car. Something was wrong.

I put on my boots and went out in my pyjamas. It was so cold the handle of the car door burned my hand. Inside the car, the air was thick and sweet with the smell of liquor. Dusty sat slumped against the wheel. The night air hit him in the face. He lifted his head and blinked; his eyes were wet and out of focus. He wasn't sure who I was.

"Come on, Pop. Get out of the car. You have to come inside. It's freezing cold." I reached in and shut off the headlights.

"What the hell do you think you're doing? Why don't you leave me alone?" I glanced at the houses of the neighbours; there was no one peeking from behind drawn curtains. I pulled his arm around my shoulder and dragged him from the car. He leaned on me, and together we stumbled up the steps.

I helped him slip off his toe rubbers. I took off his coat and scarf and led him into the kitchen where it was bright and warm. And then I went back outside; if his instruments froze they'd warp, they'd split, and there'd be misery in the morning. There was barely enough money for house payments. New instruments were beyond reach.

I lugged it all in: the big bass in its zippered canvas case, the music stand, the banjo and trombone, a satchel full of mutes, and the briefcase swollen with sheet music.

He was asleep at the kitchen table. I put a hand on his shoulder. "Come on, Pop. It's time for bed." He lifted his head and blinked. He knew who I was now. He wasn't asleep. There were fierce tears in his eyes. He swept my hand away.

"Leave me alone, god damn it. It's no use."

"What's no use, Pop."

"Leave me alone. I want to die."

I stepped back. I was ten years old. I didn't know what he meant. He'd never lied to me. I believed every word he said. It would have been easy enough to die; there was a rabbit gun and a deer rifle in the hall closet, and an army-issue pistol in his dresser drawer behind his box of cufflinks, along with a bundle of wartime letters, some old papers, and his brother Tony's watch.

I was forbidden that drawer. But there were nights when my brothers were asleep and my parents were out working when I'd sneak into the room and open the drawer and take the pistol out. I would hold it to my cheek and sniff the oily metal, and stand alone in the darkness of the room, and raise the gun and aim at my reflection in the mirror.

I knew about the pistol.

"Leave me alone," he said. "I want to die."

I didn't know what to say. I thought wanting to die was a sin. I'd never seen my father weep. He was stronger than I. I couldn't stop him if I wanted to. I thought I should say something. I thought I should save his life. If I said the wrong thing . . .

"You don't want to die, Pop. Please don't say you want to die. We love you. Everybody loves you. You have a good family. We love you. You've got a lot of reasons to live."

I had no idea why anyone needed reasons. I thought you simply lived.

"Shut up," he slurred. "You don't know what the hell you're talking about. How could you? Get me the bottle under the sink."

"But don't you think you've had . . . ?"

"Jesus wept! Get me a drink or get the hell out of here. And get my cigarettes from my jacket pocket."

He'd been angry at me before. He'd often spoken sharply, but not like this. I did as I was told. I lit his smoke and he splashed whisky in his glass and on the table. He held the glass in both hands. He stared at it. He could barely hold up his head. He didn't drink. He began to tell a story.

I sat and listened until he finished, until he couldn't talk any more, until I thought he was too tired to harm himself, until he was sober enough to stumble off to bed. He told me about his brother Tony. When he was finished, I believed what he'd said about wanting to die. I wanted to tell someone; I was afraid of what might happen if I didn't. But

I kept his secret. I began to look at him differently. I felt sorry for him.

And I no longer trusted him.

~

Tony sat at the kitchen table.

It was warm near the stove. There was always someone in the kitchen if he wanted some of his father's wine brought up from the cellar. Tony could still walk without difficulty, and the girls made a fuss over him; he was the Black Prince, regal of manner, thin and tragic and handsome in his uniform, a war hero.

Tony let them fuss.

He sat at the table quietly, in his battle dress, with puttees. Nothing made sense. The baby gurgled in his crib. Wood crackled in the stove, sharp as gunshots smacking into trees. Teresa dropped a pot. Tony gripped the table with both hands; he had to, to prevent himself from diving face-first to the floor. Teresa saw and understood.

"Oh, Tony, did I scare you?"

He glared. He trembled. He wanted to cry out. He was not all right. He was all wrong. He heard shells whistling overhead. He saw trees exploding, men pinching the splinters from their necks, horses panicking at the first scent of the gas.

"Get me some wine from the cellar, please."

In command now, the Black Prince again. Angela in the garden, Matteo down at the docks, the rest of the gang out.

Teresa let the cellar door slam; the baby, his new brother, born while Tony lay face-down in the mud in France, woke up.

A shell exploded in front of Tony's eyes; the mist of someone's blood floated in air, fluttering like a red gauze curtain in the breeze. A soldier sat in the muck and put his hand to his red belly; the man next to him stared at his own bloody arm lying in a puddle of water.

The baby cooed. Tony shuddered. He thought, this child is going to die anyway. He will grow up and become a soldier and go to war and he will find himself lying in the mud beside a man whose cheek has been peeled to the bone by a chunk of shrapnel.

The baby cried.

Gas would come creeping down the hill, oily and heavier than mist, smelling oddly of onions. It would roll down the hill and burn the baby's lungs, and it would take him a long time to die, and he would die with the smell of onions in his nostrils. Why not save us all some time? If there were no more babies, there would be no more war. No more soldiers, don't you see?

Teresa shrieked.

Tony was standing at the stove, a stick of bone-white birch in his right hand; with his left, he held the baby against his hip. The door of the woodstove was open onto a little hell: yellow tongues of flame, and little curls of smoke.

Tony looked at his sister, didn't see her. All he saw was something which looked like smoke and could have been gas. He pushed the stick of wood into the flame, making room inside the firebox. He took the baby, lifted him, held him in front of the furnace door.

Teresa saw madness, dropped the wine, raced across the room, eyes on both her brothers. Holding Tony's dull gaze. *If there's time, if there's time, if he doesn't* . . . In a fury, she pushed Tony in the chest. He dropped the baby to the floor. Oddly, the baby did not cry.

Teresa picked the child up off the floor and rushed out the back door into the garden. Angela looked up from between the rows of beans. Teresa was crying. "Ma, it's Tony, something wrong with Tony. He was going to stuff the baby in the stove!" Angela took the child. There was something wrong with these men who went to war; they came back mad. She gave Teresa the hoe. They watched the kitchen door.

Tony was still standing in the kitchen, looking at the stove as if he'd never seen it before. He closed the door against the flame. He straightened his uniform, sat down, and began to tremble. He did not stop trembling for two weeks.

No one spoke of this again.

The Second Night

The question of insurance coverage has been settled during the day. My father is entitled to a private room. He has been moved. The room is grey, there is a metal bed, a plastic chair, a closet, and a bathroom. His pants and his suspenders are in the closet. He will not put them on again. There are peculiar cords, and tubes for various gases, dangling from the wall near the bed.

There is a sign posted on the door:

Body Substance Precautions
Body substance includes oral secretions, blood, urine and feces, wound or other drainage. Wash hands. Wear gloves when likely to touch body substances or mucous membranes. Wear plastic apron or gown when skin/ clothing is likely to be soiled. Wear mouth/eye protection

when likely to be splashed. Recapping needles not recom-
mended. Discard in designated container.

The language is awkward but the sign is a clear warning
to me: I must prepare to see my father's spittle, the dribbles of
his blood, and puddles of his shit and his urine.

The windows of his room are large. If Dusty had the
strength to raise his head, he would see the last elms in the
city and beyond them to the lake. He knows this neighbourhood; he delivered mail around here for years. It was a
good route, with quiet streets and large houses. In the summer,
the walk was shady and cool; in winter, the Christmas tips
were generous.

No one has died during the day, and although there is a
dismal and never-ending supply of them, no new old men
have been admitted. The nurses are silent this evening. There
is nothing much for them to do now that the drugs have been
handed out. I sit up, reading in the half-light. I am ready to do
my job.

If Dusty wakes, if he is afraid, I will reassure him.

Under his hospital pyjamas, he wears his maroon T-shirt,
the one with the flying-horse insignia of his old army divi-
sion, the First Airborne. He waged a private war in England
with his trombone and his prick. He'd won his wings, but he
was haunted by the war he never had. He wears the T-shirt
now. It gives him strength.

He is as sick as it is possible to be.

I have learned that there is a thick slab of cancer on his
chest, there is a lump of it the size of an egg in his armpit, a

hard fist of it clutching his kidney. He makes the least impression under his thin sheets; it is obvious that his testicles have been removed, a needless humiliation. The therapy is too new; too late to have done him any good.

The doctors said there was some scarring on his heart, he may have had a silent heart attack, a mild one, years ago; he might not even have noticed when it happened. I thought I knew when.

Christmas, not long after I'd left home for good. I was visiting, the house was full of cousins and bottles, and there was food on the stove and carols on the radio. Dusty was holding court at the kitchen table, but he was a little too drunk to tell a proper story. He kept losing the thread; he seemed confused. My brothers and cousins rolled their eyes in amusement. I felt a vague contempt for them, and for him.

I was standing next to the sink when he caught my eye, and pushed his glass forward with a finger. He wanted another drink. I shook my head; I wouldn't do it, I thought he'd had enough.

He glared; nobody was going to tell him when he'd had enough, not in his own house. He pushed his chair back and tried to stand. His face went ashen and he sagged backwards, briefly, and slumped back in the chair. I'd never seen anything hit him like that. No one noticed but me.

For a moment, I thought about calling an ambulance. Then I thought should tell one of my cousins to get the phone, to dial 911 right now, god damn it, while I helped him lie down.

And then I thought, Let's see what happens.

Nothing happened. He sat quietly for a time, and no one noticed that his face was grey or that he'd stopped talking. Dusty was drunk again, that was all. Eventually, he slurred and raised his head and said he was thirsty. I made him a whisky and water, weaker than usual. If he wanted a drink, he could have one; to hell with it. The scar of this on his heart.

The pain is muscular and aggressive tonight. It lifts him up and throws him down a dozen times, as if his flesh were made of rags. He drifts in and out of a morphine stupor. He will not admit he is dying. He will not have an easy death. I have the responsibility to watch.

I've earned the right.

He learned what his brother Tony had done, eventually. He learned about it long after he had learned to love him. The knowledge that Tony had tried to kill him was so powerful that he couldn't remember who told him, or when. But I think it would have been Teresa: *Tra-la-la, I saved your life.* She'd have said it with a little laugh as if to say the horror didn't matter. It must have been she who told him. He wouldn't have believed anyone else. She was his saviour.

She would save him again.

Old Matteo still had the farm in those days, but he'd built a house in Fort William, because that was where the steady wages were. One day, Angela sent her youngest boy to the store for a gallon of vinegar on a late-summer day when she was making pickles, turning the garden vegetables into *giardiniera* and *sottaceti*. Dusty was seven years old. The sun was hot, his hands began to sweat, the heavy jug slipped out of his fingers and broke on the sidewalk in front of the house. Vinegar splashed his shoes, his socks, his shins.

There was never much money, certainly not enough to pay for things twice over. Angela snapped and grabbed my father by the ear and hauled him into the house. And she was sitting on his chest, shrieking and weeping and beating his head with a stick of firewood when Teresa once again came to the rescue and snatched him away.

If Dusty had been too young to remember when Tony tried to stuff him into the woodstove, he was old enough to remember when his mother tried to kill him. He never forgot.

He shifts in bed, he lifts his head and looks around the room. He seems charged with a peculiar energy. I am startled, and almost disappointed, to see him suddenly alert. I'd thought he was about to die at any moment. When the pain returns, it will hit him harder and hurt him more. But for now, it seems as if he's cast off hurt as easily as he's cast off his bedclothes

"Oh, Joe. God damn it, it's cold in here."

"Do you want something hot to drink?"

"I was dreaming. Can you get me a cup of tea?"

"Hang on," I tell him as I pull the covers up to his chin. "I'll go make some." He'd been dreaming. Listening to his dreams was better than going to the movies: he'd fought against the legions of Genghis Khan armed with nothing but a sword; he'd been carried over the forest in the claws of an eagle; or my favourite: as he slept, he floated high above the clouds, tethered to the earth with a slender silver cord.

I bring him a pot of tea, and I put a bit of sugar in his cup. He smiles, and makes a gesture with his hands, as if he were taking the top off a bottle. There's a mickey of rye in his drawer. I spike the mug. He wraps his hands around the tea and holds it. He doesn't really want tea, I think. He wants to warm his hands, and he wants to smell the whisky.

"You have to show them who's boss. Animals aren't stupid." He talked like an old junkie, sometimes, resuming conversations which had been abandoned minutes, or hours, or days ago.

"What's that?"

"My uncle Joe had a horse named King."

"You dreamed about a horse?"

"Yeah, King. A hell of a horse: when he wanted to pull, you couldn't stop him. But there were days when he didn't want to pull, and you couldn't budge him with a pry bar. Joe paired King with another dray horse, Charlie. A hell of a team, they could have moved a mountain.

"Charlie wasn't as strong, but he was a steady worker; he just wanted to get the job done. When King didn't want to pull, Charlie would get fed up and bite him on the shoulder. Never worked. Eventually, Joe got fed up with having half a team, half the time. Help me drink this, would you?"

I lift the cup to his mouth. All he wants is to wet his lips. I might as well join him. I pour myself a double in a plastic glass. The sweetness of the liquor. I don't have to work in the morning. All I have to do is sit in a chair, read my books, listen to him talk, and watch him die.

"There was a Finn lived down the road from us, he always had his eye on King, the way that horse could pull. So when Joe had finally had enough, he sold the horse. But he told the Finn, 'I'm warning you, sometimes this horse won't pull.'

"The Finn was one of those oldtimers who thought he knew best. He said, 'Yah, yah, you leave that one to me. I can take care of a horse who won't pull.'

"One day the Finn was taking some hay off his field with his new horse, when King decided he'd done enough work. He quit right there. He just stopped.

"The Finn thought this might be a good time to teach the horse a lesson. He took a handful of hay from the wagon, set it under King's belly and lit it with a match. King moved all right. He took three steps forward, and then he stopped."

And then Dusty stopped.

He wanted to catch his breath, of course, but it remained his habit to stop talking at the moment when you were keenest to know what happened next.

"What happened next?" I asked.

"What the hell do you think happened? The goddamned wagon caught fire. Stupid Finn, smart horse. I don't know what happened to him after that. But I'll tell you, if it was my horse, I'd have shot him."

He wouldn't have, of course. Dusty liked to say he'd do a lot of things he had the heart but not the stomach for. Saying it was almost as good as doing it, and in most cases a lot safer.

"You know, in spite of the trouble with King, there wasn't much Joe couldn't do with a horse. Maybe he got more out of King than most men would have. There's supposed to be a big house in the old country, Casa Silvaggio. Maybe it isn't there, maybe it didn't exist, maybe it's called some other name now, doesn't matter. Silvaggio would have been a big man. He'd have been rich, him and the whole damn gang."

He lifts his teacup by himself now. His hand is shaky. I won't help unless he asks me. I don't want to fuss. His Adam's apple bobs, as if he were drinking water. I know the lovely feeling: the sweetness of the whisky, the heat of the tea, the long hard swallows, and the warmth.

"I don't know if I told you this before. You aren't going to believe what I'm going to tell you now."

"Try me."

"Joe was skidding logs in the bush with one of the horses, I think it was Charlie. You know what it's like in the deep bush in the winter, when it's late and dark and there's a lot of snow? It's tough sledding. Well, the sled got caught up on a stump.

"He had a full load of pulp, big logs; you saw those old photos when we went to visit the farm. Joe was by himself, remember. The sled was hung up bad, it nearly tipped. You can imagine getting snagged underneath like that; no way could you pull free.

"Well, Joe couldn't leave the horse in the bush and go for help. If anything happened the horse would freeze to death. But he didn't want to leave the load. He'd have just as much work to do to free it tomorrow. So he took an axe and he started to chop away at the stump. It was cold, and it was hard going, the stump was frozen and he was working in close quarters. He had his shoulder up under the horse's ribs, you know, to give him leverage.

"But he slipped, just as he was taking a swing; damned if he didn't cut that horse's foot clean through at the fetlock. The hoof was just hanging from a piece of skin. The pain should have driven him crazy, but he was numb from the cold, and he couldn't bolt because he was still in harness.

"Well, a horse costs money. You don't have a horse, you can't make a living in the bush, you've got no way to get ahead. So Joe unhitched the horse, which is what he should have done in the first place; and he led him home on three legs through the snow, hoof dangling from a piece of skin.

"Pops went over to take a look. He said, 'Joe, you'd better shoot that horse, he's no good to you now.' Joe said, 'I'm not going to shoot him, no sir. He's a good horse, I'm gonna fix him up.'"

"'You can't fix him up, he's gonna die.'

"'You watch me, son of a bitch.'

"And he took Charlie into the barn and he rigged up a sling under the horse's belly, to take the weight off the front foot. And he stitched that god-damned hoof back on. Don't ask me how. You sever tendons like that, you figure they snap back up inside. He must have cut into the leg and hooked the tendons somehow, pulled them down.

"I'm telling you, sonny, he stitched that hoof back on the end of Charlie's leg, and that horse stayed in the barn all winter long, rigged up in that god-damned sling. We used to sneak into the barn and look. Kids, eh, curious. Great big horse in a sling, frost snorting from his nostrils, shadows falling on the far wall, the bloody hoof all bandaged up.

"Joe kept him slung up until the spring. Fed him and watered him by hand. Nobody said you could do it, everybody said it was impossible, the foot was going to get infected, the leg was going to fall off, it was cruel to sling a horse up like that, you'd just have to shoot it in the end. The vet came out and took a look; he left scratching his head.

"Now, the obvious thing to have done, when he was back in the bush like that, he should have unhitched that horse and come back the next morning. Unload the pulp. Free the skid, load her up again and you're on your way. That would have been too easy.

"But I'm telling you, that horse walked again. And he worked again. Not like before, of course. He favoured that hoof, but he worked hard to the end. God damn it, I'm tired."

He drifts into sleep.

The Third Night

———————————

You know how this story will end.

He is lying in a hospital bed. He has been dying for some time. He is weak and painfully skinny, his muscles are slack, he is unable to support his own weight by himself. His hips poke squarely through the sheet. His cheeks are sunken. I can see the bones in his feet, the sharp bones in the backs of his hands. His mouth is partly open and he makes a loud noise when he breathes, sucking the air into his throat.

His cancer fattens; he's starving to death.

Perhaps I will not get to hear all the stories I have come for.

He shifts in his sleep and then wakes in the half-light, confused by a mixture of pain and morphine. The smell of hospital is unmistakable. He knows where he is, even if he doesn't quite know why. Suddenly, he raises his head and he looks at me with a sneer, as if I am a vulture.

"What the hell are you doing here?"

I could remind him that he is dying. There's no point. He will not live much longer. I do not feel the need to say it aloud, to hold his head under the cold wet truth of his death until he gasps for air. I am not as cruel as that.

But neither do I feel the need to divert him from a moment of terror. He knows at some level who I am and why I have come. He ought to know. I am his son. He knows I love him. Just as he ought to know I wouldn't save him if I could. He has always known.

He shakes his head, and his eyes adjust to the shadows. He sees me now, and breathes easily; he smiles, and like he has done so many nights before, he picks up where he left off.

"Joe Silvaggio had a load of grain."

This is the real beginning of the story of how my family came here:

The sky is blue, the sun is hot, the poppies in the ditch are red as drops of blood. My great-uncle Joe Silvaggio is on his way to the mill with a load of grain. He holds the reins with an easy hand. In Ripabottoni, in the high hills of Molise, there is only one road. The horses know the way.

Joe Silvaggio lights a black cigar and waves at three men cutting wheat in a field. Let them work with their backs, he thinks. I have a team of horses, a man with a team of horses doesn't have to bust his ass.

One of the contadini wipes his forehead and waves a greeting. He takes his scythe in his arms as if it were a woman and waltzes in a crazy circle across the stubble. Silvaggio waves dismissively.

"*Ciao, ciao*, your padrone calls the tune!"

The man stops dancing.

In the air, there is the salty smell of horse and leather harness and the sweet smell of freshly cut grain. Silvaggio clears his nose and spits, reaches in his jacket pocket for a flask, rinses his mouth with grappa, spits and drinks again; this time he swallows. The horses move on.

One day, Silvaggio thinks, I'll be a padrone. I'll have my father's horses, and his house. Peasants will dance with their scythes in my fields, and if they want bread, they'll learn to step lively. He thinks, I already have this team of horses. I have a handsome wife. She is a Fiorito; rare in this village, a Fiorito without a *sopranome*. She is neither Pelicino, little bird, nor Cimone, tree stump, nor Cocciolongo, longhead, nor Seraphina, angel. Her branch of the family has withered away; the risk of intermarriage is too small to be important.

She is my beauty, my Filomena. And I have grafted her to me, and she will bear me many sons before I'm through with her. And my sons will be handsome and powerful men, and if by chance I have daughters they will be beauties, and I will break the heads of their boyfriends. These are my pleasant thoughts on this hot day.

He hears another team coming hard on the road behind.
It must be some *stronzo* who doesn't know enough to go easy
on the horses when it's hot. Silvaggio turns to look. Not this
son of a bitch, not this asshole who thinks he's better than
me. Too bad for him. I was here first.

"Hey, Silvaggio. I don't have time to smoke a cigar and
drink from a flask. I have work to do today. Move your horses
to the side. Let me pass."

Silvaggio bares his teeth. He spits in the dust, says nothing.

"Hey, Silvaggio, pull over. I'm in a hurry. Let me pass."

Madonna, Silvaggio thinks. I'd rather smoke a cigar and
drink from a flask and think my own thoughts than have an
argument, but if an argument is what he wants . . . Silvaggio
exhales a careless feather of smoke, and he smiles. This asshole, like the one I sit on every day, will follow me for the rest
of my life. The sooner he gets used to it, the better.

"I can see you're in a hurry. Unhappily for you, I was here
first; you'll have to wait your turn."

"Let me by or I'll –"

"Or you'll what? *Quaglia, figlio di quaglia.*"

The man in the cart can't believe his ears. "You're calling
me a quail?" It is too much. There is a sudden hiss in the air;
a horsewhip snaps and stings and coils like a hot snake at
Silvaggio's neck. "Who's the quail now?"

Silvaggio clutches his throat, spits out his cigar, and
tumbles from his cart. Before the whip can sting him again,
he draws his pistol. Neither man hears the gunshot. Silvaggio
hears silence.

I have a bee in my shirt, thinks the man with the whip.

He is puzzled, there is a buzzing in his ears; something hot and red and heavy is strangling his heart. No bee was ever like this. He cannot breathe.

He touches his chest, and looks at the tips of his fingers, and drops his whip in the cart. Not much blood but, oh sweet Jesus, there should not be any blood at all. He cannot find air, he cannot find the word for red. He knows, looking at his fingers, that he is dead.

Silvaggio rises to his knees. He watches the man pluck at his shirt, he watches the red wound blossom like a flower. The man opens his mouth. The birds begin to sing. Silvaggio wants to silence them.

The man with the poppy on his chest is moving his lips. He is trying to speak. Silvaggio wants him to say, "Look, it's my fault. I'm sorry. I shouldn't have hit you with my whip." Instead the man falls backwards, wordless, drowning in air, drowning in blood, drowning in grain.

Assassin of a God, I had no choice; no one lashes at me and gets away with it. Pig of a God, my neck hurts. Dog of a God, it's his fault. Holy Mother of God.

The man wriggles slowly now, like a *serpente* with a broken back lying in the road in the heat of the sun. Silvaggio looks to see if anyone is coming. He pokes the man in the shoulder: yellow grains of wheat, red drops of blood.

It occurs to Silvaggio that he is poking the man with the barrel of the pistol. Madonna. He pockets the pistol and smells the spent powder in the air and on his hands and whispers softly, "Ah, you little quail. You were in a hurry to fly; you shouldn't be in such a hurry now."

The man no longer hears.

Silvaggio brushes his trousers and looks around. Not much time. Some son of a bitch of a contadino is going to come along and send for the carabinieri. Some son of a bitch of a carabiniere is going to ask questions. And some son of a bitch of a peasant who dances with a scythe will say he saw me pass, he saw me wave, he saw a second wagon, and he heard a shot.

Silvaggio unharnesses the fastest of his horses. He leaves the wagons where they are – no time to think, no need to ask any questions. There are no questions. There is an answer.

Canada.

~

What my father said was "Joe Silvaggio had a load of grain." And then he fell back on his pillow. It is not a lengthy story now. He cannot draw it out. He is telling me to remember. He is telling me not to forget.

These are not the same things.

He doesn't have the strength to tell the story of his uncle Joe. Not tonight. He knows he doesn't have enough breath, or enough time. But he knows that I have heard it often enough that a reminder is all I need. It is the story of how my family came to Canada.

The hotheaded Joe Silvaggio killed a man. He hurried home, said goodbye to his father and mother, and packed a few tools while his wife, Filomena, packed her dresses. Together they fled to the coast, a boat, away. Filomena's brother Matteo – my father's father – came with them.

And that is one version of why I am here.

The story of the murder in the road is as true in my mind as anything I have seen, as real as any place I have been. I asked for it often as I grew up. It is the story of who I am, and where I am from.

My father does not know where he is any more. He does not know why he is here. I will not tell him, not tonight.

I watch him sleep.

The Fourth Night

*T*he pattern emerges: I arrive in the early evening, and my mother or my son or one of my brothers goes home. My father lies still, eyes closed, lips pursed, his supper untouched. Tonight is no different.

He curls his upper lip and sucks a breath of hospital air through his closed teeth. Though he has been drugged until he is practically unconscious, it is impossible for him not to detect the scent of antiseptic, dribbled urine, leaking bowels, seeping wounds, and talcum powder – the final smell of other old men, all of whom are shrinking, wasting, dying. He holds his breath. His chest does not move.

I attempt to find meaning in each tiny gesture he makes or fails to make, to see if his time has come, if this is the moment, this second, now. Not yet. He exhales. Slowly, with his eyes closed, he brings his right hand around to the front of his face. With the forefinger, he rubs his upper lip like a man stroking the ends of an invisible moustache or a cat cleaning its whiskers. He breathes now, an imperceptible sound, almost a whimper.

"What's that, Pops?"

"Meow."

With the simplest of movements and a single sound, he has given me another story, one that used to take him half an hour to tell. He hears me laugh. His hand falls limply to his chest. He smiles. He knows I've understood.

⟋

My grandfather, Matteo, and his brother-in-law, the hot-headed Joe Silvaggio, establish themselves in Canada in the early 1890s. They clear adjoining homesteads in South Gillies Township, in the Northern Ontario bush, twenty-five miles southwest of Fort William.

It's a simple deal, too sweet to be true: no matter who you are or where you are from or how you got here, this infant government of Canada will give you 160 acres of land and seven years to clear a field and put up a house and a barn. Do that, and you've earned title to the land.

Silvaggio has his Filomena. And Matteo is married to Angela Maria Delvecchio, a girl also from the village of Ripabottoni. How she came to the edge of the wilderness, and how my grandfather met her in Fort William, is a mystery.

But what happened after they were married is no mystery at all: their first child died, and then came five girls and seven boys.

The Silvaggio family is almost as large. All the girls, Silvaggio and Fiorito alike, are pretty and vivacious. All the boys are rock-hard and handsome, with flashing white smiles.

The two families work side by side; the farms provide enough to live on, more or less. The Silvaggios earn extra money cutting pulp. Matteo is thinking of leaving the bush and building a house in town.

Late one morning, on a day in late spring, five or six years after his last child – my father – has been born, Matteo says, "I'm taking the boy for a ride. I think I'll go to see my sister." Angela says nothing, and continues making bread. It is a good thing to have fewer men underfoot when there's work to do in the kitchen, especially this littlest one, the one she'd had when she thought she was past having children.

Matteo puts on his heavy coat, goes outside, and hitches the horse to the wagon. When Angela is in a dark mood, it is best to get out of the way quickly. "Let's go, *ragazz'*." Dropping the final *o*, in the manner of Molise. He lifts Dusty up, sets him on the seat, wraps a blanket around his shoulders, and gives the reins a flick. Cold air, white birch, the last hard snow, and a hint of warmth hidden in the sunlight.

"Spring is coming soon," he says aloud; he says "*Primavera*" to himself. This is Canada, be Canadian. *Una via nuova.* A new way. *Una vita nuova.* A new life. Speak English to the boy. But as he drives he speaks to himself in the language of the old country:

This son of a bitch of a bush, if you don't work hard, if you don't cut it back, it will take your field in a season or two, it will swallow your house in less than a lifetime, no matter how well you build. These are not the high hills of Ripabottoni. Here, no one builds houses with stone. These fields have no memory. There is nothing but air and sky, trees and water.

Matteo stuffs his pipe with tobacco, strikes a kitchen match with his thumbnail, and lights up. Puffs of blue smoke trail from his nostrils, puffs of hot breath trail from the nostrils of his horse.

The boy leans into his father and closes his eyes; he can feel his father's warmth. He hears the rattle and slap of harness and halter, the nicker and whinny of the horse, the checkered rhythm as its thick hooves slap the icy road. When the boy takes a breath, he imagines that he can smell what lies under the snow: water and grass, thistles and mud.

After half a mile on the concession road, Matteo turns up the narrow lane that leads to Silvaggio's farm.

A bower of poplars, a house, a barn, and a hasty collection of simple wooden outbuildings. Old tools leaning against cold trees. A sheet of clean snow draped over the potato field. A collar of dry snow curled around the blade of a rusted plough. Hard paths beaten to the barn, the outhouse, the woodshed. A good but an unforgiving farm.

Joe Silvaggio steps out to greet the wagon. He holds the stub of a cigar in his teeth and the stub of a short axe in his hand. He is shirtless, the sleeves of his long johns rolled up to his elbows. He is wide of shoulder, square of head, and handsome when he grins.

He is grinning now. He's been chopping at the frozen hill
of shit which has built up in the outhouse over the winter.
Sure, he ought to have cleaned it in the fall. But what does it
matter when work like this is done, as long as it gets done?
Better to do it now, before it melts; shit smells less bad when
it's frozen.

The two men smile and nod. There is little between them
except Filomena. Little, save a hilltop town in Italy, which no
one in this wild place could imagine. Little, save the knowledge of what had happened on a hot day on a narrow road a
long way from here.

There is little between them.

Safe now; safer here; safest not to speak of it at all.

They had broken the land, blown stumps, cleared roads
together. They'd helped each other with their harvests, and
for a time it seemed they competed with each other to see
who was the better man in bed; their children were many, and
the births narrowly spaced.

"I hear you got a deer," says Matteo.

The boy's heart flutters. He is only a child, but he knows
the look of a deer in the field: skittish, pink of tongue, hoof
held high, an alert intelligence. And he knows the look of a
deer when it is dead. He's peered into the dull brown eyes,
run his hands over the cold hard horns; his stomach has
turned at the stench of butchered guts. He knows about the
need for meat.

Silvaggio twists his moustache. "A stupid animal. Lucky
for me. I came out for a piss. Not so lucky for the deer. It was
kicking the snow, looking for something to eat. Over there,

by the barn. I gave it something to eat, all right. I gave it one shot. Bang."

"One shot," says Matteo. A man could walk all day in the woods and not see anything to shoot. Silvaggio needs to piss, and as a result he has meat on his table. Madonna.

"Hello, boy. Are you glad to see your uncle? Come and give your zio a hug!" Silvaggio lifts the boy and holds him tight for a moment, rough cheek against smooth. He knows why his brother-in-law has come: he wants meat, I have meat. A deer in the spring is a skinny thing, but it is better than no deer at all, and I'm the better man today.

There's no hurry; I'm going to savour this.

"Come on, it's cold out here, let's go inside."

Matteo thinks, the deer around this place are not like the deer in the hills around Ripa; they are bigger, they taste stronger. Everything is bigger here; bigger, stronger, wilder.

Silvaggio says, "I'll give you some meat to take home. Come in, we'll have a drink first. Are you hungry?"

"I could use a drink," says Matteo.

The kitchen smells of thick sweet heat, of condensed milk and coal oil, of coffee and fresh bread. Filomena kisses her brother, cuddles her nephew and tells him he's getting big. She sets a cold lunch on the table: tongue, sausage, cheese, and wine. A pot of tea. A cup of milk for the boy. She is happy to see Matteo and his son. It's a hard life here, but everything is easier with children. The children remind us of what? Of innocence. Of life before . . .

She puts a plate of cookies near Dusty, so he can help himself. The two men talk about the weather, about cutting wood, about the likelihood of getting work from the township later in the year, when the frost has passed and it is safe to grade the roads. They talk about their animals.

After lunch, Silvaggio lights a little cigar; let him wait, let him wait. Matteo draws on his pipe; he waits. Silvaggio pats his belly, closes his eyes, and eases a gentle belch.

When Matteo's pipe is finished and the air is blue with smoke, he decides he's had enough of waiting. He calls for the boy; damned if he is going to beg. "Time to go," he says.

"What's the matter with me, I almost forgot," says Silvaggio, a little too eager, a little too loud. "Come on, I'll cut you a piece of that deer. Did I tell you I got him with one shot?"

The deer is hanging upside down in the barn, gutted, with its hide still on. It takes the boy a moment to adjust his eyes from the brightness of the sun on the snow to the darkness of the barn. He can smell hay and cowshit and the corpse of the deer. Somehow, split and hanging upside down, it is not a deer, although it is unclear why it's not. The boy wonders if the corpse of the deer frightens the horses in the barn.

"It's a fine one," says Silvaggio. "It makes me feel good just to see it. A gift from the fields, *dio grazie*. What do you say, how much do you want, shall I give you a haunch of the stupidest deer in the world?" Silvaggio slaps the side of the animal. It swings slowly, side to side. Matteo needs the meat.

"Whatever you can spare."

"Son of a bitch, what am I thinking? I'd forget my asshole if it wasn't tied on tight; you wait here." Silvaggio returns a moment later, stopping first to poke the head of an axe in the snow by the doorway. He wipes the blade roughly clean with a handful of straw; he takes a short grip on the handle, steadies the carcass and hacks at it with a grunt and a grin.

Matteo is silent. Son of a bitch, he thinks. He cuts my meat with the same axe he uses to chop his shit. Does he think I'm stupid, does he think I'm blind? But he holds his tongue; brother-in-law or not, it's foolish to confront a man who holds an axe when your own hands are empty.

Silvaggio throws the haunch of meat in the back of the wagon, exaggerating its heaviness. Matteo purses his lips and grunts as he gathers up his son. And when he has turned the wagon down the lane, and is clear of the Silvaggio farm, he tosses the meat as far as he can into the bush.

A fox will eat shit. A man will not.

One morning a month or so later, when the weather has turned warm, Matteo is lying awake in bed, still thinking about the deer. He cannot go back to sleep. He knows if he thinks carefully, an idea will come to him. If you think carefully, you can easily get the better of a hothead. Silvaggio, who enjoyed the fact that he'd killed a man, and enjoyed knowing that Matteo knew. For the sake of the family, it would always be unspoken between them.

Hey, I killed a man, I can kill another. I'm a man who has killed. But if either of us comes to grief, both our families suffer.

Matteo stirs in bed, leans his bony hip into Angela's soft backside. She moves away from him and pulls the blankets tighter. He hears a howling from the direction of the hen-house; one of the barn cats is speaking its love for the world.

You and me, cat, we make the hens nervous. Matteo cocks his ear and listens to the clucks and murmurs of alarm. Nobody can get any sleep around here any more. He gets up muttering. *Porco dio. Dio gatto.*

"Where are you going?" whispers Angela.

"That god-damned cat has sung its last song."

Matteo, in his nightshirt, takes the .22 pump from the closet. He chambers a shell and carefully opens the kitchen door. He steps outside. He sees a cat in silhouette on the roof. He thinks, I've got you now, Romeo. He is not a sharpshooter, but there isn't a man who lives in the bush who can't shoot straight when it counts.

One shot, and the echo of a shot. An abbreviated screech, and then the scratch of claws on shingle, and a soft thump in the grass. Matteo walks behind the henhouse to make sure of his kill. The night is sharply quiet now. The cat is still. The ground is hard, and Matteo is cold. Ah, *stupido*. Why didn't I put on my boots? There are needles of stubble and buttons of stone beneath his feet, and a ribbon of the northern lights tied in a knot above his head. He is wide awake now, he breathes deeply and pauses; which is better, the nascent smell of grass in the earth, or the thick smell of hay in the barn?

When Matteo is by himself, away from Angela and the children, his mind wanders, and sometimes he feels as if he were back in Ripa. Not because of the land. Land is nothing here, every two-bit son of a bitch in this place can have some land, as much as he wants, just by asking the government. Even lazy men who don't know how to farm can have quarter-sections with trees and water, they can live by selling a little wood and hiring a man to build a house. Why, if a man had this much land in Ripa. . . .

But this is not Ripa, where land is dear because it's scarce. Where land is often rented for generations, let out for so long that the man who owns it must buy it back if he wants to use it himself. That's what's wrong with this place: there's so much land it has no value.

He shivers and decides: the smell of grass is sweetest; grass is so sweet, it makes cowshit smell good. A man's shit smells like death. A man's shit freezes in winter and piles up in the outhouse until some son of a bitch decides it's time to take an axe. Hey, what's the matter with me? In the shadows, the cat lies curled up like a rabbit.

The idea comes to him then.

He picks up the corpse and brings it back to the house. Little drops of blood as bright as beads of glass; all blood should be so bright. He leaves the cat on the floor of the inside porch, and chuckles as he climbs into bed.

"What is it?" asks Angela.

He says, "Meow."

All men are crazy, she thinks.

In the morning, Matteo takes the cat outside. There is a pair of nails driven into the bark of an old poplar. He hangs the cat by its hind legs, and begins. He slits its belly, strips the guts, peels fur from flesh.

Dusty watches from the kitchen window. The cat is naked now, its long muscles pink as chewing gum; the air around his father is filled with tufts of fur. He remembers petting that cat, scratching its back and making it purr.

When Matteo is done with the cat, he returns to the house, and whistles as he washes his hands at the sink. The house cats move away from him.

"Come with me," he says to the boy. "We're going for a ride."

They arrive at the Silvaggio farm just before lunch. "Well, now, you must like the cooking over here. How did you like the deer?" asks Joe Silvaggio.

"Pretty good," says Matteo. "But today, it's my turn to supply fresh meat." Matteo hands his brother-in-law a package wrapped in brown paper. There are smiles all around – I do a favour for you, you do a favour for me; this is how life works.

"A rabbit, a nice one," says Silvaggio. "That's some pretty big rabbit." He hefts the package, implying that a rabbit is not as big as a haunch of deer; it's not big enough to balance the scales, but it will do for now. He uncorks a jug of chokecherry wine and takes two glasses from the sideboard. Filomena puts a cast-iron frying pan on the stove. The two men talk, and soon the smell of hot oil in the pan mingles with the smell of the tobacco.

"You go ahead, I'm not hungry," says Matteo. "Angela made us an early lunch. Perhaps some bread and jam for the boy. I'll take another glass of wine."

Silvaggio tucks in with knife and fork. He eats eagerly. "Hey, this is pretty good rabbit. You sure you won't have some?"

"No, you go ahead. It's good, eh? Eat your fill."

Silvaggio grunts. He chews the tiny bones until they are bare. He thinks, nobody has to tell me to eat my fill. He spits the bones out into his hand. He lines them up on the edge of his plate. He pushes his plate away and pours a cup of tea. "I couldn't eat another bite."

"It was good?"

"I said so, didn't I? I said it was good."

The two men sit in silence. Silvaggio lights a cigar, Matteo lights his pipe, and they smoke while Filomena clears the table.

Then Matteo strokes his moustache. "Meow."

Silvaggio sits up straight. "What did you say?"

Matteo draws a finger over his moustache the way a cat draws a paw over its whiskers. "Meow."

Silvaggio stares at his brother-in-law; has the man gone crazy? Is he making fun of me? Matteo smiles and strokes his moustache once again and says, "Meow." And then Silvaggio understands that his belly is full of cat. He sees at once that he has been paid back in full because of that dirty axe. So that's what Matteo meant by "Eat up, eat your fill."

Silvaggio's face turns bright red. "You son of a bitch!" He jumps up from the table. "Where's my gun?"

Matteo grabs his son and runs out the door. He throws the boy in the wagon, reaches for the reins, and slaps them hard against the rump of the horse. He is laughing, but not too hard; he is making a sharp turn onto the concession road when he hears the first shot. Buckshot splashes the gravel behind the wagon.

My father told this story whenever we were hunting rabbits along the trails in back of the old farm; he told it whenever he heard a cat at night, or when one of our house cats had kittens. He tells it now, as he is dying, not in so many words, but just as eloquently. He drew his finger across an imaginary moustache. He made a sound like a cat.

Eyes closed, he smiled.

And then he is suddenly awake. He looks at me as if he's never seen me before, as if he thought he was alone. His eyes widen, he wants to speak, he is frightened now.

It's okay, Pops. It's okay.

The Fifth Afternoon

*T*he house I grew up in is not my house any more.

I can see my mother's attempts to make it livable: her stiff curtains, her crystal bud vases, her tiny porcelain figurines in their pastel bonnets and hoop skirts, her rarely used teacups in the china cabinet next to his rarely used beer mugs.

My father's reclining chair, frayed and formed by the shape of his body, dominates the room. Beside it, within reach, is an end table with a rack of unused pipes, two books of crossword puzzles, a tin of Player's tobacco, a black glass ashtray, a package of cigarette papers, and a machine for rolling smokes.

I pour myself a breakfast whisky in the kitchen and return to the chair, determined to spend a moment in his world. He is not going to sit here again. I roll a cigarette by hand and, standing, light it. Then I sit in his chair and lean back, and put up my legs up and take a second stiff gulp of my drink and a mouthful of smoke.

I can smell him in the chair.

It was where he often slept, or rather floated an inch above sleep, while soundless late-night war movies played on the television, as if he were filling in the gaps in his own sub-liminal war.

There were nights when I would creep in late and turn the television off, which woke him more surely than the sound of my footsteps or my whispered "Pops, you awake?"

In the last year of his life, the chair would have been more familiar and more frightening each time he sat down. The soft slump of its cushion held the imprint of his healthy form. He was shrinking rapidly; he was lost in his old impression.

I look around the room. What did he see from this corner of the room? The television in front, the kitchen beyond, to his left the sidewalk and the street. If he chose to, he could see the fat white smoke which drifted over from the paper mill, but it is not always necessary to look; its smell is pungent and almost always present.

Above the entrance is the wooden crucifix with its little gilt Christ, arms outstretched, hands pinned to the wood. I gave the cross to my father as a Christmas present when I was young and full of fervour. I can see him reaching above the door frame, ready to tack a small nail into the wall. He strikes crookedly and says, "God damn it!"

The cross is hollow, I know it well. It slides apart like a wooden pencil case, revealing a compartment for two white candles, a vial of holy water, and a tiny scroll filled with instructions, "For use at the bedside of the dying."

The cross is meant to be laid flat on a table near the death-bed. The Christ can be slid off and made to stand upright in a grooved slot. The candles are to be lit when the priest comes, and the holy water is to be sprinkled during the per-formance of the last rites; the scroll contains prayers.

I gave it to him when I was ten. What must he have thought, to get this as a gift, and what must I have been thinking to give it?

I'd wanted, briefly, to be a priest. But I'd also hoped that, if he were reminded daily of Christ on the cross, he would not squabble with my mother. I'd hoped that he would not drink. I suppose in some way I'd been thinking of this moment, when I would be sitting in his chair, holding a cig-arette made with his tobacco, drinking a glass of his rye whisky, waiting for him to die.

It is almost time, after all these years.

I rise from the chair and lift the cross from its nail. It opens stiffly. The wood is dried out, brittle. Inside, all is as I remember. A time capsule of death. Except that the candles have warped and turned a pale yellow, the rolled-up instruc-tions have crumbled, and the holy water evaporated years ago.

I do not want to think of death.

In the heat of an afternoon in June, I think instead of Christmas.

Dusty's love of holidays was equal to his love of drink. He always bought himself some little gift, a child's toy, and set it under the tree. "What's this? For me? Whatever could it be?"

A kaleidoscope, a spinning top, a wind-up duck that waddled across the floor and frightened the cats, or one of those plastic birds that dips its beak to drink when it sits perched on the edge of his glass. His laughter was gleeful; he was more innocent than we were.

We gave him conventional presents: a bottle of aftershave, a tie, sometimes a flat fifty of Export "A" cigarettes. Things he needed, things he'd use. Nothing pleased him so much as the toy he bought himself. His endearing selfishness. His right to be surprised.

He'd have wrapped his little gift, and tagged it, "To Dusty from Santa." After all the other presents had been opened, he'd pick up this last one and hold it to his ear and give it a shake. "Well now, what do you suppose this is?" He was reliving his childhood.

Of course, he knew what was in the little bright packages. He knew, as surely as he knew what was in the presents he'd collected as Christmas tips from the people on his mail route: if a package was small but heavy for its size, it was a mickey of rye or Scotch; if it was a solid rectangle the approximate size of a book, it was a box of chocolates; and if it was a hard, thin square, it was a tin box of cigarettes.

"Reach into my bag, there are some envelopes; bring them here."

Envelopes at Christmas contained money, sometimes two bucks, sometimes ten, on rare occasions a twenty from one of the rich families in one of the big houses. Some years he hauled in as much as two hundred dollars, the payoff for a year's worth of whistling while he worked. A bonus for remembering faces, trading quips, and scratching the ears of dogs. A payoff for his *Italianitta*.

When Christmas approached there was more and more mail, and he worked later every night, and came home slower and drunker. I worried that he might smash the car. I waited at the window, eight o'clock, nine o'clock, ten o'clock. I waited until I saw a pair of headlights make the turn and I recognized our car. When he was drunk he drove with exaggerated caution, fifteen miles an hour, straight as an arrow down the centre of the empty street.

As I grew older, I became angry at him for the way he worried my mother, for the way he worried me, for the way he worried my younger brothers. I cultivated a young man's indifference, a mask for my contempt.

The winter when I was sixteen, I got temporary work at the post office delivering mail during the Christmas rush. I was assigned to his route. Nepotism may have been the basis for the hiring of temporary help, but it was usually avoided when it came to the assignment of routes. He must have pulled a few strings. It would be easier if I screwed up on his walk, rather than on one of the others; he was saving himself from embarrassment, and looking out for me. He stayed inside to sort the mail, and I carried a sackful of Christmas cards out into the hard white cold of morning.

There was always snow then, and it was always knee-deep, and the sidewalks were always unshovelled. Letters are slippery in the cold and hard to handle when you're wearing gloves; I went out barehanded. Thanks to previous walks around the route with Dusty, I knew which apartment buildings had foyers in which I could stop and warm my hands.

I was a Santa Claus of sorts. I had a sackful of holiday cards, support cheques from the government, and magazines for old men in striped pyjamas and old women in flower-print housecoats and fuzzy slippers.

One old man surprised me by pulling his front door open just as I bent to slip his mail through the slot. I found myself about to drop a handful of envelopes on a pair of yellow feet. I looked up. He was unshaven. His pyjama shirt was open. He held a cigarette between orange-stained fingers. I knew he lived alone; the house smelled of liquor and sleep, of tobacco and warmed-over bacon fat.

I straightened, smiled, and handed him six cards. Who would send cards to an old man like this? He must have had plenty of relatives; he didn't look like a man with friends. He looked me in the eye, oblivious to the cold, as if the sight of me was an affront.

"Where's Dusty?"

I said there was so much mail that he'd stayed inside to do the sorting. The old man scowled and wondered what the hell he was going to do with the Christmas tip. He always gave Dusty a tip, Dusty was his friend, they went way back.

I said I'd deliver the envelope with the tip. He looked at me quizzically, as if I were tricking him. And then I smiled and said, "Dusty's my dad."

"You're Dusty's boy? Well, Jesus Christ, why didn't you say so? You better come in and have a drink."

It was eight in the morning.

"No, I couldn't, really."

I had a long day ahead of me. The mailbag weighed forty-five pounds when it was full. It cut into my shoulder and made it hard for me to keep my balance on the slippery steps and icy walks. And the load got lighter half an ounce at a time.

"Whaddya mean, you won't take a drink?"

The old man was suddenly insulted; he'd been waiting since early morning for my father; more to the point, he was waiting for an excuse to crack the bottle and take his first drink. What would Dusty have done?

"Oh, well, that's very kind of you. Sure, I'll just have a short one."

"That's better. What's your pleasure?"

He disappeared into the house before I could answer. I stepped inside, took off the mailbag, and pulled the door closed behind me. He returned with a bottle and two glasses and poured a double for me, and a double double for himself.

"Merry Christmas, har, har!"

We touched glasses and threw our drinks down the hatch. And then he poured another and I couldn't jerk my hand away because he'd have poured the liquor on the floor and there would have been an incident. I drank the second drink slowly, two sips.

"Your dad's a helluva guy." I nodded my head. "Yar, he's a

helluva guy." I grinned. "God-damn good musician! He plays a good trombone."

"Yes, sir, pretty good."

The old man plucked a pack of cigarettes from the breast pocket of his pyjamas. I declined a smoke. When there's work to do, you do the work. After, when the work is done, then you can stop and take a smoke. Although sometimes you have to stop and take a drink. And then you can drink what you like, you can drink as much as – the heat of the house was getting to me. I thanked the old man, and said I had work to do.

"Oh, Jesus, don't let me keep you from your work. A man's got to do his work, har, har. I don't work any more. I got hurt. I'm too old. I'm too sick to work." His eyes began to well with tears.

I buttoned my coat in a hurry and shook his hand, refusing to splash pity on anyone so early in the morning. I wished him Merry Christmas and stepped into the cold. He closed the door, and then cracked it open and called me back.

"Wait a minute, you forgot this!"

He handed me the envelope with Dusty's tip. "Are you sure you won't take another drink?" he asked as he closed the door in my face.

Twice more that morning, old drunk men were waiting to pour Dusty a Christmas drink, and twice more I took his place and drank what was meant for him, and the cold hit me in the head at the same time the liquor did, and I was spinning drunk by lunch.

I was Dusty's boy. And now I understood why he was so

often drunk at this time of year. He couldn't say no. His drunkenness at Christmas was just one of the family rituals. There were others.

Every year the merchants in the west end of Fort William held a draw on Christmas Eve: they gave away turkeys, trinkets, certificates for merchandise, and a grand prize of money. Plenty of money. We bought a book of tickets every year and lived in hope for the week leading up to the draw. On Christmas Eve, entire families went down to watch the winning tickets pulled from a drum.

My father was always late to come home from work on Christmas Eve, but not always unreasonably so. Often there was so much mail he'd have walked his route twice, and when he finally came in his beard would be weighted with ice, his eyebrows white with frost, and his fingers red and stiff as claws.

Too late, too tired, too cold.

He took off his wool hat and his great double-breasted reefer coat with the brass buttons, and he sat at the kitchen table and warmed his hands around a bowl of soup.

"Here, Joe. You look lucky tonight. You take the tickets and go to the draw. Go on, now, and win us some money."

Me, take the tickets? I was nine years old. I quickly put two pairs of socks on my feet, wrapped two scarves around my neck, and carefully slid the tickets inside the pair of gloves I wore inside my mitts. I wanted to keep the tickets next to my skin. I didn't want to lose them.

Win us a prize, Joe!

The street was quiet; there was no sound but my footsteps squeaking on packed snow, and the whistle of the razor-cold wind. I lowered my head and hurried along. From the corner of my eye I could see bright light pouring from the houses on each side of the street: living-room curtains open, other people's trees lit up inside. The wind filled my eyes with tears, and the lights blurred and became more beautiful.

I wanted very much to win the draw. I didn't want my parents to argue about money. I made the sign of the cross when I passed in front of the church. I prayed for luck and apologized to Jesus because I prayed for luck: *I know it's wrong, but honest, Jesus, the money isn't for me, it's for my parents.*

The intersection of Brown and Frederica was blocked off with bales of hay. A wagon and a team of horses stood in the middle of the street, as if ready for a hayride. A hundred people surrounded the wagon, stamping their feet.

I was freezing, my cheeks burned hot, my fingers tingled. The sky was black and clear and pricked with stars. The windows of all the shops in Westfort were dressed in red and green, and white plumes of breath rose above each head in the crowd, as if they were cartoon word-balloons: *Let me win.*

We waited for the mayor. We waited and we eyed each other; one of us would win, the rest would not. We tried to glare the luck of others away. It better not be you, you bastard; it better be me who wins. Now and then, one of the horses would shit and everyone would laugh and point at the steaming lumps.

Men began to clap their hands impatiently. They swore

under their breath and into their beards, their scarves. Inside my glove, the tickets had turned soft from the sweat of my palms. A man elbowed me aside and said with a soft and absent slur, "God damn, it's cold. Where the hell's the mayor?" Another man, also drunk, answered, "He's not freezing his ass in the cold, that's for sure." A woman glared at them. Someone said, "I think he's here. Make way for the mayor, here he comes."

A long black car pulled up; the purr of the engine made the horses fret. More muttering: only a city slicker with a soft head would drive his car carelessly in front of a team of horses in a crowd.

Ernie Reed stepped out of the back of the black car, he smiled and shook a few hands and, with the help of the crowd, he hopped up onto the wagon and waved and wished us all Merry Christmas. I watched my neighbours forget how cold they were and cheer. *That Ernie, geez, he's just a regular guy.* A regular guy whose pearl-grey topcoat had a velvet collar. A regular guy wearing grey suede gloves, spotless and clean. A regular guy with a homburg on his head. He was sleek and soft; a regular rich guy.

It isn't hard to remember how I felt. I hated feeling as if all I had was hope. I hated knowing that everyone who had come out in the cold on Christmas Eve had been drawn by the same hope; hope was useless.

And I thought it wrong that a man like the mayor, who didn't work hard, should have an easier life than a man like my father, who worked very hard. I knew how badly work hurt my father, it made him meaner and harder. And I knew the pain of working for poor wages gave him an easy excuse to drink.

The mayor pulled his gloves tight and made a little speech. One of his lackeys spun the drum, and the mayor reached inside and called out the lucky number: not mine. Again the drum spun: not mine, not mine. I didn't win a thing, not the turkey, not the merchandise, not the trinkets, not the money. Nothing.

I walked home with the useless tickets in my glove. I wanted to rip them to shreds, but then I thought I should bring them home to show my parents, because there might have been a mistake, because someone might call, you never knew. . . .

I walked past the church again on the way home and did not pray this time. I did not make the sign of the cross. I felt betrayed again by the love of God; if you pray, all things will come to you except the things you want, when you want them. Or when you need them.

When I got home I opened the door and was hit in the face with a blast of heat. The furnace was stoked. Our Christmas tree, such as it was, was ablaze with tinsel and a string of coloured lights. My father had warmed up enough to have stripped off his shirt. He raised his glass with a shout: "Hello, Joe, whaddya know? Are we rich?"

I couldn't say a word. My face was numb from the cold. I didn't know what to say; I couldn't begin to know. There was no need to say anything. He told me to take off my boots and wrap my hands around a hot cup of tea. All thoughts of the draw were put aside and, mercifully, I began to think about what I might find under the tree in the morning.

The draw was not important. I knew it didn't matter but I felt foolish for having had such flimsy hopes. When no one was looking, I plucked the soft warm tickets from the inside of my gloves and threw them in the garbage.

The Fifth Night

I asked for the old stories often as a boy. I wanted to know
who I was, who my father was, and where my family had
come from. I needed clues. These old stories were the foun-
dation on which the family had been built, they were the
very material of which each of us – my father, my uncles, my
cousins – were made. My great-uncle had killed a man in a
fit of temper; my father and his brothers were hot, swift,
and unpredictable.

A patina of confusion dulled certain details. There were
missing pieces and inexplicable facts. Some of the tales were
as improbable as opera. And there was a darkness in the way
my father told a story which fired my imagination.

He rarely explained; he described. I pressed him for details.
He refused to invent. For most of us, repeated memories lose

their sharpness in time, and remembered faces tend to soften and grow indistinct, like the portraits on the faces of overused coins. But I trusted Dusty.

He knew the structure of the family narrative, and whenever he told me what he knew, he laid it out the same way every time. I trusted the sound of his voice; if he faltered, he started again the same way, until he recovered the rhythm.

There was magic in his repetition. He gave me what had been given to him; he gave it the way it had been given to him. He spoke like a veteran of an ancient battle fought long ago, in the days before tales were written down; he was the last survivor sitting by a fire remembering the bravery of heroes, singing the old stories because songs are easier to remember.

I often asked him why he didn't know more. "Little pitchers have big ears," he said. His mother and father, his aunt Filomena and his uncle Joe refused to talk about the past. For a reason: some people have long memories for grievance. You never know who's listening.

As I grew up, I imagined the details of the stories for myself. I wore Silvaggio's pride and took his place in the wagon. I wondered how would it feel if some son of a bitch came up behind me and tried to force me off the road. I endured the heat of the day. I invented the peasants in the fields, and I made light of them. Like a traitor, I stood in a wagon with a whip and wondered why Silvaggio wouldn't let me by. I flinched when the shot rang out.

I sought indirect ways to learn more.

I asked my father what he knew about Ripabottoni. He said it was somewhere in the mountains. What was it like? He thought there were wolves and wild boar in the woods, herds of sheep on the sides of the hills, and hard wheat in the high valleys.

I went to my uncles; they brushed me off. I was ignored, or glared at, or hushed: "How the hell do I know? Why do you want to know about that old stuff?" They were born here; the past is the past, it didn't concern them.

And a sin remembered is a sin.

I thought all the old sins were my inheritance. I stared at the old sinners in the family album and willed them to speak. Joe and Matteo standing in their thick black suits. Gold chains hanging from the pockets of their vests. Thickly curled moustaches. Faces set hard with defiance and pride.

My grandmother Angela Maria Delvecchio, stiff and unforgiving. My great-aunt Filomena, a hint of tenderness in her smile. The women in their quaint black hats and old-country dresses, waists cinched, with gold crosses around their necks and children on their laps. I was not one of them, they died before I was born.

But they gave rise to me.

On the fifth night of his dying, he still does not want to eat. I hector him, and try to take the measure of my hope with his teaspoon. One tiny bite, one tiny bit of strength, a minute more of life.

He turns up his nose at the smell of hospital roast pork, will not open his lips, refuses the watery potatoes, pale carrots, and wrinkled peas. He shakes his head at the rusty salad, the glass of lukewarm milk, but he takes a little apple sauce. As much as will fit on the tip of a spoon; baby food in a baby's portion.

He does not swallow.

A minute passes, and another. Then finally, I see his Adam's apple move, and he dabs the corner of his mouth with a tissue. I resist heaping praise on him, as if he were in a high chair.

I can't shake the feeling that I've done this before, but not because I fed my son with a spoon when he was a baby. I still keep a note in my desk drawer, scribbled when I was four-teen. I had dreamed my father was an infant, mute and help-less, dreamed that he was sitting in bed. And in the dream I sat at his side and fed him with a spoon.

I had that dream the year he bought the apple tree.

I dreaded the sporadic attacks of his green thumb. My older brother was beyond him now, my little brothers were too young, so whenever Dusty got the urge to garden, I was the one who did his bidding. I dug the soil, collected slugs and potato bugs in an old tin and drowned them in boiling water. I carved dandelions from the lawn in the spring, which he made us eat in salads. And I worked a load of horse manure into the earth while the flies danced around me in the sun.

We lived in a house built to accommodate the veterans who came home from the war and wanted to start families. It was a two-bedroom stucco bungalow, pink and white, on a street of bungalows.

Dusty couldn't afford it. He had no job when I was born; we'd been living in a borrowed shack at the foot of Mount Mackay. The doctor told him I'd die if I spent another winter in the bush. He said, "What the hell do you want me to do about it?" The doctor arranged for him to get a mortgage.

Dusty didn't know the first thing about fruit, or planting trees. But he directed me to dig a hole in the middle of the back yard, where the tree would be the most visible from the kitchen. No matter if it was entirely in the wrong place, in the way of everything.

In his mind, there was an ideal, a golden mean of apples.

He thought it was possible to achieve this simply because he yearned to do so; his will was made not of iron, but of yearning. He made me help him because, if the tree bore fruit, he'd have done his duty as a man and as a father – he'd have taught me all there was to know about growing apples.

If the tree withered, I'd be invited to wonder if the fault lay in the weather, and to consider if some tiny but crucial fact had been overlooked. Perhaps it was the wrong month of the year or phase of the moon or time of day to plant this kind of tree. Implicit in this was the notion that any outcome depended on luck and the purity of one's desire; as for skill, it helped, sure, but you couldn't trust it. He lived a life in which all results were random.

He filled the bottom of the hole with fertilizer, loosened the root ball, lifted the tree and sunk it with a grunt, stood back, had me straighten it this way and that, and then he held it steady while I filled the hole with dirt, packed it under his guidance, flooded it, let the water soak in, and flooded it again.

Eating apples in our imagination.

I was told to fill a five-gallon bucket with water and pour it at the base of the tree every morning for the rest of the summer.

I was his accomplice in apples. One night when I was very young and he and my mother were bickering again, I awoke in tears, inconsolable because I thought with a child-ish selfishness that it somehow meant they didn't love me. He got up, dried my tears, and sat me on his knee.

"Don't you know you're my little apple?"

I had a stake in that tree.

But there was no fruit of any kind the first year and none the second, in spite of the buckets filled and hauled and poured.

Over the second winter, he seemed to give up on the tree, to abandon his desire; it had betrayed him. He was no longer interested in talking about the apples of the future. After supper he stayed inside and drank his tea. He refused to look out the kitchen window. He sat in his chair and read the paper. He gave up.

In the spring of the third year, there was a profusion of pink blossoms; oh well, there had been blossoms before. The little tree seemed especially busy with bees; there had been bees before. But this time, the blossoms turned into fruit over the summer: we were going to have apples, plenty of them.

The tree was young, and the fruit it bore was fat and round and golden. The apples grew so large and there were so many of them, it seemed as if the smaller branches might break. My father stood with his hands on his hips and a smile on his face, a man of the soil rewarded.

When it was time, he culled two and bit into one; and as he bit, he swore and swallowed and bit again, as if in disbelief. He danced a turnaround jig on the grass, like a man who'd rolled a pair of dice on his last dollar and won more money in the tumble of a moment than could be carried in a sack.

"God damn it, that's good!"

He ate as if he were sinking his teeth into a heaven of his own creation. He gave an apple to me. I held it in both hands and bit; nothing sweeter since. We ate, and juice ran down our wrists. These were long-odds apples, dumb-luck apples, an accident of bees, apples proof of magic. The neighbours shook their heads. What the hell kind of magic is this? No one had seen anything like it, apples bigger than softballs. Dusty smiled, as if he'd known all along that he'd bought a magic tree, that it was only a matter of time, of faith, of yearning.

The following year there were fewer apples; they were still as sweet, but the tree seemed to be resting, catching its breath somehow. There were no apples at all after that. The tree was somehow, suddenly, barren. I watered it, he coaxed it, I stopped giving it water, he fed it fertilizer, and we wondered whether each new cure was killing it.

I'm sure my father whispered little apple prayers; I'm certain there were nights on the bandstand when he aimed his trombone in the direction of the tree and blew sweet notes at it through the cigarette smoke, across the darkness of the city. Nothing doing.

The tree was barren, and it died. It didn't matter; done once and done well was well done forever and never needed to be done again. Dusty had those apples in mind as long as he lived, and the fact that they existed briefly was proof enough for eternity.

A cheap but useful trick, now that I needed one.

"Remember the apple tree, Pops?"

It was as if I'd whistled the opening bars of a familiar song. He couldn't resist. He opened his mouth and tilted his head in remembered pleasure. I gave him some more apple sauce. He swallowed, and dabbed at the corner of his mouth with a folded tissue.

He dabbed at his mouth until he fell asleep.

In the morning, I saw the sun rise behind the hospital: slowly, light diluted the darkness the way water dilutes ink. I saw the soft grey underbellies of the clouds. I saw the wet sheen on the leaves on the tallest trees. He was going to die.

There was no hope, and nothing to do.

The Sixth Night

I grew up believing there was a mark on me. I knew it came through my grandfather by way of Joe Silvaggio, and through my father to me. But I discovered there was another mark on us through my grandmother's side of the family. This was no myth; there was proof.

One night when Dusty was at a dance job and my mother was waiting on tables at the supper club, I snuck into their room, opened his dresser drawer, and carefully pawed through the things hidden there.

I found a pocket knife and opened it; the blade was dull and loose, the handle cheap. I folded it again and put it back, exactly as I had found it. I picked up his military medals; the weight of them was heroic, even though I knew he hadn't had much of a war.

I left the pistol where it was. Behind it, however, there were some newspapers. I had never really looked at them before. The gun got in the way. It was not wise to tamper with talismanic objects. And I knew if he suspected me of going through his things, he'd have whipped me with his razor strap.

Usually, whenever I opened his dresser drawer, I did so in darkness. I left the bedroom light turned off in case, for some reason, he came home early and saw the light, a giveaway. This time, however, I turned it on and read.

The newspapers contained an account of an old murder in Spokane, Washington. A man named Delvecchio had died of a bullet in the brain; he was shot to death by a man named Joe Delio. A hard story, a cruel death, a mystery. My grandmother was a Delvecchio.

Was there a connection to us?

I read the yellow text for clues, and learned this much:

Joe Delio was the king of the Italian colony in Spokane. He was a padrone: if you were sick, you went to him for help; if you were broke, he lent you money; if you needed work, he'd see what he could do. He was a man of respect. He was making his way in the new world.

The padrone had many business interests. Among other things, he owned a bar. But he could not devote all his attention to selling sour beer and pickled eggs, so he chose a partner.

Tony Delvecchio was young and strong, hard-headed and unafraid. The two men had strong ties; their families came from the same tiny village in the hills of Italy. Ripabottoni.

Delio lived in an apartment behind the bar. Delvecchio lived in a house across the street. At first, the partnership prospered. The two men had growing families, and their wives became friends. But the padrone began to harbour suspicions about his young protégé. There was a series of little slights; some nights, the receipts from the bar seemed light; there were stray remarks, unexplained silences. Delio thought perhaps Delvecchio was envious; perhaps he wished for a larger share of the money; perhaps he wished to become a man of influence himself.

Something was wrong.

If you do a favour for a man, you expect that he will to do a favour in return; it's the way of the world. But if you lend someone a hand, and he fucks you in the ass and laughs behind your back, you put a stop to it or else you are a fool.

One night, Delio rang for three glasses of beer. Delvecchio was working behind the bar. He brought a tray. Delio took a glass of beer and gave it to his wife; he declined to take one for himself.

According to the news stories, Delvecchio was confused. Hadn't his partner asked for three glasses of beer? He offered the tray to Delio; once again, the padrone declined. "You help yourself," he said. "You go ahead. You like to help yourself."

Suddenly the air was charged.

Delvecchio asked Delio why he would call for three glasses of beer and give one to the woman, but refuse to take one for himself. Once again, Delio said, "You go ahead, you help yourself."

Help yourself, help yourself. Was this a joke?

"Why won't you drink with me?"

Delio spoke slowly, carefully. "I don't like to drink with a man who helps himself at my expense, a man who thinks I'm stupid enough not to notice, a man who thinks I can't count."

"Madonna, you think I'm a cheat?"

"Since you said it, now I'm sure of it."

The two men spat curses at each other, curses which, once uttered, could not be taken back. And then Delvecchio lost his head and pulled a pistol from his apron; blind with rage, he fired at his partner's head. He missed.

It was his last mistake.

Delio rushed Delvecchio. There was a struggle. Delio reached for the gun, he twisted his partner's hand. There was another shot. Delvecchio staggered backward with a bullet in his brain.

Delio's wife told police, "in broken English and between fits of weeping," that Tony Delvecchio fell back against the living-room wall. His eyes were open; something other than blood trickled from the hole in his head.

He lived for one more hour.

Above the last beats of his heart, Tony Delvecchio would have heard his killer running down the stairs. He would have heard Signora Delio weep and shriek and flee.

Delvecchio could no longer see. But then he heard his wife's voice. Signora Delvecchio cried her husband's name and the names of the saints and collapsed by his side.

Delio ran to the bar next door, where he knew his brother-in-law was drinking; the two men jumped in a car and headed for the hills. The padrone had Delvecchio's gun.

Perhaps the king of the Italian colony was feared more than liked; perhaps he had helped himself by prospering on the misfortunes of others. From the *Spokane Spokesman-Review* of December 14, 1903:

> Immediately after the shooting friends of the dead man were very scarce, but now every hour is bringing fresh ones to the surface. His friends are busy as ants securing evidence to implicate Delio for the murder of Delvecchio. But they are extremely secretive, and nine out of every ten of them stoutly insist that they cannot speak English. To reporters and policemen alike, when questioned, they reply with a shrug of the shoulders and a monosyllabic "Dunno."

The not-so-subtle language of the time. The reporter meant, simply, that most of these god-damn dagos can speak English when they want to, but when it comes to protecting their own, why they clam right up.

There was talk in the papers about the failure of the police to react quickly enough to catch the shooter, given that the police station was only four blocks away, even if the shooter was only an Italian; but that talk was quickly overshadowed by excitement of the manhunt.

Delio leapt from the car on the outskirts of Spokane and fled on foot through the bush, through the snow, intent on following a rough trail north to British Columbia. Two days later, hungry and half-frozen, he turned up in Valley,

Washington. He stumbled into a hotel, ordered a plate of food and a bottle of beer, after which "he was so tired he could hardly drag himself upstairs and lock himself in his room, though he managed to shove his bed against the door to make himself doubly safe against attacks."

Not safe enough; the innkeeper was a police constable. He recognized the fugitive from a description in the paper, even though Delio kept his head down, his collar up, and his hat pulled over his eyes. Or perhaps because the fugitive kept his head down, his collar up, his hat pulled over his eyes.

The next morning, at four o'clock, Delio snuck out of the hotel when he thought no one was looking and fled into the woods. The innkeeper saw which way he was headed. He knew he'd have no trouble tracking him in the snow.

Two hours later, as the sun began to rise, the posse caught up with Delio. The padrone was lying in the snow, half-hidden by a clump of brush, protected by a fallen log. The leader of the posse called for Delio to give up. But the king of the Italian colony was a king; he refused to surrender to these Americans, ignorant men who know nothing about blood and honour. He would die like a man.

He stood and emptied the pistol at his pursuers. They cut him down with a volley of bullets, and he "fell with his face buried in the snow and the revolver with which he killed Delvecchio clasped in a death grip."

The murder was no longer front-page news. And the two fresh widows, wiser than their husbands, took over the bar and went into partnership for themselves.

I folded the paper carefully, making sure to replace it just so. I didn't want to arouse suspicion. Over the next few weeks, I asked innocent questions. Where did his mother come from? What was she like? Did she have any relatives? What happened to the rest of her family?

Dusty eventually told me about the murder, not knowing that I already knew. He added that the nephew of the slain man was the great hockey player for the Detroit Red Wings, Alex Delvecchio, who grew up in Fort William. Alex Delvecchio, related to me by blood! Suddenly it was difficult to cheer openly for the Montreal Canadiens.

Dusty hadn't known his mother's brother, Tony Delvecchio, even though there were pictures of him, stiff-necked and arrogant, in the family album. But there it was, out in the open: his uncle had been murdered in a saloon.

This was not a story I could brag about, nor share with my friends, or my schoolmates. I had to keep it to myself, the stain of it. Dirty murdering wops, dirty murdered wops, it was all the same: hotheaded sons of bitches.

In a way it seemed to balance the flight of Joe Silvaggio from Italy. One of my great-uncles had killed a man in a fit of temper, and one of my great-uncles had been killed in a fit of temper. The truth is, these stories were a little too close for comfort. They were the far end of a very familiar line. We were well-acquainted with the fit of temper; we had our own schemes and passions, our hunger for money, and our grief.

When I was growing up, December 1903 was not so long ago. "Wops" were one step up from Indians and blacks on the social scale, and I never saw a black man in Fort William until sometime in the 1960s.

The stain of murder and the stigma of race.

Once, according to my father, a man came to Fort William from the old country, a tough guy. He took a set of rooms in the Coal Docks, in the east end of town. He carried himself with a swagger and began to make himself known. He wasn't related to anyone, no one knew who he was, but he wore a red kerchief knotted under his ear, just so; a sign he was connected.

One day the stranger went to the fruit store, took the sweetest oranges, and walked out without paying. The next day, he went to the butcher shop and demanded the best meat. When the butcher asked to be paid, the stranger said, "If you know what's good for you, you'll wrap my veal and you'll keep your mouth shut. You want something bad to happen, you just keep talking."

At first, no one protested. But gradually, people began to talk. They discovered that the stranger wasn't connected to anyone. He'd been bluffing. Police eventually found his body under the bridge at the foot of Syndicate Avenue. His throat was slit from ear to ear, perhaps with a butcher knife. The red kerchief was stuffed in his mouth.

Who did it? Who knows?

The moral?

No story of Dusty's was delivered with just one moral, and the story of the stranger with the red kerchief at his throat had several, which my father communicated with a shrug, a raised eyebrow, a drained glass. Don't be afraid of who you are, but don't try to pass yourself off as something you're not. Don't throw your weight around. Never mind stupid people who can't pronounce your name. Don't take advantage. Don't lie. Be yourself. And above all, don't talk big because if you can't back it up, you have no one to blame but yourself.

I kept my mouth shut about our murders.

The Seventh Night

*F*ather Maurice arrives early in the evening, after supper. He is a mild priest with a pale complexion, fine hair, and a round face, the sort of man who smiles hopefully, no matter what the circumstances. He smiles at my father.

Dusty stiffens at the sight of the black suit and white collar; he is stoned on morphine, embarrassed but almost pleased by the feeling of floating weightlessness. He is happy to be helpless. He is trying not to hallucinate.

Had he been completely lucid, I'm not sure Dusty could have told me the name of this priest. He didn't go to church often, and when he did it was almost as if he went in the abstract; call it a hedging of old bets. But now he sniffs and turns away; he sees the collar and recognizes "priest."

Father Maurice smiles again — actually, he never stops smiling. His face is frozen in a perpetual and idiotic rictus. He does not ask my father how he is feeling. He opens instead with what must be his standard pitch.

"Well, Lawrence, you must be thankful. You've lived a long life and now it is your time. Your sons are here. You must begin to prepare yourself to leave."

If this priest had known my father, or if he'd tried to learn a few facts before he came, he'd have called him Dusty and he'd have chosen his words carefully. What he'd have said was, "Tough it out, soldier."

Dusty turns his head slightly; when he regards something with distaste, he prefers to view it at an angle, his lips pursed, his right eyebrow arched. If he could spit, he would.

I know what he is thinking: "What a load of crap. For the love of Christ, will somebody do me a favour and get this lugubrious prick away from me?" I nearly laugh.

But the lugubrious prick of a priest does not understand that a point is being made, he does not appreciate that an old man in a morphine stupor on his deathbed can make a point with a sidelong glance. Then Father Maurice does the unthinkable: he touches my father's arm and makes the sign of the cross over him.

Dusty cannot duck the blessing, but he recoils. If it is not extreme, it is still a form of unction. He has just been told that he may as well give up now, all hope is gone, he is dying in his bed. It is a moment of unthinking cruelty.

Dusty always had an uneasy relationship with priests.

I remember lying on the floor reading comic books by the heat of the register the winter of the year I made my Confirmation. Dusty came home after delivering mail during a bitter day-long snowstorm. His hands were numb, his nose was running, his eyes watered; he had a wet cold. He slammed the door behind him and said, "Son of a bitch!"

My mother asked him what was wrong; she was expecting to hear my father rage against the weather.

"That god-damned Corrigan!"

I looked up, frightened. Corrigan was the monsignor of St. Agnes Church, our church. It shocked me then to hear a priest being cursed. My father sneezed and pulled off his coat, kicked off his snowy boots, and pulled a bottle of cheap port from his mailbag.

"What's Corrigan done now?" my mother asked. "And please don't swear in front of the boys."

"Ah, for Christ's sake, that's not swearing. I was at the liquor store picking up a bottle. Who's ahead of me in line? That son of a bitch of a priest. And he's got two bottles of Johnny Walker in his hand. Two bottles of Scotch, and all I've got is this bloody porchclimber.

"I look at him. I look at both his bottles. And he just smiles at me. 'Aheh, aheh!' he says, in that voice. "Aheh, aheh. For my throat. I've got a bit of cold.' The son of a bitch!"

My father was good at casting himself as an underdog, but even I got his point. Two-Gun Corrigan – so called because of his shoot-from-the-hip, shoot-from-the-lip sermons – was a hard-edged, red-nosed whisky priest. When he preached from the pulpit, white-hot sparks of spittle flew from his mouth. My father dismissed him, but he kept an eye on him, the way you'd watch a snake.

I learned to do the same.

When I went to church, I was in the habit of kneeling at the railing of the choir loft. I liked to stare down at the bald spots of the important men of the parish. They were rich, we were poor; they were respectable, Dusty drank. And so they excluded my father from the honour of being an usher, nor was he allowed to take up the collection. My revenge was to take pleasure in mocking their vanity.

I studied the absurdity of their comb-overs. They may have had money and new cars and fat Knights of Columbus rings on their fingers; my father had a fine head of hair. I cuckolded these men from on high. I stared at their wives; the slope of this one's shoulders, the long pale curve of that one's neck. I was a connoisseur of the wisps of hair that fell carelessly from beneath their hats.

This morning's mass was rich in promise. Corrigan stormed up to the altar from a side door, trailing altar boys in his wake. His Latin was slurred and swift. He was drunk. The sermon was going to be mercifully short.

I wasn't much interested in a sermon. I was looking for Mrs. McRae; she was always worth watching. She wore a hat with a wide white brim, and a dress that revealed a creamy pillow of cleavage and her expansive, muscular back. I could see the straps of her slip, I could detect the clasps of her bra.

If she dressed a little too showily, she was given some latitude by the rest of the parish because she was a widow with three daughters, and if a revealing dress was what it took to find a father for those girls, why then all was forgiven, and all was understood.

I found her much more sensual in appearance than any of her girls, who were my age; the thought made me blush.

Corrigan cleared his brogue of phlegm, slapped his missal, and broke the spell. He paused, and opened the sermon softly. "Those among us who are true followers of Christ are aware they must support the works of Holy Mother Church. We do this freely because what is given in this world will be returned to us a hundredfold in the next.

"The bishop is trying to build a new Catholic high school in Fort William. I have asked you time and time again to give as much as you can, because I know you want your sons and daughters to be educated all the way to Fifth Form according to the faith."

He was as sure of this as he was of the sunrise.

His voice rose, his face reddened. "But every week I must go to the cathedral and make my report to Bishop Jennings. And do you know what the Bishop says to me? He says nothing! Do you know how it feels when, every week, week after week, I have to tell him that the people of this parish have once again given less than the people of St. Ann's? Less than the people of St. Stan's?"

His eyes narrowed into slits.

"It isn't for us to decide for ourselves what must be done. The Church in its wisdom decides, and you – each one of you – must find it in your hearts to respond with generosity, for good work is its own reward."

He hammered the pulpit with his hand. "I don't want to say who is to blame. I don't want to single out any one group." Oh, but he did. There was no stopping him. I saw my father stiffen.

Corrigan did not like Italians. In particular, he did not like Fioritos. He'd refused to say the funeral mass for my uncle Tony, who'd returned from the trenches of France an atheist. Corrigan despised my uncle Dave the communist free-thinker, my uncle Dominic the profligate, my uncle Frank the brawling union man. He sneered openly at my father for his late nights, his fondness for women, his love of the bottle.

Corrigan had deigned to bury my grandfather, old Matteo. But even that was not without incident. He'd said the funeral mass and heaped the honey of his praise on my grand-father's head: Matteo Fiorito was a humble man who had come from the old country prepared to work hard; he'd raised a dozen kids, cleared two farms, endured the death of chil-dren, cut wood in the bush, built a fine house with his own hands, sponsored other Italians, and sent sons to both world wars. Even if, the tone of his voice suggested, those sons were inferior men.

He told of how old Matteo had walked to church winter and summer, through rain and snow, and had taken Communion with his late wife, Angela, every morning for more than twenty years before she died.

And then in the presence of my relatives, all of them, and in front of all the other mourners, Corrigan spat contempt at each of my uncles in turn. He said they didn't deserve to have had the love of such a fine, god-fearing man as Matteo. He said they were not good sons, they were not good men, they ought to feel ashamed because they did not go to church, they were schemers and dreamers, they were cruel to their children and unfaithful to their wives.

He said they were not worthy to carry Matteo's coffin.

He'd hit a nerve. He couldn't possibly have known. It was a lucky shot. My father and his brothers had in fact botched the carrying of the coffin; it was a tight turn from the front room into the hall of the house on Francis Street, and grief is blind and drunk and you could never get any of my uncles to push or pull in the same direction at the same time. They'd dropped their father in his coffin.

How could Corrigan have known?

My uncle Dominic leapt to his feet. His fists were clenched, the cords in his neck stood out, his eyes bulged white. "I don't give a good god damn if he is a priest, he can't talk about us like that. It's disrespectful to Pop. Why, I oughtta go up there and punch him in the mouth."

My uncle Frank grabbed his brother's hand, put an arm around his shoulder, looked him in the eye and sat him down, whispering harshly: "Pop's dead, and it's bad enough the way it is now; let it go." Storming the altar and punching a priest was too much, even for a Fiorito; at least not in church, and not during the old man's funeral.

Corrigan broke through my reverie with fresh and bloody thunder about the building of the high school. "Good work costs money." He thumped the pulpit with the heel of his hand. "The parishioners of St. Agnes do not give." Thump. "Are not giving." Thump. "And have not given enough." Thump. "The people of this parish are failing, failing, failing in their devotion." Thump, thump, thump.

He paused to catch his breath, his rheumy eyes ablaze. The church was quiet. We were at fault. We bent our heads, we looked into our hearts, we found ourselves wanting.

"I don't want to lay blame," Corrigan continued. The hell he didn't. "I don't want to single out any one group." Here it comes now. He swivelled his head, there was white spittle in the corners of his mouth; he was out of control now. He aimed his waxy yellow finger. "But it's all you Italians out there!"

He hammered the pulpit one last time and knocked the missal and the lectern to the floor. There was a gasp as the church sucked in its collective breath. Corrigan stared at his hands; the palms were splotchy red; the stigmata of the alcoholic.

His assistant, old Father Bannon, stepped forward and retrieved the fallen missal; he brushed the cover of the holy book with his hand, and kissed it. He pushed the pieces of broken lectern aside with the tip of his black slipper. No one else moved.

And then a small dark Italian man stood up in his pew. He levelled a stare at Two-Gun Corrigan, whose weapons were now empty. The small dark man held Corrigan in his sights and then he turned, chin high and ramrod-straight, and walked out of the church.

Not taking Communion was as good as making a public admission of sin; walking out before the body of Christ had been served was practically grounds for excommunication.

The dark man's wife followed dutifully, herding three children before her. I was overtaken with a shiver.

Corrigan waved a hand dismissively and began the acts of transubstantiation. He nudged the altar boy with a sharp elbow. From the railing of the choir loft, I heard him whisper, "All of it!"

The boy — I knew him from school — emptied all the wine from the cruet into the chalice. Corrigan threw his head back a little too far, he held the cup to his lips a beat too long, he took too much pleasure from each drop. He couldn't help himself: "Ahhh." And he smacked his lips over the precious blood.

My father snorted. Dusty drank Alberta Premium when it was the cheapest whisky on the shelf; if he was really broke he drank Old Sailor port. But Two-Gun Corrigan drank Communion wine for breakfast and Johnny Walker Black for supper. And if a priest could spend the pennies of the poor on the very best hard liquor, all the rest was hypocrisy. Case closed.

Corrigan wiped the inside of his chalice with a fury, and roughly brushed away the crumbs of the body of Christ. He served Communion with belligerence, shoving the host into each communicant's mouth with a blunt thumb and forefinger. My father rarely took the sacraments. I saw him watching Corrigan closely, relishing the moment.

Ite, missa est.

It was usual for the priests to stand at the back of the church and shake hands with the parishioners after mass. Not today; not Corrigan, and not Bannon. Neighbours gathered outside in small groups, whispering. *Did you ever?* No one had. I overheard someone say, "Well, you know, he's not exactly wrong about those people." I walked home with my father. I was vaguely ashamed, but I knew my father was pleased, and that this pleasure was the sweetest flower of his rage.

Corrigan's attack on the Italians occurred not long before my oldest brother turned wild and began to run with a gang. One night, after a series of drunken brawls, he and two of his leather-jacketed friends broke into St. Agnes Church, lit a fire on the stairs leading to the choir loft, snapped the lock off the poor box, and made away with the money.

It was not much of a fire, really: a few pages torn from a prayerbook, not enough smoke to announce a pope, not enough fire to destroy the house of God. But it was a fire, nonetheless. It was not much of a theft: a broken lock, a few coins missing; there was rarely much money in the poor box. But it was the poor box, nonetheless.

The police came to our front door. My mother was shocked; the skin of her neck turned red, a sure sign that she was mortified. She'd have to be the one to tell my father. The policemen were gruff and judgemental. No, the priest would not press charges. Yes, my brother would be watched carefully from now on. The next time there was trouble, he wouldn't be so lucky.

Dusty came home, took my brother into the basement, and beat him with a blackthorn stick – "I'll teach you a lesson you won't forget, you son of a bitch!" There was talk of sending him into the navy, or to reform school. The real sin, in my father's eyes, was that my brother had given a spoiled priest the moral advantage.

For the rest of the summer my mother was afraid to go to church on Sunday. She could make easy excuses. She worked late on Saturday nights, and she came home tired. But she was afraid not to go to church. It was a sin to miss mass. It was a long summer.

I was about to enter high school. Corrigan had promised that any parents who wanted to send their children to St. Patrick's High School – tiny, underfunded, with excellent academic standards, but which only went to Grade Twelve – could borrow the tuition money from the Church. If he could have excluded my family from the offer, I think he would have. A year at St. Pat's cost an enormous ninety dollars, a month's mortgage payment. We simply couldn't afford it. But I had good grades, and I deserved to go. I would go, damn it.

My father was caught. I was bright, and he wanted the best for me, but he refused to present himself, cap in hand, at the rectory. He would not beg from the priest who had refused to bury his brother, who had spoiled his father's funeral, who had damned the Italians of the parish as cheapskates. "I'm not going to put up with any of that crap." The subject was off limits for weeks.

Finally, my mother sent me to borrow the money. She mustered enough courage – small blessing – to call the rectory and say that I was on my way. I brought my Grade Eight report card with me, in case there was anything to prove.

The rectory smelled of Corrigan's stale cigarettes, the housekeeper's floor wax and her tuna casseroles. I was admitted and told to wait in the hall. The housekeeper knew who I was. I could tell by the frost in her voice. I sat and fidgeted while bloody Christs stared at me from crosses. And then I was summoned.

Corrigan was wordless and unblinking behind his oak desk. His hair was white, his soutane was white, his beady eyes were bright. He was sleek and ruddy from too much food, too much whisky, and not enough work.

The tips of his fingers were stained yellow. I'd smelled the tobacco on his salty hands at mass on Sundays and high holidays, and especially on the feast day of St. Blaise, when he'd press the ritual candles against my throat and mumble a blessing to prevent me from choking to death on the Friday fishbones. The candles at my throat and the smell of his fingers made me gag.

Corrigan had slapped me once on the side of the head when I had been slow to ring the bells during an altar-boy practice. I got slapped enough at home. I quit being an altar boy. Now he stared at me. I was helpless again.

Finally he let out a sigh of distaste, opened the ledger on his desk, wrote a cheque and tore it neatly from the book. He did not get up. He did not wish me luck. He held the cheque between the tips of his fingers and looked at me. I wasn't sure what I should do.

After what seemed like an hour and must have been a scant few seconds, I stood and approached him. I tried to steady myself; I trembled. I tried to thank him; my voice cracked. My brother was going to hell. I was going to high school. I took the cheque and turned on my heel. The door of his office wouldn't open. I shook the handle, I pushed and pulled, and then I was suddenly free, and I ran down the steps into the August sunlight.

Not exactly free.

Ordinary pain is easy enough to endure: a cut finger, a turned ankle, a bruised elbow. There is a deeper pain, the kind of hurt that teaches you who you are, that draws something vital from the core of your being and renders you limp and defenceless. This was what Father Maurice delivered to my father with his smiling benediction.

Dusty did his best. He looked away. But he trembled because he now understood that the bed on which he lay was his deathbed. He was going to die. The priest had said as much.

Before Father Maurice was fully out the door, I spoke, loudly enough to be heard: "Fuck that, Pops. You're doing fine."

Dusty had always thrown himself up against the world and bounced off, grinning. He would drink until he was so drunk he couldn't stand, and then he'd sit down in his chair and drink some more. He'd sleep with his head on his arms and his arms on the table, yet he'd wake at six in the morning and, nourished by no more than a cigarette and a cup of coffee, go to work at the post office. He never missed a day because of the bottle. But when he came home, his sweat smelled like liquor.

He'd spend every cent he had and then turn out his pockets and laugh when he came home. He could be weak or belligerent; he could be unexpectedly tender.

And then he got old, and his demons died before he did. They hadn't managed to kill him, they'd simply disappeared before he had a chance to kill them. He was approaching his death with the attitude of a high-wire artist walking across a chasm; it will be fine if you keep a clear head and you don't look down.

The priest was a gust of wind.

The Eighth Night

I had plenty of time to think while he slept.

His cancer had grown slowly over a period of several years. I tried to pinpoint when it first took him. I couldn't. He began to shrink the way all old men do, and as Dusty got smaller, the cancer swelled. His skin turned white, and his shoulders seemed to disappear. His voice, which had always been sharply declarative, became tremulous.

He refused to shrug off his vanity. His hair thinned, so he wore his beret constantly. When the cords of his neck stood out like the strings of his bass, he wore a knotted handker-chief, red.

The more he shrank, the deeper he rooted in his closet for clothes he hadn't worn in years. He'd go downtown wearing a shirt from the sixties, a pair of pants from the seventies, now and then a fifties tie. An old man's act of defiance; if this shirt was good enough then, it's good enough now. He wore old pants as if there were memories in the pockets. He began to look like his father. Is there a lesson in this for me?

I left Fort William a few years after my first marriage ended. I was offered work in the Arctic, returning once or twice a year for visits. I wasn't always happy when Dusty insisted on meeting me at the airport, but not because he'd begun to dress like an old peasant, and not because he seemed to know every other old man in the airport and felt the need to stop and chat with them all.

I took secret pleasure in his gladhanding: he enjoyed a kind of fame, in that everyone knew who he was, and he had constructed a world in which everyone he knew was connected to everyone else; he thought it his job to connect me to them.

"This is my boy Joe."

And I'd shake hands with some harmless old codger in a security guard's uniform, and listen idly while the two of them remembered friends who'd died.

"Who was that, Pops?"

"Oh, I used to go out with his sister. What the hell's her name?" Glaring at me, as if he thought I knew and wouldn't tell him. "She was married to Nels Antonelli. Nels lived down the block from us when we were kids. We joined the army together. One time, when we were on leave . . ."

He could start a story in the morning and, allowing for natural breaks and the quotidian ebb and flow, he'd still be telling it at night. Every single detail of my father's life was alive in the present tense.

I didn't want him to meet me at the airport because I didn't like it when he drove. He was never very good in a car. He'd forget what he was doing. His mind wandered in and out of a continuous strip of film whose frames were filled with people and places and old events, and it was his duty to narrate. He seemed to think that if he drove slowly, it would be easy for others to guess his intent, even if he didn't know where he was going himself.

Towards the end of his life the speed of the film slowed down. He drove like a man on a cart, holding slack reins in his hands: no rush, the road is familiar. The horse will bring us home.

His horse: memory.

One afternoon when he was taking me back to the airport, he stopped the car in the middle of Nipigon Avenue, on what used to be the western edge of Fort William. He sat still, he said nothing. I raised an eyebrow. He pointed to a group of kids playing ball in a field.

"That used to be bush, all of it. You could knock the partridge out of the trees with a stick. Pops used to bring them home by the sackful." A long pause. I could see old Matteo, walking down a gravel road, his moustache drooping, lost in thought. "He brought them home and fried them up, put them in a crock and covered them with lard." A long pause. "They'd keep all winter."

You couldn't hurry Dusty through a story. I'd learned a long time before to use his inevitable pauses to give rein to my imagination. While he paused, I could see old Matteo walking slowly down the dusty street with a bag full of birds in one hand. I could see the house he built in town, two storeys tall with half a dozen bedrooms. I could see the empty lot next door on which he paid taxes, in order to use it as a garden. I could see the kitchen, the woodstove, the frying pan, the cold dark basement.

Dusty would sulk for days if I grew impatient with his timing. The middle of the road be damned. He waited for me to ask the next question, the right question, even though we both knew I knew the answer.

"When was that, Poppy?"

"Oh, golly." As if it had just occurred to him. "That must have been in the twenties. If you wanted something to eat, you took one out of the fat and heated it up in a pan on the stove." A long pause. Now he walks through the house where he grew up, goes down into the cool basement with its barrels of wine, and the torpedoes of salami hanging from the rafters. He reaches into the stone crock, pokes a finger under the layer of lard, takes a small browned bird upstairs into the kitchen and crisps it in a hot cast-iron frying pan. "Delicious."

And then a horn behind us startled him. "By Jesus!" He jumped in his seat, looked over his shoulder, tramped on the gas, hauled hard on the wheel and made a squealing left turn in the face of an oncoming car. An angry horn faded in the distance as we came to rest in the refuge of a side-street. And then he laughed. There hadn't been any traffic in that memory.

He wore suspenders to keep his pants up. He watched war movies late at night and drank whisky from a waterglass. He smoked thick handmade cigarettes, no more than six a day, and he'd fall asleep in his easy chair.

He was a little smaller, a little more frail, every time I came home. He was weak, and I was stronger. He lost so much weight he regained the face he'd had when I was a boy. He was handsome again, briefly.

Then his features sharpened, and he took on the look of death. He became gaunt, like the old men in the family photo album. He wore slippers and shuffled about the house as if he were preparing to take his place among them. All those old people in the albums, dead.

His parents, dead before I was born. His grandparents, tiny, wizened, and dead before I was born. Silvaggio dead. Delvecchio dead. DiFabio and Caporicci, on my grandmother's side; all dead. My uncles, most of them, dead. Not one of them left to tell me what I wanted to know.

My aunts and uncles practised a kind of *omertà* while I grew up. They'd never been to Italy, didn't want to talk about the old days, had never seen their father's village in the hills of Molise, had lost their language. Ripabottoni is not easy to find on any map.

Nor is it easily recovered in memory.

Why do you want to know that old stuff?

Dusty was a master story-teller, but he was a lousy conversationalist, and utterly useless on the telephone.

"Hi, Pop, what's new?"

"Nothing."

A long pause.

"How are you feeling?"

"I'm feeling good; why the hell wouldn't I?"

A long pause.

"How's the weather?"

"Weather's good."

A long pause.

"Okay, put Grace on."

If I had news, if I'd changed jobs, if I was planning a trip, I preferred to tell her first, and let her tell him to his face. But there were other times when I'd finished talking to her and I'd ask to speak to him again, and out of the blue I'd throw a question at him in the hope that the suddenness might spill a new detail, shake loose a forgotten scrap of one of the old stories. He understood why I sometimes came at him from odd angles, sometimes at odd hours. But there were rarely any variations in what he recalled.

He lived in the moment of his memory: everything that had happened to him continued to happen. The older the story he told, the younger he was as he told it.

On the edge of the hospital bed now, with his bare arms poking through the blue gown, and his skinny thighs showing bone, he suddenly snaps awake and looks at me again as if he doesn't know who I am.

"What the hell are you doing here?"

The Ninth Night

*H*e seems to have recovered, slightly.

There has been a stream of visitors during the day. He has not been in company, nor has he been the centre of attention, for months. His spirits have risen; vanity is a tonic.

I arrive for my shift at his bedside as the nurse shoos out the last of the visitors and brings him the evening's hormone pills and morphine. She is healthy; her uniform fits snugly across her hips. The smell of her perfume goads my father deeply; he puts on his biggest smile and says, "Hello, Doll-face." A reflex action. She's too busy to pay attention. Dying men flirt when they have the strength; they flirt like bees, automatically, drawn by the fleeting smell of flowers. She's seen it all before. She ignores him. My father sags, a defeat. He surrenders to the task of swallowing his pills. The effort weakens him. You can see how he thinks: she hasn't responded; I must be dying.

The morphine does its work.

My father had six brothers and five sisters; he was the youngest of the family. I have three brothers, one older and two younger. I grew up with male cousins. And I knew that I stood in a line which passed directly from my grandfather to my father and my uncles to me.

Matteo's sons were hard, rangy, and undisciplined men. They liked to laugh, they weren't afraid to scrap. They did what they wanted to do, when they wanted to do it.

When they came for supper they made my mother nervous. Dusty poured them drinks; sometimes they drank everything in the house. They played cards and bickered and laughed and told familiar stories, or they'd simply sit and smoke and not say a word. Either way, I sat still and kept my ears open. Living or dead, I knew them by these kennings:

Tony was the oldest. He was buried alive in the trenches of France, not once but twice; his lungs were scarred by mustard gas, his heart was swollen by rheumatic fever, his injuries took thirty years to kill him. He died before I was born. He was telepathic; there are letters and stories which prove as much. He came home from the war and tried to kill my baby father. He was a bootlegger; they called him the Black Prince because he was grave and handsome.

Dave had a face as sharp as a knife. I was afraid to turn my back to him when I was young. He'd been a paratrooper; he'd taken a bullet in the thigh while knocking out a tank in Italy. He rarely spoke. He played the banjo. His wife was smart, earthy, and beautiful. They were communists.

Dominic was amoral and profligate. He could open a man's wallet, a woman's legs, or a boy's heart with his gap-toothed smile. He once sawed apart the house he was living in, hauled it a hundred miles down the road, and hammered it back together again just so the next son of a bitch wouldn't get it. Never mind that the house wasn't his.

Frank started a credit union just after the Depression with a handful of friends and all the money they had in their pockets, hardly enough for a bottle of whisky. He'd worked on the Great Lakes as a first mate and as an organizer for Hal Banks of the Seafarers' International Union. Later, when Banks forced him off the water, Frank hit the road with a drinking buddy and a magic act.

Vic was sweet and quiet. Of all the brothers he was said to be most like old Matteo. He kept his own counsel, there was a sadness in his eyes. He moved to the West Coast with his wife and their adopted children when I was young. And when he left, I felt as if it meant the end of the family.

Joe died in a car accident in Cleveland. I have a photo of him standing with his foot on the running board of an old roadster with some flapper friends. I was in my twenties when I first saw the picture. Instantly, I thought, "I had a suit like that, but I don't know who those people are, and I can't remember that car."

My uncles, each of them, lived in the moment. I never

heard one of them express a regret or a second thought when sober. Each of them could drink a bottle dry, play the mandolin, and sing every verse of that old hit, "Abdul Abulbul Amir."

They had high, broad foreheads, good voices, strong straight noses, and prominent cheekbones. I have a photo of my father and his brothers standing on the steps of the family house in the west end of Fort William. Temperamentally, I am as unlike these men as it is possible to be. But I look like them. And I am one of them.

I grew up wondering how much of them was in me. It was hard not to wonder, because I was recognized by strangers everywhere I went. "Are you Dusty's boy?" "Are you any relation to Frank?" "Oh, you're a Fiorito, are you?" When I was young, I didn't know what to say. When I got older, I learned to answer the question with a question. "Who wants to know?"

In my early twenties, I worked briefly in the paper mill. We weren't a mill family. If you weren't related to anybody who already worked at Great Lakes Paper, you were given the lousy jobs. I was put on the four-to-twelve shift, hauling logs from a conveyor belt. One night after work, someone offered me a ride from the plant gate as far as the Westfort Hotel.

The hotel was not on the way home, but I was thirsty and I'd worked hard and I'd earned the right to a glass of beer and that was how I thought of it then: a drink was a reward. I'd just put in a hard eight hours with a picaroon in my hand. I was tired, my arms were sore, both my hands were bloody, and I smelled like sweat and sap and rotten bark.

I needed a reward.

The Westfort was a tough hotel, not where I normally drank my beer. It was a hotel where thugs bunked, where construction workers drank, where old alkies came to rest. It was one step from the gutter.

To hell with it. I tucked my lunchpail under my arm, took a deep breath, and entered with a swagger. I needn't have bothered; there was nobody there but a few old men unwilling to go home, and a few soft-bellied young drunks hatching schemes and rehashing lost opportunities; shoulda, coulda, woulda.

I slid into a chair at an empty table, as far from the others as I could manage without seeming antisocial, a lightning calculation; bar regulars tend to be sensitive to slights from strangers.

The waitress breezed past my table trailing a scarf of perfume through a cloud of smoke. She held a tray of empty glasses shoulder-high and smiled. I smiled back. She raised an eyebrow. I gave her what would have been a peace sign on the street, or anywhere else at that time, but in the Westfort a V sign simply meant two draught. She swung her hips as she walked away.

I opened my lunchpail, unfolded my newspaper, and rolled a smoke. A bit of a gamble. Only hippies, poseurs, or retired bush-workers rolled their own smokes. The waitress brought my beer and spilled some change on the table. I picked up the coins and smiled with a millworker's gallantry. Keep the change.

The tips of my fingers, the flat of her palm.

I thought I'd have just enough time to finish the cross-word and get in one more flirt before I had to catch the last bus home. I threw a dash of salt in a glass of beer, watched it bubble up lightly, drained it in one long swallow, slapped the paper into eighths and scanned the room; in that neighbour-hood, some people thought you were putting on airs if you read an out-of-town paper.

But nobody was paying me any attention.

After a time, I saw an old man with a crop of white stubble on his face. He seemed to be heading in my direction; he could have been on his way to the washroom, he could have been aiming himself towards home, or he could have been taking a run at the shadow-demons on the wall; none of my business.

I buried my nose in the paper.

Somebody bumped my table. I looked up. The old man's face was pink from exertion, his cheeks were veined blue and red. If the table hadn't been there, and if he hadn't been holding on with both hands, he would have fallen in my lap.

Maybe he'd run out of steam, maybe he was lost, and maybe he was just old and drunk. I smiled mildly, as if it was normal – please, feel free to lean here as long as you like, I'm a swell guy, it doesn't bother me – and returned to my puzzle.

He growled through a throatful of phlegm. "You son of a bitch!"

Excuse me?

"You son of a bitch. You look like a Fiorito. I don't like you. I don't like your old man. And I don't like any of your uncles. Fuck them. And fuck you. I'm going to smash your fucking face." He pronounced the word "fucking" as if was spelled with three *f*'s.

"Oh," I said.

I'd never seen him before. He knew who I was. And this was going to be bullshit, with my last name written all over it. If he swung a fist at me, I was going to have to take it. For a moment, I thought about hitting him first. But you can't hit an old man in a bar, especially if he's so drunk he can hardly stand. It isn't fair.

He wanted a piece of me. Was it worth asking why? Should I laugh in his face? Would asking slow him down or make things worse?

He could have had reasons for his anger.

Maybe my uncle Dominic had borrowed the old man's tools and left them in the bush, or sold them and drank all the money. Maybe he thought I was a commie like my uncle Dave. Maybe my uncle Frank had cold-cocked him with a ham-sized fist during a fight on the docks. And maybe Dusty and his daughter had . . . The possibilities were endless and delicious. But not comic. I was about to pay for a sin I hadn't had the pleasure of committing.

The old man was breathing hard. He gathered himself, he tensed his muscles and clenched his fist. He was trying to find his balance so he could hit me in the face. I didn't have a graceful way out. I was going to have to take one on the chin.

We had an audience. The rummies, the bartender, the waitress watched us with interest. I thought about sliding to my left, to keep some distance between us. The prospect of being chased around a table by an old man was both funny and humiliating. Whatever the reason, it wasn't my fault but it looked like my responsibility.

I decided to get up and take it like a man.

But then, with slow-motion suddenness, another old man lurched towards us through the smoke, equally grizzled, equally bald, equally drunk. "Don't you touch him, you old fucker. He's a Fiorito, and that's good enough for me. Keep your god-damned hands to yourself. If you want him, you have to come through me."

The first old man stopped in mid-swing. The second old man barely had the strength to speak. He stumbled forward with a drunk's inevitability of purpose. I wondered how he was going to be able to defend himself, let alone rescue me.

I wondered why he'd bother.

That was the other side of the equation. Maybe, on a day when the banks wouldn't look at him, this old man got a mortgage on a little house at the credit union my uncle Frank started. Maybe my uncle Dom had covered his back in a bar brawl. Maybe he was old enough to have served in the army with my uncle Tony. Maybe he'd gotten lucky at a dance one night long ago, when Dusty's horn made his girl hot and wet.

I'd never seen this old bugger before, but he, too, knew the shape of my nose and the expression on my face; he knew I was a Fiorito. That was all he needed to know; he came stumbling to the rescue. The two old men clutched each other and began a feeble tango to the rhythm of their curses.

"You old fucker."

"You can't call me an old fucker, you old fucker."

I was suddenly, quietly surplus. The waitress shot me a flat stare: what kind of troublemaker would goad two old men into a fight for the sake of his own amusement? A Fiorito, that's who.

My fault, because of who I am. My fault, because of where I grew up. My fault, because of my name. My fault, written on the bridge of my nose.

The bartender cinched his apron; he nodded towards the door: *Time's up, buddy.* I shrugged and drained the last of my beer and offered an innocent smile, as if to say these two old men were no concern of mine.

"You let me go or I'll . . ."

"You hold still, I'm gonna . . ."

"Okay, boys, let's break it up."

And I walked home: I was the product of something clannish and visceral, and I had nowhere to hide because of my face, because of my nose, because of my father and his brothers.

My uncles lived in the eternal present tense; for them, eternity was nothing more than the time it took to lose a hangover. There were no unexpired grudges. Nothing was forgotten, no one forgiven. You had to keep track of the score. Fuck 'em if they can't take a joke.

Dominic said, "A man can call you a wop, but he better have a smile on his face. If he's smiling, you smile back. But if a man calls you a dago, you hit him hard."

Dusty said, "Hit 'em first and hit 'em hard."

Dave said nothing; he smiled.

It wasn't the first time this had happened.

I was in my teens, still tender, not quite old enough for summer work. I'd spent the afternoon in the pool hall playing snooker with a pal, two bits a game, loser pays. I won some and lost some.

I was riding the bus home, watching the houses go by and replaying the games I'd lost when a woman with a bag of groceries yanked the bell cord. The bus pulled over, she got off. The driver eased his way onto the street again, and there was a scream of tires and the bus lurched forward and I heard the sound of breaking glass and metal scraping the pavement, and it was only then, out of sequence, that I heard a dull thud, like a slammed door. I looked back. We'd been rear-ended.

My elbow had been parked in the open window. My arm hurt now, nothing serious, a bruise. The other passengers, a dozen or so men and women, got off. The back of the bus had been caved in. The front of the car that had hit us was crumpled like a sheet of paper. Its windshield was a web of opaque veins at the centre of which was a jagged, red-rimmed hole. A hole big enough for a man's head.

There was a man slumped in the passenger's seat. His head was a red stump. His features were a mask of blood, and the blood was running off him in rivers. He'd been pitched through the window; the soft parts of his face had been scraped away by broken glass.

The driver of the car sat with his arms wrapped around the steering wheel, as if he was sleeping. The driver of the bus called an ambulance. He wanted us to stay where we were. He needed witnesses, he wanted us all to go to the hospital, he wanted to make sure none of us was hurt. I wasn't really hurt. I felt queasy, and I needed air.

I walked away from the confusion.

I took a shortcut down the street where my father had grown up — the street meant nothing to me, certainly I never knew anyone who lived there. But, for some reason, I thought this would be as good a time as any to walk past the house my grandfather had built.

I walked slowly, my hands in my pockets, timing my steps to the cadence of the small prayers I said for the man whose head was a pulsing red stump. I heard the ambulance in the distance as I passed my grandfather's house.

I noticed an old man sitting on a porch across the street, taking in the sun. The sound of the siren must have awakened him from a dream. He smiled, nodded his head up and down, and poked his cane in my direction. I looked around; was he pointing at someone in my grandfather's house? I shrugged the question, Who, me? He waved his cane again. He was saying something I couldn't quite hear, so I crossed the street to listen. He was sitting in an old armchair no longer good enough for the living room. He leaned forward and took a closer look at me. And then he made a pronouncement.

"You are a Fiorito."

"How do you know?"

"I can tell by the shape of your nose."

I was speechless for a moment. I thought about stopping to talk. I wanted to ask him who he was and what he knew about those of us who have this nose. But if I asked him questions, I'd have to reveal the depth of my own ignorance about my family to a stranger. I broke my silence.

"You're right," I said. "I am."

"Are you Dominic?"

"Do you know Dusty?"

"Eh?"

"Dusty, the youngest."

"I thought you were Dominic."

He was confused now. Perhaps his life had been passing in slow motion before his eyes, and he imagined himself a young man sitting on the porch on a summer day long ago, as Dominic walked by. Or perhaps he thought I was Dominic playing a trick; and had I been Dom, I might have. Instead, I almost laughed in the old man's face.

"No, no, I'm Dusty's son."

He shook his head and smiled. It didn't matter what I said, I was Dominic to this old man. "Dominic, good, good."

No one was impervious to Dominic's grin, which he gave spontaneously and without reserve; this old man could still see it, even though I wasn't grinning.

When Dom looked you in the eye, appraising you in a way, he made you feel defenceless. As a boy, I felt my only defence was to give him the biggest smile I could muster in return; this was long before I understood that no one who smiled at him escaped untouched.

Dusty has enjoyed a good day, according to my mother. He's eaten most of his supper for the first time since he was admitted, but she is the one who is invigorated by the meal of beef in gravy.

I tell her to go home and get some sleep. She kisses Dusty on the forehead and I haul a book and some papers from my bag and settle in for the night. I ask Dusty if he wants to read a magazine. "No, thanks," he whispers. His voice is small and full of gratitude, as if I'd offered him some incalculable kindness.

After a time, and out of the blue – old habits die hard – I tell him I'd been thinking about Dom on my way to the hospital.

Dominic, who'd stolen cars and liquor, forged cheques, fought as many men as he wanted to or needed to, and fucked as many women as he fancied as many times as they'd let him. It didn't matter if she was beautiful or young; all that mattered was that she was willing. And sometimes it didn't even matter if she was willing, not until long after he'd taken her stockings off and had his fill of her and was lighting his cigarette, soothing her tears, sniffing his salty fingers with a leer, pouring her a drink and confessing his love: foreplay to the second round.

He drank hard, and the more he drank the thirstier he became. He spent his spare cash on pleasure, and cash in his pocket was, by definition, spare and his to spend. His children, my cousins, did without.

Dusty began to talk.

He tells me how Dominic once managed to steal a boxcar full of lumber over a period of a summer, literally piece by piece, from the sawmill where he worked. He sold the lumber for five thousand dollars in the days when that much money would buy a house. His family did not have a house; they lived in a house no better than a shack.

He did not bring the money home.

He split the money with a confederate, hired a room in the Victoria Hotel, and called for friends; he ordered a supply of room-service food and liquor while his family went hungry and wondered where he was.

He drank and ate and fucked every penny away. And when the money was gone, and he was too sick to care for himself, and too sick to work, he dragged himself home and lay down until he was well again.

I don't know what makes a man so mean. And I have no idea why any man would work so hard for what he thought was easy money. But he'd seen hard things done by others; he cut his own corners and drew his own conclusions.

As a boy, he once worked for a butcher. He delivered meat on his bicycle, not always to customers. "Hey, Dominic, we're having a party tonight. Why don't you see if you can pinch something for the barbecue?"

He was strapping and handsome. Sometimes when he delivered a parcel of sirloin, he asked the mistress of the house for a glass of water; sometimes he was invited in and given extra payment.

One Saturday morning, Dominic woke up with a shiver. He was always cold after a late night, and his nights were often late, and Saturday was always a busy day.

There was no time for breakfast at home, which meant he'd be hungry enough to pad his wages with a steak when the butcher's back was turned, his own version of a thumb on the scale.

Dom rode his bicycle down Francis Street, past the train station on Syndicate. He turned east on Victoria Avenue, and then north; he cycled silently past the bars and the quiet brothels along Simpson Street. And then he raced over the bridge to the coal docks, and the butcher shop.

The ring of keys in his pocket slapped coldly on his thigh as he hopped off the bike. He was thinking of coffee in the pot and bacon in the pan. He wanted coffee now. He'd make a pot as soon as he opened the damn door. He thought of having coffee, and of spreading fresh sawdust on the floor around the butcher blocks. He thought of bacon in the pan.

The door of the shop was locked, as it should have been, when he arrived. But there was a light on in the back of the store. Either the butcher had neglected to turn it off last night, or else he'd come in early. Unusual in any case. Dominic turned the key in the lock and thought quickly. Was there something he'd done or forgotten to do which he'd have to cover with a lie? He couldn't think of anything, and so he prepared himself to look innocent, an act which made him feel vaguely uneasy. He opened the door.

There was no sign of the butcher. The butcher's cat emerged from the shadows with a switch of its tail and an interrogative yowl. Dominic scratched the cat's ear and called the butcher by name. No answer. The cat wheeled suddenly and high-stepped away. Dom took off his cap and his jacket and hung them on the coat tree. He walked through to the back of the shop and into the cold room.

The butcher was sitting on the floor, legs splayed in front of him, his head slumped forward as if in sleep. There was a bottle of plum brandy on the butcher block; the bottle was half empty. Not unusual; the butcher liked a drink, although he didn't usually fall asleep on the floor. Usually, when he got drunk, he curled up and slept on the sausage table.

The front of the butcher's apron was red. Not unusual, either. No butcher's apron is white for long. But not many aprons get as red as this. The butcher's chest was soaking wet, his lap was soaked, he was sitting in a puddle of blood so dark it was black. Dominic was cold now, colder than he'd ever been. The cat returned and stepped daintily around the edge of the dark puddle.

There was a long knife, the handle loose in the butcher's hand, a boning knife, the blade of which had been sharpened so often it had been whittled to a sliver.

A cold, red sliver now.

Dominic stepped close, not wanting to believe what he saw. He took the knife from the butcher's hand and shook the man by the shoulder, half afraid, half expecting him to wake and scream. The butcher's head lolled to the side. He wasn't going to wake. And he couldn't possibly scream.

He'd slit his own throat.

He'd known where to cut, and he'd used his most efficient knife. He'd cut surely and with a butcher's knowledge of the anatomy of veins and cords. He'd reached across himself and started his cut at the left side of his neck, under the ear, drawing the knife deeply, quickly in a straight line, so fast there'd been no time to lose his nerve. Blood had spurted everywhere at first, and then it had run thickly, slowly down his chest.

For the briefest of seconds, the butcher's head rolled over to the side and Dominic saw a red flash of flesh. He saw what no man ever ought to see. He saw death. And threw up into the sawdust. He threw up into the butcher's blood. And when he had finished throwing up he heaved, drily, until his sides ached and he saw that he still held the boning knife in his hand, and his hand was sticky with blood and vomit, and he thought, briefly, that the knife fit his hand easily.

He rose and set it on the edge of the maple block and turned to leave. And then he stopped. He thought about the knife again. He picked it up once more and put it back in the butcher's hand, the way it must have been held. And he went to the phone and called the police.

This is as much as Dusty could manage.

It is more of the story than I've been told before, and at the same time less. What my uncle Dom saw may not have been transformative, but certainly it was central to some of his notions: *No blood matters but mine. If I cannot feel the pain of others, then that pain does not exist.*

And if Dom had peeked at the inside of the butcher's neck and did not change as a result, then he must have known he was past changing, and would never change again. And so, to hell with it.

I think my father thought about that for a long time. He

told this story, like all his others, more than once; now he would never tell it again. I suspect he sympathized with the butcher, a bottle to drink from and a sharp knife to stop the pain. Just like that.

Dusty knew Dominic was odd; he understood there was something missing, something wired badly in his brother's head. When they were kids on the farm, Dominic had challenged everyone, brothers and cousins alike, to beat the backs of his legs with a rod or a stick or a belt, refusing to acknowledge the hurt, taunting them to hit him harder. He breathed the pain as if it were air, he drank it like water.

Dusty knew something was wrong.

After he abandoned his family for the last time, my uncle Dom hightailed it to the West Coast, where he found work as a millwright. He didn't exactly settle down, but he more or less stayed in one place. He would return to Fort William for a brief visit every couple of years with a new woman on his arm, each a variation of the one before: big and blowsy with red nails, long legs, a big ass, a tight skirt, and heavy breasts; a woman who smoked hard, drank greedily, and laughed at bawdy jokes.

My mother would put on a feed of spaghetti, Dusty would pour sweet wine in careful measure, and everyone would eat their fill; best behaviour, all around. And then after supper, Dom would disappear again for two more years.

The last time I saw him, he had one of these women in tow. He and my father drank rye and ginger ale, and I listened to them tell stories, and the woman disappeared into the kitchen, ostensibly to help my mother. My mother didn't want any help, especially from a woman in danger of dropping cigarette ashes in the spaghetti sauce.

"Supper's ready!"

Dusty got up to wash his hands. Dom sat beside me on the sofa, swirling the last of his drink, squinting at the last of his smoke. It was him and me; he drained his drink and he grabbed my knee with his giant hand and looked me in the eye. His smile was lewd and lubricious. He leaned over and said, "Joe, I'm in love; it's wonderful." He threw back his head and laughed, and as he laughed he was watching me to see if I laughed, too. I did.

My mother called "Supper's ready!" a second time.

Dominic grinned at my old man.

Dusty knew enough not to grin back.

Dominic died shortly after that last visit; the noise of death was growing louder for my father. He went to the funeral in British Columbia with Dom's son Jimmy, and he came back from the funeral chastened and licking his wounds.

As usual, he'd mixed death with too much drink. He was unable to control his sorrow, and he'd had words with my uncle Vic: no old slights forgotten among the brothers, and new slights were piled on top of the old ones easily; every time they met, there was a risk that scar tissue would grow. Vic's wife intervened; she and Dusty had words. She told him not to come back.

Jimmy brought back a shoebox full of Dom's ashes with him on the plane, and he had Dom's pot still and copper fittings packed in his luggage; curiously, the metal never set off any alarms.

Jimmy spread the word that he was going to scatter the ashes on his property, on the side of a hill looking out across Lake Superior.

The day of the wake was perfectly sunny, the lake and the sky one colour. A light breeze, a few white clouds. And not much liquor; among the gathered cousins, some refused to drink, some had learned the hard way not to. Dusty drank and so did I.

When the time came, we walked along a path through the low bushes to the side of the hill. Jimmy said a few words, something about the size of Dom's appetites, his lust for life, and the way the old man seemed to mellow towards the end. He'd finally made an attempt to settle down, a small comfort, of no real use to anyone except the last of the big women. Jimmy said nothing directly about the grief Dom caused; no point now. But he said Dom had seemed to like the view of the lake the last time he came to visit. Then Jimmy scattered a few ounces of grey ash, and passed the shoebox around.

I watched Dusty carefully. He was smiling slightly, lost in a memory; he stood still for a moment, then bent low and spilled a bit of his brother and handed him to me. I was surprised by the weight of the ash and the size of the fragments; I recognized what I thought were bits of knuckle, and one or two teeth.

There was a carpet of cedar and black spruce in the valley and a smell of the bush in the air. I recognized another scent. Dom's ashen heart and the last nuggets of his bones were falling on juniper. I grinned and was about to say it smelled like gin here; Dom would have grinned, too. I inhaled deeply and shook a bit of him from the box. As I did, a gust of wind lifted the ashes of Dom's smile into my mouth.

I don't know who else noticed.

Dusty noticed.

When I reminded my father, he chuckled weakly. Just as he had when I'd reminded him of the two old men in the bar, and how they'd fought over me. Odd, to think of this as he lies dying.

Dusty's boy?

Not much longer.

Matteo died before I was born.

I have seen his face in photos. I know what he looked like. As a young man, he seemed slight and narrow of shoulder. He was bashful and proud, not used to the good suit he wore for the camera. He was a hard worker. Everyone loved him. He didn't say much; there wasn't much to say. He made good wine. He could dress a hog, make cheese, and cure sausage. He could clear a field, blow a stump, plant a garden, and build a house. He wasn't very good with horses – one of his old mares kicked away the traces in the midst of ploughing the big garden in town. Old Matt went after it on foot. He found it tethered to a fence halfway across town. Then and there, he gave the horse to the man who'd caught it and calmed it down. These are the things I was told.

In the photos of him as an old man, he has a stout belly, his shoulders slope, his moustache droops, his smile is wry and full of rue. He sold his labour at the expense of his life; work wore him out.

Dusty used to say the old man could pull a six-inch nail from a board with his teeth; he could bite through a piece of baling wire. He was born with strong teeth. He had the teeth of Ripabottoni.

My own teeth were soft and full of holes and some were missing. Why didn't I have teeth like Matteo's? Dusty's teeth were no good, either. When he had all the back ones pulled, he lay on the couch in the living room for three days straight, with a bottle of whisky on the floor, moaning, drinking, spitting blood into a handkerchief. I'm sure my mother suspected he'd had the teeth taken out deliberately, so that he could drink as much as he wanted.

As a child I thought my grandfather, with his nail-pulling, wire-cutting teeth, must have been, if not a superman, then some sort of extra-man. In my teens, when my father would trot out the story of his father's teeth, I'd sniff and think it was faintly ridiculous. You might be able to fool a child with that story, but not me. And we'd have words.

The summer I turned twenty-two, not long after I abandoned hope of permanent work in the paper mill, I got a job as a labourer for the City of Fort William – my first permanent job. Coincidentally, working as a labourer for the City had been Matteo's last job.

I showed up on the first morning at the City Yards in clean clothes and new boots, with a shiny lunchpail, sure signs that I was green. My hands were soft, in spite of my adventures at the mill. My fingernails were white and neatly bitten. There was no dirt, no oil, no thick pads of skin at the base of my fingers. I couldn't keep a callus for more than two weeks.

Worse, I knew I couldn't do the things that most of the men there could do: snug the head of a hammer with a shim, hone the blade of an axe with a rasp, replace a spark plug, change a fan belt, or use a pickaxe without hurting my back.

I stood still and let my eyes adjust to the darkness as I looked around the giant garage. The drivers were tending to their trucks. I could hear laughter, low voices, but I didn't know a soul. The air reeked with the smoky dregs of jokes, the smells of motor oil, fresh gasoline, stale sweat, truck tires, solvents, dull tools, cigars, rubber gaskets fresh from their boxes, and sweet Thermos coffee.

I heard it again. "Hey, you! Fiorit'!" The dropped *o* again.

Who the hell could it be this time? I turned towards the voice. Three old men sat together on a wooden bench, their black lunchpails parked between their boots. Cigarettes burning slowly. Fingers stained with nicotine, nails blackened, hands frozen into claws from years of work, fat, hard men with caps on their heads, dirty overalls, and ancient boots. Unshaven, squinting through the smoke. So old, you couldn't tell how old they were. I felt as if I'd been spied upon, caught unawares.

"Yeah, that's me. How do you know who I am?"

They smiled; yellow teeth, where they had teeth. The one in the middle said, "We knew your grandfather." The one on the right said, "We worked with him here, before he retired."

"That was a long time ago," I said.

It was all I could manage. I ought to have talked to them but I couldn't. I didn't want to tell them I knew nothing about old Matteo; embarrassed to admit I knew so little.

The old man on the left wasn't about to let me go. He sat up straight, flicked the last of his coffee from his cup, screwed it back on top of his Thermos, and said, as much to his friends as to me, "Matteo, son of a bitch, he could pull nails from a board with his teeth." He held an imaginary board in front of his face, bared his own teeth in a grimace, nipped at the head of an imaginary nail, tugged and spat it out.

The other two men nodded, talking back and forth to each other: "Nails from a board"; "With his teeth"; "Oh, those teeth; he could cut a piece of baling wire with those teeth"; "Strong teeth, a strong man."

All I said was, "He died before I was born."

If I had asked the old men questions about my grand-father, once again it would have meant that I didn't know. If I didn't know, it meant no one in my family had told me.

I couldn't explain that my father had been the youngest child of a litter of thirteen, that Matteo was an old man by the time my father was born, that Dusty was an afterthought, largely ignored by the rest of the family, that nobody had time for the baby. It didn't matter. If no one had told me, it meant we were a bad family, we'd given up on who we were, where we were from, why we'd come.

I knew why we'd come.

Silvaggio.

Maybe it was better not to speak, after all.

The Tenth Day

I hopped in the car and drove around the old neighbourhood. Westfort. I drove past the church, past the garage behind the house on the corner of Francis and Brown, where I had my first cigarette at night, past Mrs. Antonelli's little candy store, where I went one day to buy gum and her fat son emerged from the back room, in her apron, a fistful of dough in his hands. Before he was aware of my presence, he whined, "How do you make it into round balls, Ma?" When he saw me, he turned red in the face.

I drove to the footbridge at the south end of Brown Street. It was just as rickety, just as high as I remembered, and just as useful a place to stand and drop stones on passing trains. I crossed the swing bridge over the Kam River, and saw the rotten wooden pier where we caught pike in the dirty water downstream from the mill.

Most of the grain elevators have been torn down. When I was a boy I lit my first cigarette with a wooden match; on the box was the legend, "There is enough grain stored at the Lakehead to make one loaf of bread for every man, woman, and child in North America."

A single laker is moored alongside the dock of Great Lakes Paper. Dusty had shipped out on the lake boats briefly as a teenager. His brother Frank had been a first mate, and Dusty got work on the strength of his name. He cleaned up the galley, swabbed decks and scraped rust, he painted bulk-heads and he battened down the hatches. It beat working on the highway.

He went ashore one night in Detroit with a couple of pounds of stolen butter stuffed in his pea jacket and a ham tucked under his arm. He intended to barter food for drinks; food was better currency than money during the Depression.

He ended up in a dive down by the docks. He ordered draught beer and spread his booty on the bar while the bar-tender turned his back and drew a glass. The bartender raised an eyebrow at the sight of real butter and real ham.

"Where'd you get this, kid?"

"I took it from my ship. Cookie won't miss it. I'll sell it to you for drinks." With a broad smile, the bartender took the food into the kitchen, returned to the bar, and set up a glass of hard liquor.

Dusty was feeling pretty good; he grinned at himself in the mirror. He was a man among men. The bartender wiped his way down the counter, and then returned and poured another glass of Scotch. He must have taken pity on the kid.

Bathtub liquor was not a fair trade for real Canadian butter.

"Psst, kid. You want a reefer?"

Dusty didn't quite hear. "What do you mean, do I want a reefer?"

"Not so loud, damn it! You don't know who's listening. I said, 'Do you want a reefer?'" Dusty thought hard for a moment. What a queer deal; every damn deckhand on every boat on the lakes wore a reefer. "What the hell do you mean? Why do I want a reefer? I'm already wearing one! You blind, or what?"

"Jesus Christ, shut up!"

The bartender grabbed Dusty by the arm, dragged him along the bar and hauled him into the kitchen. The ham was parked on a butcher block. A big black cook was slicing it for sandwiches.

"Look," said the bartender. "You're just a kid. I'm grateful for the butter and the ham. But you're out of your league here. Reefer, laughing tobacco, mary-jane. You never heard of that?"

Dusty shook his head; he had, but he hadn't.

"All right. Here's the way it's going to be. You could get into trouble for stealing the ham. And so could I, for taking it. You're going to keep your mouth shut, starting now.

"I'm going to take you out front. I'm going to pour you one more drink. You're going to drink it and then you're going to get the hell out of here as fast as you can and go back to your ship, and if I ever see you down here again I'll kick your ass good."

Dusty did as he was told.

A week later, his ship was lying at anchor in Chicago. He was strumming his banjo on deck. He was singing to himself, staring at the stars and looking at the lights of the big city. In the distance, two red and green lights seemed to be moving towards the ship. The lights belonged to a mahogany launch which soon pulled up alongside the laker. A voice called out, "Hey, up on deck. You, with the banjo."

Dusty looked down. In the launch was a little guy and a big guy wearing snap-brim hats and suits with wide lapels and padded shoulders; they were not yachtsmen.

"What do you want, mister?"

Said the big hat, "You play pretty good, kid." Said the little hat, "Yeah, kid. You sing good, too. How'd you like to make a little money?"

Dusty said, "Geez, I dunno."

Big Hat said, "Look, kid; our boss is having a little party. But we don't have any live music. The boss, he likes to hear a banjo." Little Hat said, "It's all you can eat, kid, and all you can drink. And dames, if you stay on your toes." Big Hat said, "It's money in your pocket, kid. More than you're making now." Little Hat said, "If the boss likes you, there's plenty of work."

Dusty hesitated. Here was a chance to make some money playing the banjo, a chance to play professionally in the big city. Money and dames. He could jump ship easy enough.

He'd never get another job on a ship if he did.

Big Hat barked, "Make up your mind, kid. We haven't got all night." Little Hat added, "Well, what's it going to be?" Dusty saw one of the thugs reach into his suit pocket. A gun? Dusty hit the decks. He heard laughter, and peeked over the edge; Little Hat was lighting a cigar. Dusty crawled away, dragging his banjo behind him. He felt like a coward. The Hats turned their launch about and roared off across the water.

Dusty stood up when he thought it was safe. Maybe he should have jumped ship. His life would have changed forever.

He wasn't finished with Chicago.

He had a pint of Black and White Scotch in his duffle bag; it was the real stuff, bought on the Canadian side for four dollars, but thanks to Prohibition it was worth three times as much on the American side.

The next afternoon when his watch was over, he and four mates took a cab into town intending to sell their liquor and see what kind of trouble they could find. The cab dropped them off in front of a steak house, the Stockade Inn. They entered and ordered a round of soft drinks, which they spiked with their own liquor, to keep expenses down. The manager got wise in a hurry. He approached the table.

He said, "You boys better leave."

Dusty piped up – he was always piping up – "Hey, mister, we're not causing you any trouble, are we?"

"No, boys, you're not causing any trouble. But every one of these tables has to pay its own way if I'm going to make any money. And I'm not going to make any money with you sitting here drinking out of your own damn bottle."

"Geez, mac. I'm sorry."

Dusty handed over his mickey. "Why don't you have a drink on me." He intended to give the manager a simple snort. The manager misunderstood; he uncorked the Scotch, took a whiff, and pocketed the bottle.

"Kid, that's the real stuff. It's been a while since I've tasted anything this good. And that's the first time in years anybody ever gave me something for nothing." Dusty's heart sank at the loss of his bottle; he couldn't demand it back. There was nothing to be done. "Well, mister, thanks for being swell with us."

The manager paused, as if he were considering something. Finally he said, "You boys come with me." He led them through the dining room, down a corridor, and into an office. He closed the door and barred it shut with a length of steel.

Dusty must have had a question written on his face because the manager smiled and said, "A little precaution; you never know who's going to come busting in here, the cops or the Mob."

Dusty shivered; if it was the Mob, and if they came in now, and if by some streak of dumb luck it was the thugs in the hats from the launch, and if they recognized him as the kid with the banjo . . .

The manager opened his safe and took out a bottle of Black and White Scotch, identical to the one Dusty had given him, complete with excise stamp. He uncorked it.

"Here, take a taste of this and tell me what you think."

Dusty knew a bit about liquor. He spat and sputtered, "Geez, this is rotten. Where'd you get this stuff?"

The manager spoke softly. "You heard of Al Capone? Let's just say he's got the world's best salesmen. Once a month they come in here and tell me what I'm going to buy, and how many cases, and how much I'm going to pay, and it's always cash on the barrelhead."

The young sailors were nervous now. Dusty's habit when he was nervous in a group was to be bold. "Why don't you tell them to go take a running jump in the lake? That's what I'd do"

"Kid, if you talk like that in front of the wrong people, you're the one who'll wind up at the bottom of the lake. Or maybe you think you can swim with your arms broken, I don't know."

The realization that he was a stray remark away from a tangle with a mobster made him suddenly weak. He was in over his head; he felt like a hick.

The manager said, "Look, I'm going to do you boys a favour. I can do myself some good with your little bottle. In return, I'll set you up with some steaks. But then I want you to get the hell out of here and go back to your ship. You're nice boys, but you sure as hell don't belong down here."

He took them out front and left them in the hands of a waiter with instructions to bring on the works. They drank schooners of beer and ate fat steaks, and were lighting cigars when the manager came by. "Boys, there's a cab outside. I want you in it now."

He walked them out, and put an arm on Dusty's shoulder. "Kid, you're just the type to land in a jackpot without even trying. Stick this in your wallet. If you get in trouble while you're here, you'll get to make one phone call. Dial this number. But you better not get into trouble. Because if you ever do have to make that call, I'll wring your neck myself."

Dusty took the business card. "Is this you?"

"Me, hell. That's my lawyer. He's got a fix at city hall. But if you have to use it, you'll be sorry. You just keep out of trouble." The manager told the cabby to take the boys to their ship, and to return to the restaurant for his fare.

Dusty always told these stories one after the other.

The coda was optional: When the ship arrived in Montreal, he took a deep breath and walked into the recruiting headquarters of the Mackenzie–Papineau Brigade. He thought, on a lark, that he'd enlist and go to fight against the fascists in the Spanish Civil War. He'd show Tony he could be a soldier. He'd left home in a reefer, but he'd come home in uniform, with a bright scarf at his throat and a medal on his chest; he'd be a little hero of the lost cause. The recruiting sergeant smiled. "Go home, sonny. You're too little to be a soldier."

I asked him, drunk and sober, why he'd tried to enlist. He didn't always answer. But when he did, he said the same thing he'd told me the first time I asked.

We were working in the back yard, in the garden. I was doing the digging, he was running string lines for the rows of beans. I put the question to him, thinking I knew the answer. I was in my teens, about as old as he'd been then. The Spanish Civil War was a good and noble cause. He was young and itching to test himself. I expected him to tell me he was looking for adventure, that he wanted to throw himself into a current larger than the St. Lawrence.

He was kneeling in the dirt. He was as sober as a man can be in his garden on a sunny afternoon.

He said, "I wanted to die."

The Tenth Night

---

*D*usty needed comfort; there was none.

He hoped he would get well, or at least well enough to go home one more time. There was no point in bursting such a fragile bubble; the doctors had pronounced sentence.

For more than a week of nights, I have seen the pleading in his eyes: *I know it's bad, but if you know I'm not getting out of here, please for God's sake don't breathe a word of it to me.*

Unspoken is the blunt fact that no man has ever risen up whistling and walked away from the bed on which he now lies. Old men have died by the dozen on this mattress. Dusty is resting on a pallet made of their thin shadows. For God's sake, don't say death.

He sleeps fitfully while I read my books; when I turn a page and look at him, I listen to the sound of his moans and imagine the cancer in him is a living thing. It is swimming for joy in his blood, it is racing under his skin and biting at him up and down his limbs, it is worming its way into his core and sucking his vigour; as it becomes stronger, he grows weaker.

He's fighting hard. He knows without saying that the fury of his struggle is the measure of himself, and so he fights until he is exhausted, and then he sleeps, and the cancer gnaws at him as he sleeps.

He is too weak to endure the sympathy of others. To accept sympathy, he would have to admit that he is weak; to admit the extent of his weakness would mean he has accepted the end.

I choose to divert his attention.

If Dusty feels young when he tells the old stories, if he feels like a boy when he remembers, then I will force him back to his youth. I will lead him, I will urge him, I will push him into the brightest corners of the oldest stories. If his life is going to flash before his eyes, he ought to rehearse. And I will witness the rehearsal.

I push him to speak of his father.

The last light is fading; a thin rain has fallen, and the branches of the old elms are fresh green against the sunset. If it weren't for the pinching scent of disinfectant, and if I were able to open the window, the night air might smell like a beginning.

He's had a spoonful of supper; his lack of appetite has discouraged him. His stomach is dull, there is no hunger on his lips, no savour on his tongue. The nurse has taken his tray, and left him with a glass of water and his hormone pills.

He takes a small nap. And then he wakes, needing the

bathroom. I help him to stand, and give him an arm to lean on as he walks. A step. A step. He's weak, it's hard for him to walk. He whispers, "God damn it, I have to catch my breath."

He stands in front of the toilet; I catch him gently when he lists to the side. He sits reluctantly and I wait by the door. Another failure, to have to pee sitting down.

I help him up from the seat when he's done. He leans his shoulder against the wall. He hikes up his hospital pyjamas. He tries to tie the drawstring; he gives up and clutches the waistband with one hand, leaning on me as I lead him from the bathroom. I try to help him into bed. He pushes me away. He wants to do it himself. He is angry, but not at me. He can't do it alone.

When he regains the bed, he is fully, if painfully, awake. I ask him about his old man. I ask him what his father said about Ripa.

"Oh, I guess he told us about the old country. I don't remember everything. I'm so tired now I don't remember much. How the hell could I remember? I was just a kid. It didn't mean a thing to me. All I ever wanted was a slice of bread and jam and a glass of milk. He told me once he killed a lamb." The rhythm of his speech; a different tone of voice, sometimes two, in each sentence; he always made his best music with his voice.

The story of the lamb is one I had embroidered over time with a vivid and logical imagination: If this had happened, then that must also have happened; if that, then what else?

Matteo is a young man from a poor family. His mother and father are peasants. He has a brother, Vito, and a sister, Filomena. The Fioritos are the least branch of a large family. They have no land, no wealth; they have nothing but native wit and the value of their labour at a time when labour is cheap.

One Sunday in the square in front of the church, Matteo sees his father, Giusepp'Antonio, talking to the padrone. Matteo's father stands, cap in hand. The padrone calls to the young man, takes his arm, and says, "I have a job for you tomorrow. I need someone to take my sheep up into the hills. Your father says you are good with animals, so you will know what I want you to do. Take the flock and watch them fatten."

The padrone slaps Matteo's cheek, hard.

Hidden in the sting of the slap is a threat: worse than this will come to you should anything happen to my sheep. He slaps Matteo's face a second time, softly now, laughing as the young man flinches. Everyone laughs; Matteo's father also laughs. The padrone turns and goes to have a drink with his friends.

Matteo's father walks home with his son. He thinks, now the boy is getting his start. If he works hard, the padrone will think well of him, and a man who is well-thought-of will always find work.

The padrone thinks, I am doing everyone a favour; this young man has nothing else to do, he needs to be out from underfoot, there's no place for him in town, he'll just get into trouble if he isn't given a job. He is a peasant, he is the son of peasants, let him use a peasant's skill; fear will keep him in the hills where he belongs.

Matteo does not think. He stops himself from thinking.

His heart pounds; he knows his father has had to plead for this opportunity. He thinks, if I fail, I fail for both of us.

In the morning, armed with nothing more than a stick, a knife, some string, and his wits, young Matteo drives the padrone's sheep along the road leading to the hills above the town. This is the first time he has had such a responsibility, but the job is simple enough: follow the sheep by day, sleep with them at night, be a sheep himself – one whose smell is strong enough to keep a wolf at bay.

The padrone's sheep are dirty and skinny after the long winter. The herd trembles as it walks along the road. Now and then Matteo smacks one of the sheep on the rump with his stick and it runs forward; then, afraid to be alone, it falls back into the herd again, and each sheep bleats to hear the others bleat.

Matteo drives the herd before him. Dust, and the smell of the animals, rises in the air. He is shy and unsure of himself; he misses his mother already and he has yet to reach the edge of town. He is a man, not a boy, but he wants to weep.

He looks behind him.

The village rests on the edge of a hill; the stone houses are like a shawl falling from the shoulders of a girl. Matteo thinks of the girls of the village. He thinks of Angela Maria Delvecchio. She has gone to America, some kind of big America, some new wild America, somewhere north of America.

He would have given her a note when she left, but he cannot write. He would have spoken to her, but there was nothing to say. Surely, he thought, she knows how I feel. Surely, she took that knowledge with her. He looks behind him to see if anyone from the village is watching him. No one watches.

In his pocket he carries the heel of a loaf of bread, a bottle of water, and a piece of hard cheese made with sheep's milk; it is a strong cheese which smells of sheep when the weather is warm. He'll have to snare or trap his meat if he wants more to eat.

As he walks, he brushes his cheek. The padrone's men laughed when he flinched; fuck them in the ass. He remembers the lack of expression on his father's face, a warning. Keep your head, or lose it.

The herd before him scatters suddenly, swept apart by a wave of fright caused by . . . caused by who knows what. A shadow in the shape of a wolf. The scent of something in the air. Just as suddenly the herd knits itself together again, and the sound of its bleating is a comfort.

Matteo talks to himself as he walks. He talks, as is his habit, to an image: his father's first son, the infant also named Matteo, who died at birth, whose life was taken suddenly by an illness beyond the ken of the old women who keep the cures.

The first night in the hills he looks up at the stars and asks himself this question: "Do I have the soul of my dead brother, because I was given his name? Am I in him, and is he in me?" He prays for his dead brother. He prays for himself.

In the darkness, he holds a lamb in his arms and leans against its mother's ribs; he is moved by the rhythms of animal breathing, he warms himself with wool that has yet to be shorn.

He fears the idea that a wolf may come near. He tries not to sleep but the heat of the bodies of the animals makes him drowsy. He feels the pulse of their beating hearts and he closes his eyes, trusting the herd to wake him should danger come near.

In the morning, he wakes to the sound of the sheep. He eats some of his bread, he follows the herd as it grazes. He naps in the afternoon, when the sun is warm and the sheep have had their fill of grass. Now and then, he wakes with a start when he senses – what? Nothing.

He stares at the clouds, he sniffs the wind, he sets a snare for rabbits. He throws a fistful of gravel at a yellow songbird; the bird flies through the rain of stones unharmed, as if it were made of sunlight.

By the third day, Matteo thinks like a creature of the herd, which is to say he doesn't. He feels the heat of the sun, he shivers when it's cold at night, he smells the stones, he tastes a blade of short sweet grass. The ewes accept him as one of their own, and they brush against his legs.

Below the hills, the village is the colour of ripe wheat. The trees in the distance are green and dark. The road leading from the village is dusty, and the ditch along the road is dry and speckled with poppies, red as drops of blood. He can see wisps of smoke rising from the village, he knows there is soup in the kitchens. He is always hungry.

It happens on the first day of the second week.

He has managed to snare only a single rabbit, his bread and cheese are finished; his hunger is more powerful than fear.

One lamb more or less, what's the difference? The padrone has too many sheep for one man.

He chooses the littlest one, the one he has held at night for warmth. The lamb trusts him, and allows itself to be picked up. Matteo carries the lamb away from the herd, and hides behind a rock. He does not want the other sheep to see.

He kneels by the lamb and strokes its head; then he covers its eyes with a hand and quickly slits its throat. He holds the creature tight while it kicks and bleats, he holds it until its eyes grow dim and the blood no longer pumps freely from its neck. He holds his breath; the lamb shivers as it dies. In the distance the herd is restless, and moves away.

Matteo opens the belly of the lamb and cuts out its liver, slick and darker than the darkest blood. His hands are warm and wet and sticky. He places the meat on a rock and cleans his knife with a handful of grass. He eats the liver greedily and wipes his chin with the sleeve of his jacket. Wool on my back and lamb in my belly; I am no better than a wolf. I am worse than the wolf; this herd trusted me.

The liver is all he can eat; he does not know what to do with the body of the lamb. And then he slings it, guts and carcass, down a ravine; perhaps it will attract a wolf, and then who is to say what might have happened?

In the village below, dogs sniff the air.

Matteo rehearses what he will say when the time comes for him to bring in the herd: There was a wolf at night. No, there were two wolves; one I hit with a stone, and it ran off like a coward, but the other was too fast for me, and it made off with a lamb. It was bigger than a wolf in any fable. I drove it off, I chased it with my stick.

He knows he will be caught.

He knows the padrone will smile and stroke his cheek. "Ah, Matteo, it's too bad about the wolf, but I am glad to see no harm came to you. The opposite, in fact. The air in the hills must be good for you. Am I mistaken, boy, or have you gained weight?" And then the beating.

His parents will be required to pay for a lamb whose meat and hide is rotting in the hills.

⟊

Dusty has had enough talking. He is exhausted.

The story he tells me is true beyond a doubt: my grand-father took a herd of sheep into the hills; he killed a lamb and ate its liver because he was hungry. Not long afterwards, he left Ripabottoni.

He may have fled because he feared punishment. He may have fled to find Angela Maria Delvecchio. He may have fled because, while the padrone was considering the problem of the lamb, Matteo's brother-in-law, the young hothead Joe Silvaggio, killed a rival and was forced to flee; and so Matteo may have been sent to accompany his sister, Filomena, who was Joe Silvaggio's wife.

He may have come for all these reasons.

He crossed the ocean and entered the United States by way of Ellis Island. He stayed briefly in New Jersey. There were rumours of relatives; there was, or was not, a small farm in his name. He travelled north to Montreal. Rumours of relatives again. He stayed a year, and learned to read and write English.

He crossed the country as a waterboy serving the crews who were laying the track for the Canadian Pacific Railway. I have heard that someone, somewhere, has a photo of a rail gang, showing a knot of boys standing slightly apart from the men; among the young ones is Matteo.

He made his way to the railhead at Fort William. He found Angela Maria Delvecchio; I am convinced this was not by accident. He took a deed on a quarter-section homestead twenty-five miles southwest of town and, using his saved wages, he began to farm.

Suddenly, Silvaggio is by his side.

Matteo and Angela get married. They are the first couple wed in the new cathedral, St. Patrick's. The Irish priests are not happy. Matteo and Angela are Catholics, yes, but they are also dago peasants who can hardly speak English; they ought not to have the honour of being first.

As a young woman in her wedding photos, Angela had a firm gaze; as an old woman, you'd have crossed her at your peril. Matteo was meek; she was the hard one. I think he was swept across the ocean as a result of his appetite for a lamb, and his appetite for her. He ate quickly, without thinking, and what he had eaten was as heavy as a stone in his belly.

Dusty sits up in his bed now and stares out the window. There is nothing to see but reflections in the glass. It's dark, it's late, it's quiet. He is alone, even though I am in the room with him.

He is impossibly frail: his elbows bulge out from his arms, his knees bulge out from his skinny legs. His stomach is swollen. He cannot understand the reflections in the window. And then he moves his head; he has been staring at himself.

I give him a glass of ice water, hold the straw to his lips. It is all he can do to swallow once. I remind him that we had been talking about his father. "He was always tired, Pops was. But he used to tell this story sometimes. Is there any whisky?"

"Sure there is. What story, Dusty?"

"There were some monks who lived in the hills. They kept a garden, and they had cows for milk. They also raised grain and where there's grain, there's rats. So the monks decided they needed a cat. At first, the cat was very busy. But soon, he found an easy way to get his supper. He'd jump on the table while the monks were praying and he'd eat the soup from their bowls. The monks got angry, but they weren't sure what to do.

"One of the monks said, 'I have an idea.' He fetched a broomstick and a sack, and then he went off to find the cat. He put the cat in the sack, and he beat it with the broomstick as hard as he could, and then he said, 'Ahem.'"

"He waited a moment, and then he beat the sack again, and once again he said, 'Ahem.' He beat the sack, he said, 'Ahem.' Finally, he let the cat out of the bag. The cat took off for the dining room. Supper was ready. The cat jumped up on the table to get some soup. The monk said, 'Ahem.' And the cat jumped down from the table, and he never jumped back up again."

Dusty is about to laugh; instead, he moans, an ache in his own bones. He closes his eyes, purses his lips, tilts his head back. His hands are curled tight as claws.

The work of memory exhausts him again.

The morphine lags a couple of steps behind his pain, as always. If memory can relieve the heat he feels in the marrow of his bones, if memory can lift him from the knowledge of the nearness of his death, then I will continue to make him remember.

Exhausted, he sleeps.

The Eleventh Day

*T*here were other clues about my grandfather. When I was a boy, they were hidden in the dark corners of the basement among Dusty's old packsack and the boxes full of rocks which he thought might bear ore; they were hidden in the darkness among the busted transformers for electric trains, the tools on the workbench, the coal scuttle, the piles of papers and magazines, the stack of kindling, the crosscut saw, the axe, the hatchet, and the spiders.

There was a clue in an old whisky bottle on a high shelf; it was corked and filled with water, and contained a hand-carved crucifixion scene: the holy cross, a tiny wooden hammer, some wooden nails, a ladder, the cock that crowed. Matteo's handiwork. He'd made it for something to do, to keep his peasant hands busy. The water had long ago turned the colour of tea.

And a clue in the old wooden wine barrel. Matteo's barrel, now my father's, in which there were leather belts and musty woollen blankets; my father's gas mask from the war; a stereopticon with pictures of a waterfall, a prairie scene, some mountains; a rusted waffle iron, useless without a woodstove to put it on.

On top of everything else, the horse collar.

Padded, leather-covered, it was not meant for a horse. It was stiffened inside with a web of heavy copper wires, and a braided electrical cord snaked out of the leather, ending in a two-fanged plug. In the twenties, the collar had been the latest cure for rheumatism.

When he gave up the farm next to Silvaggio, my grand-father moved his family into the house he'd built in town. In the beginning, before he found a job as a labourer for the City, he worked like a horse on the docks, hauling coal from the bellies of the whale-backed boats: two bits a ton, bring your own wheelbarrow.

Sell your labour, sell your life.

According to Dusty, his father often came home too tired to eat. The old man would go up to the bathroom and soak his hands in hot salt water in the sink, until the water turned cold, until it was rimmed with coal dust and tinged pink with his blood. The heat helped him to uncurl his fingers; the salt was meant to toughen his skin.

After he had a bit of supper, if his shoulders still ached, he would sling the horse collar around his neck and plug in the cord and drink a glass of wine and smoke his pipe. A man who works like a horse should wear a collar like a horse.

The current of electricity was supposed to ease the pain. He would have felt the vibration, a mystery of electrons; he would have prayed for the small miracle of charged particles. He would have thought, this is the New World, full of wonders. I have a house and a garden, I put food on the table, I have these seven hard sons and five bright daughters, I am killing myself for them. But this is not Ripabottoni. Here a man can have a job, and he can expect his children to live.

Matteo wore the collar and remembered Ripa.

Morto, morta.

When I was eight years old, beginning to get what I now know were my first migraines – I couldn't stay out in the sun or the heat for very long – I used to go down to the basement alone; that is, I went alone when I wasn't afraid of darkness, the solitude, and the spiders in the coal dust. Sometimes these were separate fears and sometimes they were one single fear, intermittent, like the headaches.

I was convinced I had a brain tumour.

I'd seen a religious show one Sunday on television. A mother and father were squabbling about money. Their son complained of headaches; they ignored the boy. They continued to squabble. And then the boy – my age – died of a tumour, inoperable by the time it was discovered. The moral: love God, pay attention to your children. Dusty and Grace ignored me; they bickered, they fought; I had horrible headaches; therefore, I was dying of a brain tumour.

The basement was forbidding, and certain things stored there were forbidden – you kids keep out of that old stuff. I went down to heal myself in the darkness. I pried off the lid of the barrel and did what my grandfather had done. I sat with the horse collar around my shoulders.

I had a mistrust of electricity since the day I stuck a broken fork in a socket and shocked myself wordlessly backwards through the tingling air. I left the collar's cord unplugged. But I sat on the cool floor and imagined.

There are objects which are invested with life above and beyond their simple presence because of their provenance, because of how they were used, and who had used them, and why.

My fool's belief in magic.

The gas mask in the barrel held no such mystery. It had not been in any battles, because my father had not been on the front lines. He never got out of England. I knew he fought his war on the parade ground, with his trombone; this was not mentioned. Now the gas mask was a toy. I wore it when I flung myself on top of invisible German soldiers on the lawn, hand-to-hand combat with my pocket knife. I leapt in the air and landed with a mighty stab; there is still a scar on my little finger, a reminder of the day the blade closed and my war was over.

The gas mask smelled of the faces of my brothers, who also took turns scrambling into and out of imaginary trenches. But when I wore the horse collar, I believed I could smell my grandfather's sweat beneath the leather. Like old Matteo, I hoped for healing.

Eventually, the collar was thrown out with the trash, along with the barrel and everything else that was in it. I wish

I had the collar now, for reasons that have nothing to do with the ache in my own shoulders.

The house is empty, or might as well be: my son is sleeping, my mother is at the hospital, my brothers are at work. I open the family albums and search for a photo.

My uncles Frank, Dave, and Vic are sitting at a table in the back yard with my father; they are drinking wine and telling stories. Dominic, Joe, and Tony are not in the photo; they are long dead.

I am as old now as they were, then.

I still look like they do.

I used to wonder how Italian they were. I wonder how much Italian there is in me; probably none. And yet my uncles sang, they made wine, they cooked when they were in the mood; and although they were not often in the mood, they cooked well enough by instinct, and made all the dishes Angela had made.

I can't sing or play a mandolin, but I make fiadone at Easter. I was raised to eat dried hot peppers on eggs fried in olive oil for breakfast. I have a taste for spaghetti made a certain way, with a handful of oregano, a bay leaf, and little hot chilis. These things mark me.

A more important marker is this: as far back as I can remember, no one but another Italian has ever been able to say "Fiorito." I understand the fatigue, the humiliation, the reasons why some people change their names. We did not, although, for a time, it was the fashion for some of the family to spell the name "FioRito," to break up the syllables, to help those people whose tongues were paralyzed by vowels.

I never gave in to the mangling of my last name, which surprises me now, because I was a timid boy. I endured the mocking of my schoolmates because I didn't know how to fight back, and they knew no persuasion but force. But from the moment I entered school, I insisted my new friends and my teachers learn to pronounce my name correctly. I stood up to Mrs. Spears, who was blue-haired, fat and ferocious, prone to dislike me because she'd endured my older brother, and had failed my wildest cousin the previous year. I got the benefit, not of her doubt, but of her certainty that I was going to be trouble, just another little prick.

And so when she called me the first time – "I see we have another Freedo!" – she glared; she'd had experience with my kind. I stood and said, "That's not how you pronounce my name." And I pronounced it for her, and there was a hush, because no one ever stood up to her.

She had mispronounced my family name for years; I had plenty of cousins, she had a long memory. She glared at me. I held my ground, waited until she said, "Very well," and told me to sit down.

I have no other recollection of Mrs. Spears. But she refused from that moment to pronounce my last name again. She called me Joseph, which was just as bad.

This battle to be called by my proper name began as soon as I entered the world, as soon as I was able to play outside with others. Kids would ask my name; I'd tell them. They'd screw their faces up and say, "Freedo." I'd correct them. They'd say, "Fa-reedo," "Freedio," "Freeto." I'd correct them patiently. The year Fritos Corn Chips were introduced, recess became unendurable. I kept to myself whenever I could.

The other kids in the neighbourhood had single-syllable anglo names, with simple, building-block consonants. Bird. Crow. Smith. Or they had double-brick European names which also posed no difficulties: Mazur, Dopko, Van Brunt. My name ought to have curved softly, like a string of pearls; instead, it strangled everyone.

Down the block when I was growing up was a family whose name was Cambly. I didn't know, until a few years after I left home, that they were actually called Campolieto; they gave up, they changed their family name. I didn't learn, until I went to Italy, that Campolieto is a small town just down the road from Ripabottoni.

I wanted to know about Ripa. My grandfather died before I was born; he couldn't tell me. My uncles were born in Canada; they weren't much interested in anything that happened before them. But I thought if I listened closely, I might learn what made them who they were, and what made me the way I am, as if my roots lay in their deracination.

I'm sitting in the kitchen eating a roast beef and onion sandwich. It's late, I've been to a dance, I'm drinking a glass of rye and water, mostly water, no ice. Whenever I go to a dance, Dusty buys me a mickey if I ask him to. He says, "All right, but

if you get in trouble, you're on your own." I am used to taking
a drink. I never lose my head. No, that's not true. There are
nights I am prudent, and there are nights I am lucky.

There's not much more than the heel of the mickey left,
enough for one more drink. My mother has come home from
waiting tables at Club 17; she doesn't want a drink, she's
kicked off her shoes and gone to bed. My brothers are asleep.
I hear the car pull up on the front lawn. Dusty, rolling in from
a dance job.

Is he drunk or sober? He unloads the car; parks the trombone behind the rack of jackets and coats; he stows the bass
fiddle in the hall closet, next to the blankets and the boxes of
old clothes.

He's sober, in a good mood. He looks at my sandwich;
he says, "What's that in your glass?" As if he didn't know;
he's asking for the sake of form. He gets a form reply. "Rye
and water."

"Make me one, too, there's a good boy." He takes half my
sandwich while I'm making his drink. We begin to talk: yeah,
Grace has gone to bed; no, the dance was nothing special, so
I finished the evening in the poolroom; yeah, I played with
Ken, and yeah, Ken's fine, and all the games were close. At
this hour, talking to the old man, there's nothing at stake. It's
easy to enjoy his company. The house is quiet; all our grievances are sleeping.

"Where'd you play tonight?"

He fishes out his cigarettes and offers me a smoke. I take
one of my own instead: Player's Light. He smokes Export
"A"; too strong for me.

He played the Finn Hall with Moe and Basil. Moe plays a sweet saxophone; Basil can walk up and down the keyboard without stumbling too badly. Dusty leans into the bass, switches to the trombone on occasion, now and then takes a vocal; "St. Louis Blues," "Georgia," and some of the lighter pop songs.

He says he ran into Tommy Beatty. He pauses and takes a drink, gives his cigarette a one-eyed squint, and draws a breath of smoke: a standard opening gambit. I know the story, I've heard it a dozen times before, but I can't resist.

"Who's Tommy Beatty?"

"The first time I ever had a paying job, I played with Tommy. He was a piano player. We got thrown in jail." He returns to his glass, and waits quietly, almost demurely; *leave 'em wanting more.*

"Thrown in jail? Come on, Pop: what, where, when?"

He is smiling now.

"There used to be a lodge on the first ledge of Mount Mackay. You know the little shrine with the statue of the Virgin Mary? The lodge was near there. Knut Hansen built it in thirty-five or thirty-six. He decided he was going to open for the summer with a dance. He knew I played, so he asked me to put a band together; he knew we'd work cheap.

"I called a few of the boys; I told them we were going to get paid peanuts, but it was a paying job, it was professional. Everybody was eager. The night of the dance, we went up the mountain early. We'd never played together before. We had to feel each other out, get used to the room. There was only one problem: no piano. I told Knut you can't have a dance without a piano." More drink, more smoke, another pause. And so I played my part.

"What did you do?"

"Tommy said he knew where he could get a piano if Knut would pay for a truck to haul it up. 'No problem,' says Knut. 'Get a truck, but make it cheap.' Tommy took us to the Royal Theatre; his father managed the place, ran the projector. Naturally, there was a piano; all the theatres had pianos in those days.

"We parked the truck in the alley and went in the side door. There was a new usherette on duty. Tommy gave her the eye. 'Come on, Tommy, there's no time for that, god damn it.'"

"We marched up on stage, wheeled the piano over to the door, loaded it in the truck, and hightailed it back up the mountain. We were working through a tune when Charley Earle and Johnny Simes walked into the lodge. Plainclothes cops, the pair of them. Grey fedoras, brown suits, black shoes. 'Nice night for a dance, boys.'

" 'Yes, sir, Mr. Earle, it sure is.'

" 'Good spot for a dance, too.'

" 'Yes, sir.'

" 'Expecting a crowd?'

" 'Hope so.'

" 'You play pretty good, son. Say, where'd you get that piano?'

" 'From the Royal Theatre.'

" 'Oh, so you admit it? All right, you're under arrest, the lot of you.'

"'What for, what the . . . ?'

"'For stealing a piano.'

"'But we didn't . . .'

"'Come along quietly now, or we'll have to put the cuffs on.'

"So once again, we're headed back down the mountain. The usherette didn't know who Tommy was, you see. She saw us take the piano, so she called the cops. The cops threw us in the slammer. Tommy said, 'Wait a minute, don't we get a phone call?'

"'That's right, kid, one call.'

"Tommy reached into his pockets. No money.

"'You got a nickel?'

"The cop wasn't too happy about that, but he dug out a nickel and Tommy called home. 'Dad, you gotta come and get me out of jail.'

"But Tommy's old man, he wasn't listening closely. 'Tommy, is that you? Where the hell are you? God damn it to hell. Somebody stole the piano from the theatre.'

"'I know about the piano, Dad. You gotta come down to the jail.'

"Well, now, Tommy's dad showed up in high dudgeon. He saw the gang of us, all herded together in a cell. 'Is that them? Is that the sons of bitches who stole my piano? What did you do with my piano? Throw the book at them, officers. Oh, hello, Tommy. What the hell are you doing in there?'

"'It was me, Pa. I took the piano, We're playing a dance up on the mountain. I thought it would be okay if I took it.'

"'Oh. I see. Well, all right then. But damn it to hell,

Tommy, you should have told me. You better let them out of jail, officers. They've got a dance to play.'

"We went back up the mountain. Knut was rubbing his hands together, worried. He'd put up ads all over town."

Drink, smoke, squint, exhale, and pause.

"What happened?"

"One couple showed up. We played one song, and they had the dance floor to themselves. And then they thanked us and they said, if it was all the same with us, they were going to go down to the Chippewa Park pavilion. Ted Embry was playing; he had a hot band at the time."

Drink, smoke, pause.

"What did you do?"

"Knut was a good sport. He paid us and we all went down to the pavilion, even Knut." He chuckled, and flicked some ash into the tray. "Ted Embry, he got himself elected president of the musician's union in the sixties; and then he got involved with some dame and his wife threw him out, and he ran off with the dues money. He disappeared. Nobody ever saw him again. Well, I'm going to bed."

There is a coda to this story.

My uncle Dominic died. Dusty went to the West Coast to attend the funeral. The next day, he went for a beer with Dom's son Jimmy. They ended up in some little roadside joint. There was a piano player in the bar; he looked familiar. Ted Embry. He recognized Dusty.

"Jesus, Dusty, don't tell anyone you saw me."

The Eleventh Night

"Can I get you a drink, Pops?"

"Nnn."

"Your pillow okay?"

"Mmm."

"You in pain?"

"Not so bad."

"Are you cold?"

"Oh, Jesus, yes."

I pulled his blanket up higher. "How about some more morphine."

He opened an eye, glared. "Nnh."

"Okay; just let me know."

He has a morphine pump now. He can get a hit whenever he wants. I pull my chair closer to the bed and place the pump nearer his hand. My mood is oddly cheerful; he's dying and I'm not. At least, not as far as I can tell. He is old, and what is happening now seems to be the natural order of things; the morphine will make everything easier.

I have brought *Cold Iron*, by Nicolas Freeling, and *Kitchen*, by Banana Yoshimoto. I will go from one to the other. There is a death in each. I will read until I cannot keep my eyes open any longer.

He speaks. "Tony came to visit."

An orderly passes the door with a bin of laundry. The bin has a wobbly wheel. The elevator bell rings; a mute tone. The charge nurse walks quickly down the hallway, frowning at some charts. Dusty is in much pain. He is fighting it; he is disoriented again. He resists reaching for the morphine. His voice is a whisper. But I have heard him clearly. And I am on full alert.

"Tony was here? Tonight?"

"Nnh."

"He's here now?"

"Nnh. Not here."

"You mean, when you were in England."

Dusty smiles, weakly, and begins to speak in a low voice. I pull my chair even closer to the bed; this is going to be better than books.

⌁

Dusty was in the army, stationed near Brighton. He was still a bandsman, but he'd qualified as a paratrooper and a dispatch rider, and he was a highly rated Morse code operator.

One day, he was sent with some others to view training films. Dusty took the desk closest to the door. The windows were open, the white screen was pulled down, and three officers stood at the head of the class. There was joking, jostling, the scraping of chairs. One of the officers cleared his throat and tapped the desk with his swagger stick. Instant silence.

"Today we will show you a brief film: 'War Gases and Spray'; how to recognize them, and what to do should you come into contact with them in the field. I say, pull down those blinds. And you there, private, close that door and turn off the light."

Private Fiorito rose with a smart "Yes, sir!" and flipped the switch. The room turned black, the screen lit up. Private Fiorito had read his briefing notes. He knew about gas. He took a special interest.

His brother Tony's lungs.

On the screen, a platoon of actor-soldiers marched across an open field, clouds in the sky, the rattle and hum of war machinery, a line of trees, and in the distance, the actor-enemy position. A single airplane appeared and swooped. "Gas Attack!" Freeze-frame.

An announcer said, "Phosgene gas is easily identifiable: you will be reminded of the smell of musty hay, sweet corn, or maize. Phosgene gas produces coughing, choking, and difficulty in breathing. . . ."

Dusty was suddenly tired. He felt his eyelids droop. The urge to fall asleep was compelling and peculiar since this was the middle of the afternoon. He was working hard and sleeping by the army's clock; he was in the best shape of his life. He was eating three squares a day. There was no reason to fall asleep. He propped his head in his hands. He rubbed his face. And he gave up.

As soon as he closed his eyes, the door opened. Tony stood in the doorway, silhouetted by the light pouring in from the hall. He appeared to be searching the room. And then he strode forward. He was dressed in his First World War uniform, and there was that big flashing grin on his face. Dusty leapt to his feet, and reached out to shake his brother's hand.

"Tony! What the hell are you doing here?"

"Dusty. There you are. I was looking for you."

Tony looked young and strong and fit, as if he were ready to go to war again. He and Dusty were about to shake hands when someone barked an order and there was a commotion and someone switched on the light.

"Private Fiorito, what the hell do you think you're doing?"

Dusty blinked and looked around; all eyes on him. The door was closed; it hadn't been opened. His arm was extended, he was shaking hands with air. His schoolboy desk was toppled over, and his papers were scattered at his feet. Tony had evaporated.

"Nothing, sir! Sorry, sir!"

There were snickers; that Dusty, what a cut-up.

"Well then. Right your desk and sit down and let there be no more nonsense or I'll have you on report." Private Fiorito L.A. H45871 righted his desk and sat down, confused.

Later that day he wrote to Tony, describing what had happened. Tony wrote back. He said, "I've been trying to reach you for a while now."

Dusty told me this story a dozen times if he told it once. It was not like any of the other stories. He never told it outside the family. He told it when there was a quiet moment, it was not for show: he never told it when I was uninterested. Always late at night, often over a drink. Tony's visit was as much a wonder to him as it was to me. No, as it is to me.

"I've told you this before," says Dusty. The room is sweet with his smell, and the air is charged; he seems to be drawing on a sudden reserve of energy, some hidden source.

"What's that?"

"He knew about Dave's wound."

While in England, Dusty received a letter from home, from Tony. In the letter, he learned that Dave had taken a bullet in the thigh during heavy fighting in Italy; it was a flesh wound, it was not life-threatening. Dave was in a military hospital, and he was going to be all right. God damn it, thought Dusty, I have to find out in a letter from Canada that my brother Dave's been wounded.

The letter was postmarked 14 June 1943.

A week later, Dusty got a note from the War Office advising him that his brother, Corporal Dave Fiorito, had been wounded in the thigh while fighting in Italy; the wound was not life-threatening, and he was recovering in a military hospital.

The date of the incident: 14 June 1943.

There is no explanation for this. Tony simply knew. I don't know where the letter is now. Maybe it doesn't exist; maybe I only imagined I saw it. But I and some of my cousins have other letters in which Tony refers to "our little experiment."

Dave knew. There are letters. Vic knew. There are letters. Dusty knew. He kept all his letters.

"Tony came to visit."

He is having trouble breathing now. He gives in; he presses the pump for morphine. He can't tell a story any more. He is reduced to a kind of shorthand. After a time, he drifts off.

But I know what his simple sentences mean.

⌒

The old men in the other rooms are asleep. My father has taken his morphine, as much of it as he can stand. He doesn't like the drug; he prefers to endure as much pain as he can. He is paying off his old debts with suffering; it is the only currency he has. He stares straight ahead. His eyes are narrow slits. He isn't blinking. His fists are clenched tightly, the muscles in his forearms tremble.

"I see you, you bastard."

"Who do you see, Dusty?"

"At the foot of the bed. The bastard's grinning at me. He's sitting there, waiting."

I've done enough recreational drugs to know that my

father is stoned. He's afraid of something, he needs comfort. I take his hand. "It's okay, Poppy, nobody's going to get you while I'm here."

As soon as I say those words, I realize they are the ones he used to say to me when I woke from sweaty nightmares as a child: *Nobody's going to get you while I'm here.*

On the pretext of fluffing his pillow, I angle my head and look at the room from his point of view. There is a darkly fluid shadow on the far wall. I unfocus my eyes and stare dully; a three-dimensional devil emerges from the wall, grinning through the bars at the foot of the bed.

An easy mistake to make when you are drugged, and you are dying, and you feel you have sinned, to think that the devil has come to perch on the foot of your bed.

"It's okay, Pop. It's no bastard, it's a shadow. There's nobody there, just a shadow. Watch me, now." I walk over to the foot of the bed and stop and waggle my hand; I follow the line of the light, I walk over to the wall and waggle my hand again. Pure relief on his face; he relaxes, he sleeps.

The Twelfth Night

*H*e is chipper tonight. He's eaten his supper, all of it, including the red Jell-O. When I arrive, he's taking whisky and water through a straw.

"Hello, Poppy."

"Hello, Joe, whaddya know? You feel up to a story tonight?"

"What kind of story you got?"

"What do you want to hear?"

"Tell me some more about Tony."

There were plenty of stories, a clue to my father in each one. Tony was the first of Matteo's children to live. He was a beautiful young man, smart and thoughtful, devilish and without pretension; he was the hope of the future.

When the First World War broke out, Tony enlisted and was sent to France with the 52nd Battalion. He fought in the worst of it. He crawled over wet fields and into shell holes; in the earth he saw the dirty bones of soldiers who'd been blown to bits the year before. He transferred to the Trench Mortar Brigade. He was blown up and buried in the trenches, not once, but twice. The second time was the worst; he'd taken a touch of mustard gas in his lungs. The doctors gave him six months to live and sent him home. He said, "We all get three-score and ten years, doc. It says so in the Bible. I plan to get my share." He didn't quite get a full share, but he lived thirty years longer than the six months he was given. He lived on the old farm for a time. He was too sick to hold down a regular job, but he made some money bootlegging. His health may have been the main reason the family moved to town, so Tony could be nearer to the hospital.

All the women were crazy about him. His dark hair, his sharp thin face, his white teeth, the way he commanded attention; he was the Black Prince

Eva Cunningham, a tall and slender girl from Toronto, was the only one who got close. She was sweet on all the Fiorito boys, but Tony was hers, he was the special one. She couldn't get enough of him. He pushed her away as he neared death. She stayed pals with his brothers.

Dusty asks for more ice in his drink.

Hospitals are good for crushed ice; there is a never-ending supply. It is a good sign he wants his drink cold; it means his furnace is stoked, it is a sign of health.

He sits up in bed and talks.

Tony couldn't do the rough work on the farm, not after the war. He couldn't handle the horses any more, he couldn't cut wood or work in the garden. But he could run a still, there were plenty of fruit trees on the farm, and he made white lightning like no one else could.

One day, he had to leave a batch of mash in the cooker and make a quick trip into town for supplies. The Fiorito men were scattered here and there, working; the Silvaggio boys were off cutting pulp in the bush around Lake Nipigon, all except Mike, who stayed on the farm to help old Joe do the heavy work.

It's tricky business, bootlegging. You can't leave a still unattended: the pressure builds up, you never know what might happen. So Tony drove over to the Silvaggio farm.

Cousin Mike was uneasy in Tony's company, but he did whatever Tony wanted; he always had. Look after the still, asked Tony. Not a request, a command. It's a simple job, said Tony. He stressed the word "simple," a little dig at Mike.

"Keep the fire banked, listen for the Provincials, and watch the pressure so the kettle doesn't blow; ease the valve from time to time. Really, all you have to do is just sit there and watch the jugs fill. I'll be back before supper."

Drip, drip, drip.

Easy for him to say, thinks Mike. You sit in the bush for a couple of hours, you get ants in your pants, you need a drink. The mosquitoes are thick, the air is still, the sun is hot; anyone would need a drink.

He drained the last of his tea and stoppered his Thermos. He tapped the gauge on the still, set the gallon jug aside and put his mug under the tap for a taste. Drip, drip, drip in the tin cup. It tasted good. Tony knew how to make liquor. Yeah, why couldn't Tony sit in the bush himself? Fucking big shot, fucking war hero, fucking mental case.

Mike rolled a cigarette and lit it with a kitchen match. He didn't need to smoke; he wanted to make a smudge around his head; fucking mosquitoes. Good moonshine.

The bush isn't so bad after a couple of drinks. Nobody gives a shit out here. You can shoot a moose. You can shoot what you want. Town's different. In town you can't shoot any-thing. You have to watch what you say. In town, who knows? People are nosy in town. Somebody in town has relatives, maybe somebody knows the old man's story, maybe some-body's run into the old man's fucking temper. You can't tell. You got to keep your mouth shut when you go to town.

Drip, drip. I'll just see if it still tastes the same.

Tastes pretty good.

Nobody talks about the old country in the bush, nobody wants to know. This is new, this is Canada. But everybody's got a secret and if it happened over there, all that really matters is it didn't happen here.

You better be careful just the same. Because you never know.

There are a lot of guys know about guys who are dead and who's to say what happened? There's an accident, maybe; somebody gets shot, nobody sees, it's my word against yours, who's to say? Mosquitoes.

Mosquitoes know everything. After a while you don't feel

them. After a while, the only ones that bother you are the ones that get on your face. You pick them off with your fingers. You pick enough of them and squash them up, your fingers smell like fish. Indians taught me that. After a while, nothing bothers you. Fishy fingers. Fucking mosquitoes. Fucking fingers smell like cunt.

Two jugs full. Better start a third one. Better build up the fire. Drip, drip, drip. Consistency, that's what you want. What you sell to the drugstore has to be the same as what you sell to the hotel, and the same as you run south across the border. It has to be smooth in the mouth and warm in the belly.

You know, there's nothing like a little nap on a hot day when you've had a drink. No Provincials around this afternoon. No cops would be stupid enough to march into the bush without a very good idea of where they are going. Fucking cunt police. Fucking prick Tony. Nobody knows where they're going but Tony.

I'll say this for Tony, he's smart.

Fucking Tony.

Mike had trapped a marten once and kept it in a cage. "Look, everybody, you see what I got? You wouldn't believe how hard it is to catch one of these devils, they're smart. And fast, so fast you wouldn't believe it."

"How fast are they?" asks Tony.

"Faster than the eye can see."

"Hey, Mike. Who do you think I am? You? Nothing's so fast you can't see it."

Fucking Tony thinks he knows about martens. He couldn't trap one if he tried. A marten is smart, but I'm smarter. I'm not the one in the cage.

"I'm telling you, a marten's fast."

"Faster than you, Mike? Gee, I guess that must be really fast."

"Jesus Christ, don't you start in on me. I could stick a finger in that cage and that marten would bite me so fast you couldn't see it move, son of a bitch."

"I don't believe you. Nothing is that fast you can't see it move."

The marten, nervous and alert, is coiled in a corner of the cage. "Watch this." Mike pokes a finger between the bars, and jerks his hand away quickly. Poke, jerk. The marten bloodies the tip of his finger. So fast you can hardly see it. "Jesus Christ, did you see that . . . ? Aw, god damn it, the son of a bitch bit me!" Holding up his bloody finger.

"Hey, Mike, faster than the eye can see. Madonna! Let's see that again. Faster than the finger can move. *Dio mio!* Hey, so fast we didn't see what happened. Come on, Mike show us again."

Son of a bitch. Fucking Tony.

He looked at the scar on his finger. Better put some wood on the fire. The bigger the fire, the faster she goes.

I'll just close my eyes for a bit.

And then his eardrums seemed to burst with shock, and he couldn't breathe. Torn leaves fell through the air like green confetti, and split branches dangled from the poplar trees.

And the noise of the explosion hit him a second time. He closed his eyes and when he opened them again he heard the hiss of steam and he smelled liquor in the air. One jug unbroken, a miracle. The still had blown up under pressure.

Mike ran home without inspecting the damage.

Filomena heard the noise of the explosion. She couldn't remember anyone planning to blow up any stumps, but the boys were always fooling with dynamite. Her first thought, an accident. She was relieved when Mike burst into the house.

She asked about the explosion. Mike said, "Never mind that. Get me a week's worth of tea, Ma. Also sugar and bacon, and flour and lard." He ran to his room. Got his jacket. Grabbed his rifle and a box of bullets; Filomena did as she was told.

Mike stuffed the food in his packsack and ran out the door. He hollered back, "I'm heading north. Don't tell Tony where I've gone. I'll come back when he cools off."

Filomena still didn't know what had happened.

When Tony returned from town, he pulled the big car into the Fiorito farmyard, and walked down the trail into the thick bush to check the still. Son of a bitch, it's blown to hell. No sign of Mike. And one jug full.

Tony walked back to the Fiorito house, packed a few supplies, took his gun. He knew Mike was gone, and had a hunch where he was headed. He wouldn't be hard to track. Two hours later, Tony had to stop. He was out of breath. He could hear a rattle in his lungs. He wasn't any good at this. Not since the war.

He was surrounded by red alder. He brushed aside the branches with the barrel of his rifle. The leaves had a thick green smell. Hard to breathe, hard to breathe.

A snapped twig.

He knelt to listen. The ground was wet, the day was hot, his knees were cold. He trembled. Would I shoot the son of a bitch? Would he shoot me? I've shot at men before. He shouldn't have gotten drunk. He should have kept the fire banked low, and filled the jugs. Would he shoot me? He might.

Once, when they were boys, Mike and Tony had gone rabbit hunting, each wearing a brand-new pair of knee-high Dutchman's rubbers. They were proud of their boots. Proud that their fathers had bought them new boots. They walked the back trails of the farm, towards the cedar swamp; plenty of rabbits there. A perfect place for boots.

Tony said, "The rubber in these boots is pretty good, it's strong. You can feel how strong the heel is. You know, Mike, I bet you could shoot your boot and the bullet would bounce right off."

"Would not," said Mike, and he made a face. Fucking Tony, full of shit.

Tony was just warming up. "You know how a rubber ball bounces, no matter how hard you throw it? Well, boots are made of rubber, too."

"Yeah, but a bullet goes too fast. It's got a point at the end. A bullet can go right through a rabbit and into a tree," as Mike knew from experience.

Tony said, "A rabbit isn't made of rubber."

Mike thought about that for a minute; Tony was right, but he had to be wrong. Tony was trying to trick him. Tony had an answer for everything, but he was sort of right about rubber, especially India rubber, which bounces really high.

"I bet if you shot at your boot, the bullet would bounce right off," said Tony again. "You'd feel it hit your boot, but I bet it would bounce right off."

"Would not," said Mike. But he didn't sound sure.

"Come on, Mike, use your head for more than a hat rack. You'd feel it hit for sure, but it would have to bounce off. But you wouldn't hardly feel it because rubber's also soft; it's like a cushion; it's springy. I bet you're chicken to do it."

Mike began to breathe faster, in spite of himself. He wasn't as smart as Tony, but he wasn't chicken.

"I bet you're chicken!"

Damn it, I'm not.

Mike thought the bullet might have a better chance to bounce if it didn't hit straight on, if it came in at an angle. He pumped a bullet into the chamber of the rifle. He pulled the trigger without thinking.

Oh fuck, oh fuck. Too late. Oh, fuck. So stupid.

Fuck.

Mike sat on the ground. He pulled his boot off carefully and looked; it was hard to see where the bullet went in. His sock was sweaty. His shin was on fire. He didn't want to look. He rolled up his pant leg. He rolled down his sock. There was a small red hole in his shin; not much blood; a thick and stinging pain.

"Jesus Christ, Tony," he said. "Why did you make me do it?"

Why the hell had he made him do it? The better question was, why the hell had he done it? "Let's get you back to the farm," said Tony.

"Pop's going to kill me for sure."

"God damn it, Mike. He's going to kill us both. But I didn't make you do it. You did it all by yourself. I didn't think you were that stupid."

Tony was out of breath.

Maybe Mike's going to pay me back for that bullet in the shin, he thought. Maybe he let the still blow because he knew I'd come after him. There's just the two of us now. He moved forward slightly. He knew Mike was close. He crouched. Let him come to me, let him come.

Not a sound. No birdsong, no breeze. Tony leaned against a birch. He needed a drink. It was hard to breathe. Now is not the time to drink. That's what started this fucking chase in the first place, not knowing when to leave a drink alone.

Tony slipped his packsack off his shoulder, easy now, and set it on the ground. Disoriented for a moment. He shook his head. These are not French woods. There is no mustard gas, there are no dead horses and no soldier's bones sticking up through the mud, no crawling under a rain of shells, no men shrieking bleeding crying. Not yet.

A twig snapped. Where?

"Tony?"

These are not French woods, but they smell the same. Leaf rot. Root sap. Death. Don't even blink.

"Tony, you gonna shoot?"

Tony shivered. Sweat on his lip. No telling where the voice was coming from. His lungs ached. He wanted to cough. No sense answering back; never give something for nothing. Shut up and listen.

"Fuck you, Tony! Where are you? Come on!"

This is a Silvaggio who has never shot at anyone except himself. He's afraid because he knows what a bullet can do. I know what a bullet can do, too, thought Tony.

The smell of alder and rifle grease. The trigger sliver-sharp against his finger. The rifle, useless in the dense brush; I should have brought the shotgun. Hell, I should have worn a rubber coat, the bullets would bounce right off. The hell they would.

"Tony, for Christ's sake. You don't want to shoot me and I don't want to shoot you. I got drunk. You never get drunk? So what if I did? You're no fucking saint. We can build another still. I'll help you build another still."

Tony listened.

I could shoot Mike. I could say it was an accident. They'd never find him. I have bacon and tea and flour and salt, enough for a week. I could take what Mike has in his pack and have enough for two weeks. I could make my way slowly up north, far away. I have matches and bullets, I can live in the bush, I can eat rabbits. I can say Mike got lost in the bush.

I can make another still.

The cops are watching, but I can send someone into town for copper pipe, I can solder up the pots, I can find a new place in the woods. I'm smarter than the cops because I know how they think.

And then he saw Mike's head, framed by the branches of a spruce tree, looking the wrong way. Mike's thick neck, his big shoulders, his rifle at his hip. Quietly and clearly, Tony said, "Hold it there."

Mike froze. "Tony! Where the fuck are you? I knew you'd find me pretty soon. I was looking for you. Come on, we can talk. I'm putting my gun down. See, I put my gun against this tree. I'm unarmed now. I got no gun. Let's talk. Come on, Tony, go easy."

Tony stood up, and the two men smiled at each other. The fight had gone out of them, but Tony held his weapon at the ready.

Mike turned up his palms and shrugged: "South Gillies–born, South Gillies–bred." Tony replied, "More strength in the back than brains in the head." Guilty and forgiven all at once.

Tony parked his rifle in the crook of a tree and sat down. Mike started a fire for the kettle; he cut lard into flour for bannock, speared a chunk of bacon with a stick and set it on an angle near the fire. There was nothing he couldn't do in the bush. Tony began to cough.

He spat a little blood.

If it weren't for his lungs, Tony might have lived long enough to tell me this story himself. There is a picture of him taking the sun in the back yard of the house on Francis Street. You could see his skinny ribs. A pack of Sweet Caps, in spite of his lungs. A bottle of Scotch beside the ashtray.

It was no accident he'd ended up in the Trench Mortar Brigade. He knew how to blow things up. There had been plenty of land to clear for crops, plenty of stumps to blow and boulders to blast loose from the soil. He learned from Matteo, and from his uncle Joe. He learned not to stand too close to the charge; any fool knows that. But he also knew – rare and precious knowledge – not to stand so far away that you were in the radius of debris. You worked out the charge. You set your caps and laid your wire. You backed off far away.

But not too far.

He never tired of the noise, the swelling and the slump of earth, the spray of dirt in the air. He'd lost the tip of his right forefinger when he was a boy, playing with a blasting cap on the woodstove; the stub was a reminder. The past leaves a trace in the present. He knew the red instant.

He'd been blown up and buried in the trenches twice. The second time there'd been a shell's whistle, then the sound of no sound, then the shudder of earth, then flying darkness and an absence of air.

The earth settled on him. He fought panic with thoughts of home. Unable to move, unable to see, and barely able to breathe, he studied time. Short slow breaths. First you live, and then you die. He prayed briefly, and then set aside all his prayers. He heard the muffled sounds of battle from some-where overhead. The toss of a coin, which way it goes. He was buried before he was dead.

And then, when it would have been easier to be dead, he was dug out of the ground. Alive.

Women loved him because he was so fragile, so handsome, so tragic; men feared his smile. We were told to be like him.

Nobody like him at all.

The Thirteenth Night

---

*H*e's eaten all of his supper again; his appetite's clearly improving. He isn't putting on any weight, but he feels good. He thinks he might go home soon. He eats, but what he's feeding is his cancer. He won't go home again. He was born in this hospital. He'll die here. Matteo and Angela died here. Tony died here.

We share a drink in the dark. There's nothing to say. He enjoys the silence of my company. He would enjoy it less if he knew what I was thinking. And then he speaks.

"Do you want me to tell you another story?"

"Which one?"

"You tell me."

"The littlest bootlegger."

I don't know how Matteo managed to afford a Chalmers Touring Car. I don't know if it was used or new, or if they all chipped in to buy it, but it was huge, and all the Silvaggios and Fioritos together weren't enough to circle it when they posed for a picture. The women held their babies; the men stood with their chests puffed out as if to say, you can call us dagos if you want, but you better not because there are a lot of us now, and we have our farms; and look, we bought this car and we have enough to eat. Our babies are strong. They're going to have a better life than us.

A better life.

Fresh from the war, with his mind on the mend, his rheumatic heart beginning to swell and his lungs unable to supply him with much air, the Black Prince turned to bootlegging.

He had set up the still. He was the brains of the operation, the one who supervised the distilling of the liquor. He rigged a tank inside the front seat of the car so he could make deliveries into town. Ten bucks a bottle, five bottles to the gallon, twenty gallons in the tank.

A bootlegger's math.

It was against the law. The provincial police had suspicions, of course. As for the regulars in the hotel, word gets around. The druggists knew enough to keep their mouths shut. But no one knew where or when it was done, and no one even remotely suspected that the car itself was a booze can.

It was time for another run. The Black Prince told his cousin Tony Silvaggio to make a delivery. Heaney's Drug Store. The Victoria Hotel. The St. Louis Hotel and the

Adanac. "Nothing doing," said Tony Silvaggio. "Not today. I've got a feeling the Provincials are waiting."

"Fuck it, then. I'll do it myself."

"What do you mean?"

"I've got a plan. Where's the kid? Dusty, do you want to go for a ride into town?"

"Sure, Tony."

Dusty was perhaps seven years old. He spent his summers on the farm. He rarely got to ride in the car; old Matteo preferred to use the horse and buggy when he was going back and forth to town.

"Will you do exactly as I tell you?"

"Sure, Tony."

"All right, take this piece of gum and put it in your mouth."

"Gee, Tony, gum!"

"Does that taste good?"

"Sure it does!"

"You want another stick?" Little Dusty wondered what was going on; he took the second piece of gum and put it in his mouth.

"Dusty, I want you to do me a favour."

"Anything, Tony; whatever you want."

"I want you to put the rest of this gum in your mouth. The whole package. Can you do that? I want you to chew it all up and keep it in your cheek. If anybody stops the car, you don't say a word. You just keep that gum in your cheek and nod yes or no. You got that?"

Dusty nodded his head.

"Good boy. Now, listen carefully. We're going to play a little game. If anybody stops us, including the Provincials, you say nothing. I'll say we're going to the dentist. And you just nod your head. Got it?"

"I got it, Tony. The dentist. You can count on me."

Tony drove away from the farm, through a thicket of red alder brush, onto an old and almost overgrown trail.

"Hey, Tony, where are we . . . ?"

"Look, kid, keep your mouth shut. You heard what I said. We're going to town. I'm taking you to the dentist, got it? Not another word until I tell you. You just keep that gum stuck in your cheek."

Little Dusty's eyes filled with tears.

"Don't you worry; you do like I tell you, and everything will be okay." Dusty nodded. Tony drove slowly now; the trail was narrow, branches raked the window, and the car was filled with the smell of the bush, pine and alder, better than any perfume.

Tony swore under his breath.

He stopped the car and turned off the ignition. The Provincials were somewhere out there on the road ahead; he could sense them. He put a hand on the kid's shoulder and put a finger to his lips. "Shh." Not a sound. The kid could hear his own breathing. Tony started the car and eased up on the clutch. "Hang on to your hat," he said. He stepped on the gas. The car bucked through the brush and onto the road, and the rear end skidded and Tony fought to straighten the wheel. And then he swore, and hit the brakes.

The police car was parked across the road, blocking the way. Sergeant Malone and Corporal McLaren lounging against it, hands on their hips, smiles on their faces. There was no way out; Tony couldn't outrun the cops going backwards. He drove slowly forward, and came to a stop in front of the police car.

"Hello, Tony," said Corporal McLaren. He was beefy, red-faced, and bad-tempered. "Now, where the hell did you come from, and where the hell do you think you're going this afternoon?"

"And you better be straight with us," said Malone, tall, white-haired, and hard. The coppers leaned on Tony's car.

"Officers, I don't know what you're talking about. I'm in a hurry here. I'm taking the kid into town. He's got a sore tooth. I've got to get him to the dentist."

"Aw, Tony, for Christ's sake, cut the crap. Who do you think you're kidding?"

"Sergeant, I don't care if you haul me in. But please don't swear in front of the kid. I've got to get him into town. I haven't done anything wrong. I was taking a shortcut through the bush. Look at him. He's got an abscessed tooth. He needs a dentist right away."

McLaren walked around to the kid's side of the car. "I think you're playing with us, Tony. You better not play with me." And then he looked in the window of the car. "By Jesus, Malone. He's not kidding. Get a load of this kid's jaw."

The beefy Malone looked at Tony with contempt; what kind of man would use a kid to commit a crime? He walked around to the other side of the car and leaned his head in the window. "Sore tooth, sonny?" Little Dusty nodded, and kept his mouth shut. Cheek swollen sweetly. Eyes wet. Frightened. McLaren said, "Jeez, Bill."

Malone said, "Hurt bad, sonny?"

Dusty nodded.

"Going to the dentist?"

Little Dusty nodded.

"You're a brave boy, sonny," said McLaren.

Malone tousled the kid's hair, and walked back to the other side of the car. "I've got a good idea what you're up to, mister. We're going to nail you soon, and when we do, we'll nail you good. But we're going to let you go this time. Get the hell out of here. Get that kid to a dentist."

The Provincials moved their car to the side of the road. Tony drove off slowly. The tank in the back of the driver's seat was filled to the brim, so full there wasn't room for it to slosh.

In town, little Dusty got a bag of candy for his sweet tooth. Back at the farm, the Black Prince laughed and coughed and counted.

"I told you it would work."

The Fourteenth Night

I sleep as much as I can during the day, in order to stay awake at night; no hope of sleep at night, in any case. I drive around town when I feel like killing time. I think about the stories that will disappear with my old man; there are too many to have written down. There are things he's seen and places he's been which will be subtly diminished without him to remember them.

I spent several years as a radio producer. I tried to interview him with my tape recorder once or twice when I came back home to visit. Curiously, for a man who spent so much time on stage, and who was such an instinctive storyteller, he stiffened when I popped in a tape and pressed the record button.

I wonder what it will be like without him.

I'll find out soon enough. I go to the hospital.

He picks up where he left off.

⟋⟍

Tony never spoke about the time he'd tried to kill my father. I don't think my father asked him why it happened. Horror had been done, horror had been the result. They didn't have to speak about it. Tony spent the rest of his life trying to make good for it.

What the hell else is there to say?

Dusty was in the army, stationed in Toronto, when Tony was taking treatments at the Veterans' Hospital. He was an out-patient, staying with Eva Cunningham's mother in a house on Wrenson Road. His lungs couldn't give him enough air, his heart was unbearably swollen. He could hardly make it back and forth for treatments.

Mrs. Cunningham was weeding the flowers in front of the house one day when Dusty got a pass and decided to make a surprise visit. He came marching up the walk.

"You must be Eva's mother. Is Tony here?"

"I am Mrs. Cunningham. And Tony is upstairs on the second floor, in the bedroom on the right."

"How is he?"

"He's good and bad. Today he's bad."

Dusty took the stairs quietly.

He sniffed the air as he climbed: not a pleasant smell – sleep, soap, and stale cooking; stale light at the top of the stairs.

Dusty would soon to be sent to England. He couldn't wait to see the look on Tony's face. Careful, now. One hand on the doorknob, a firm grip. Dusty swung open the door.

The room was black, the windows were sealed against the light. Tony lay on the narrow cot. A lit candle at either side of his head. Gaunt cheeks, hollow eyes. Not moving. Not breathing. Dusty gaped. *Oh, Jesus, I'm too late.*

His heart was pounding. He rushed to Tony's bedside and put his hand on his brother's arm. Tony was not dead yet; he roared and rose up in bed. "Don't you ever come into this room without knocking on the god-damned door. Who the hell do you . . . ? Oh, hello, Dusty. God damn it, you've got to be careful. It isn't always easy to come back."

Dusty took a breath; he managed a squeak.

"Easy to what?"

"It isn't always easy to come back."

"Come back from where?"

Tony spread his arms like a man on the cross, or a man pushing apart the sides of his grave; without so much as a sideways glance, he pinched the flame of each candle simultaneously with thumb and forefinger. Smoke, and the smell of wax, rose in ribbons from the black wicks of the candles.

"What do you mean, it isn't easy to come back?"

"I was travelling. I was on the other side."

There was a pile of Rosicrucian pamphlets on the floor beside the bed. He told Dusty about astral travelling, and said he'd been trying to fly away ever since his lungs got so bad he couldn't walk across a room without stopping to gasp for air.

But he was too tired for a visit now. "Come back and see me tomorrow, Dusty. Bring me a quarter's worth of bacon, not too fat. And get me some grapes on College Street while you're at it, black ones." Dusty turned to go. Tony reached for a pack of cigarettes. Dusty caught the movement from the corner of his eye. Tony wasn't supposed to smoke, not with his scarred lungs. But you couldn't tell the Black Prince what he could or couldn't do. He looked his brother in the eye, and lit up. "I'll do as I bloody well please, Dusty. Never mind my lungs; you just go get even with the ones who scarred them."

He drew deeply on his cigarette; he smiled and held his breath. The air was thick and blue around his head, a halo. Dusty turned to leave. He stopped when he heard the cough. Tony waved him off. The coughs came long and hard and helpless now.

Dusty went to Tony's side.

Tony waved him off. Long coughs, wet coughs. There were specks of blood in the air, a few at first and then more, there was blood on the wall now, sprays of it on the curtains, on the sleeve of Dusty's uniform.

Blood from his brother's lungs.

Dusty ran downstairs. "Tony's dying! He's coughing blood, there's blood everywhere!" Mrs. Cunningham was washing her hands at the sink. She wiped them on her apron. She smiled, sadly, as if she knew a secret.

"He'll get over it."

He got over it well enough to come home and die. A knife-edged smile on his face: I'm weak, I'm dying, but I'm in the sun and I have a drink in my hand. Nobody thought I'd get this far. Not me, when I was face down in the mud Over There. Not Dusty, who saw me coughing blood on Wrenson Road. No one. They said six months, but I'm closer to three-score and ten than I was yesterday. I won't quite make it. But I'll get close enough for the Trench Mortar Brigade.

Take me when you can.

Bastards.

My father drifts off to sleep.

Do I believe everything he tells me?

Murder is surely the reason my grandfather sought the Northern Ontario bush when most of the other Italians who left Ripabottoni in the late 1800s settled in Montreal, or Hamilton, or Spokane. The bush was as far away as he could get.

I accepted that Joe Silvaggio raced home on a cart horse, told Filomena to pack some dresses, gathered his tools, and hightailed it for Naples. I took it that Matteo Fiorito came along in order to protect his sister from her hothead husband.

Years later, Matteo Fiorito built a house in the west end of Fort William, among the English, the Scots, the Poles, and the Ukrainians; he lived apart from the other Italians.

The Silvaggios remained in the bush.

I was afraid of them and unsure of who I was. I was frightened by my hunger for the story of the murder. I have always been unsure about what it means; but it seems as if all of us are marked by this ancient, bloody act.

The Fifteenth Night

*D*usty was the baby of the family.

He wasn't planned; none of the kids was planned, but he was the least expected. He was a child, and his back was turned, when he overheard his mother say, "Just another prick."

He thought she meant him.

Perhaps she did.

When he was growing up, the west end of Fort William was a rough place, a village filled with wild children, old horses, empty fields, slow cows, and scattered chickens. The village no longer exists as it did, save in the stories he told, and in the memory of a few other old men; there are fewer every year.

Fort William was a bushtown, but it was also a developing port with pretensions to prosperity. It was filled with cheap

labour – Ukrainians and Poles, Greeks and Slovaks, a few
Italians, all refugees of one sort or another – and there was the
silent presence of the Indians from the reserve.

The town was governed by a merchant bourgeoisie,
men with big bellies and mutton-chop whiskers. Oh, well, a
padrone is a padrone, even if he drinks tea and belongs to the
Masonic lodge. My grandparents understood their place.

They were not well-educated. They were peasants, with
peasant self-sufficiency. And they had this in common with
their immigrant neighbours: they'd sailed halfway around
the world to a place where the language was peculiar, the
customs were awkward, and the structures of power were all
too familiar.

Most men do not become refugees of their own free will.

They leave their homes because they have no choice,
because they are expelled by war or by poverty, by disaster or
by – don't speak of it! – the failure of the human heart. They
flee bad luck, bad weather, the whims of kings; they race to
keep a step ahead of the world's mighty armies; they squeeze
themselves into steerage with their steamer trunks, their
wives and their children, their tools and their photographs.

They make a bargain on arrival: We are strangers here. We
know it is necessary for us to work hard, learn fast, give birth
to many children, and endure much humiliation in order to
survive. All we ask for is a chance.

Everyone who could have told me what it was like to take
that chance had died before I was born. But I know where
my grandparents came from. They came from the Middle
Ages. No lights. No machines. No modern drugs. As for the

New World, the only thing separating Angela and Matteo from the Ojibway Indians of the Chippewa reserve was the Kaministiquia River.

An imaginary line.

My grandmother was terrified of them.

She awoke one morning to find that someone had come in the night, silent as a shadow. A flitch of bacon was missing from the hook where it hung in the cold cellar. She had a vision of a throat cut in the night, and thanked God whoever it was had been hungry and not thirsty for her blood and the blood of her children.

A few nights later, the thief came again, but this time he did not come to steal. He left a hindquarter of deer, fresh and bloody, hanging from the hook where the bacon had hung.

It was a message of some kind.

It had to be someone from the reserve. I think she understood then that the Ojibway were also refugees: they'd been bumped from their own time and place into a cold and hard-edged present tense; what they knew of the world – a mixture of legends, savage habits, the memories of elders, and the incense-scented tales told by priests – was of no use to them now.

They are like us, she thought. We do not share colour or culture; we are of the same class. But that did not prevent her from telling her children that the Indians would get them if they didn't go to bed.

Dusty isn't going to get out of bed now; his horizon has been reduced to the present moment: *If I'm not dead now, and if I do not think I am dying, then there's a good chance I may not be dead a minute from now.* A minute from now was all the future he ever wanted.

"What are you reading tonight?"

"A Japanese writer."

"Who?"

"Banana Yoshimoto."

"Who?"

"Her name's Banana."

I expect him to say, What the hell kind of name is that? He can be sharply and suddenly intolerant, odd in a man who's been an outsider all his life by virtue of name and nature, and who is a democrat in his bones. Instead, he chuckles and asks if he's ever told me the story of Charlie the Chinaman.

There was a time when I'd have said, Oh, for god's sake, she's Japanese. How the hell do you make the leap from her to Charlie the Chinaman? Not any more; there is no point in lecturing him about cultural differences. I sit back in my chair and put a bookmark in Banana.

⚊⟋

He came home from school and announced that the nuns had taught him how to perform a miracle; he knew how to raise the dead.

"And how do you do that?" said Angela, ready to smack him for his blasphemy.

Dusty threw his arms open wide and said, "Rise up, Lazarus!"

Angela was a religious woman; she hushed him and told him that she'd sell him to the Chinaman if he didn't stop playing the fool.

She was a humourless woman. She did not tell jokes, she did not even understand jokes, and she greeted any and all lies with the back of her hand. Angela told him Chinamen ate rats and little boys; Dusty believed her. And so he hid himself in an unused wine barrel on Tuesdays when Charlie came to get the laundry.

Charlie wore black silk pyjamas and wooden shoes. Clip, clop on the wooden sidewalk, coming to collect the blankets, which were too big for Angela to wash by hand; she had no washing machine, and the Chinese worked cheaply.

Dusty hid in the barrel and crawled out when he thought Charlie had gone. One day he crawled out too early; he crept from the house and into the yard in time to see Angela stuffing a bag with vegetables, in time to hear Charlie say, "Cholly like cellee, Cholly like garlee." He froze. Too late. The man turned and smiled and said, "Cholly like lilla boy."

I'll bet you do, thought little Dusty. He bolted from the yard and ran down the lane and into a clump of bushes near the tracks. He hid until hunger drove him home. Angela gave him a bowl of soup and a salami sandwich, and warned him not to cause his mother any more embarrassment. Dusty said he didn't like the Chinaman.

She shook her head sadly.

Later that day, the boarder came home from work.

Listen closely now: a house full of kids is a house empty of money, therefore a boarder with monthly rent, and the myth — perpetuated by people who had wealth and status — that immigrants actually prefer to live like rats, one on top of another.

Let it pass, let it pass.

Emmanuele worked on the docks; he was a strongman who could deadlift a pair of hundred-pound sacks of flour, one in each hand, and hold them straight out from his sides, his arms as steady as if they'd been nailed to a cross.

Emmanuele was a sharp dresser, a ladies' man from Campobass', down the road from Ripabottoni. He gave Angela a bag of shirt collars and asked her to send one of the kids over to the laundry. This was Dominic's job, normally. Dominic was older, harder, stronger, and afraid of nothing. Dom was tough enough to take on a whole gang of Chinese men. But Dom was somewhere else.

So were the rest of the kids.

Dusty refused to go. Manny offered him a dime. It wasn't enough to sway him; his life was worth more than ten cents. Manny upped the offer to a quarter. Dusty gulped. A quarter was a lot of money. If he didn't take it, he'd be slapped for his stupidity. His life would be worthless in any case. He took the bag of collars.

Halfway to the laundry, he stopped. He was afraid to face danger alone. But — a bright idea — with a quarter he could buy plenty of reinforcements. He detoured through the schoolyard and drew a gang around him with promises of candy for all.

The gang fell silent as they neared the laundry. None of the kids would enter with him, which is what my father had hoped. So he made the best deal he could: *You wait here, and if I don't come out, call the cops.* At least that was something. At least the others would survive to tell the story of a poor boy's bravery.

He stepped inside the door, entering but not entering, inching forward, sniffing the humid laundry air, trying to reach far enough to drop the collars on the counter.

A voice said, "Come closer."

He froze. He knew the collars needed to be counted; there was the matter of the "tickee." He leaned closer, and suddenly he was seized from behind by a pair of strong arms.

Charlie said, "What's a matta, lilla boy? You afraid Cholly? Cholly no hurt lilla boy, Cholly likee lilla boy. You come long Cholly."

My little father wet himself.

Charlie sighed. He said, gently, "You come long, Cholly fix." He carried the boy into the back of the laundry, pulled off his wet pants, cleaned him with a warm, damp cloth.

Dusty thought he was being cleaned for the pan.

He closed his eyes and prayed, and when he opened them again he saw half a dozen Chinese men in black shirts and trousers, armed with irons. They looked hungry. They peered wordlessly through the steam at Charlie and my half-naked father. Actually, they were worried, and they had good reason to worry.

Chinky, Chinky, Chinaman
Sitting on a rail.
Along came an Englishman
And chopped off his tail.

The laundry men wore queues.

The little boy was no Englishman, but he was close enough: any little English-speaking boy might know an Englishman; any little boy's father might work for an Englishman; even a little dago boy might live under some sort of English protection; it didn't matter.

This boy was dangerous.

One of the men stepped carefully forward and gave Dusty a stick of rock candy; he reached for it without thinking and said, "Thank you." The man smiled, the boy smiled, the men in black returned to their irons. Danger, having hissed, now disappeared.

And so my father sat and watched them work, inhaling steam and starch and licking his candy until Charlie returned with his newly cleaned pants, his newly cleaned underwear. Charlie brushed my father's hair. He said he had a boy in China. He said he missed his family very much. And then little Dusty threw his arms around Charlie's neck and hugged him, fierce and fearless.

Charlie took the stick of rock candy from my father's hand and put it in a bag filled with more candy. He gave him a tickee and said, "You go home now, lilla boy, and not be afraid of Cholly no more." My father ran out the door and into the light, where the gang awaited.

The gang was not alone. They were tugging at the sleeve of a cop, urging him to break down the door. My father sized up the situation and sang out with casual bravado, "Hey, gang, what's the matter?"

The gang broke into half a dozen voices speaking all at once until the cop barked, "Keep quiet, all of you. I'll do the talking. Okay, squirt, what happened?"

Minus the pissing-his-pants part of the story, my father told the policeman what had happened and with an insider's knowledge added, "Them Chinamen are okay." The cop told the kids to run along and to quit bothering the hard-working people.

In the summer, I would lie on the grass in the shade between the houses, chewing leaves of mint and drinking lime Kool-Aid from a gallon jug while my mother cleaned the kitchen and my father sat in his shorts in the basement practising his trombone.

My own childhood was not so far removed from my father's, a difference of roughly thirty years. But he was born near the end of the First World War – cars and lights and airplanes were new – and so the difference between us was greater than a lifetime.

I stare at the clouds and worry the neighbours won't understand what he's doing. I can hear the stutter and stammer of his false starts and broken notes; it never occurs to me that adults have to practise. It seems to me that if you are an adult, you know what you were doing, or you don't do it. I think all skill is innate and comes with maturity.

He is getting ready for a dance job.

I can hear him trying to play his way into the heart of his signature song. He drags a note with the slide of his horn, he flirts impatiently with a phrase which rises and falls as it nears the vocal. He skips a measure and sings: *Just an old sweet*, damn it! *Just an old sweet*, god damn it! *Just an old sweet song keeps Georgia on my mind.*

And his horn turns to honey in the heat.

I learned about sex to the sounds of "Georgia" on Saturday afternoons, under a tent made from a scratchy grey army blanket on the back-yard grass, with a neighbourhood girl aged six, the same as me, you show me yours, I'll show you mine; her peachy slit, my little pink arrow.

Other arms reach out to me.

Other eyes smile tenderly.

God damn it. *Still in peaceful dreams I see.* Keep still; I hear something. *The road leads back to you.*

Shh.

We lived in a neighbourhood of uniforms, then. It was as if, having returned from the war, the men on the block had been reluctant to give up their creased trousers and peaked caps. Next door to us, a meter reader, grey-blue; down the block there were firemen and cops, blue-black with red piping; across the street, two more postmen in grey and black; and old man Collins.

Old man Collins was a conductor on the railroad. He went to work in his black uniform, disappeared for weeks at a time, and came home at odd hours on odd days, always pleasantly drunk. He was a giddy man, and he told harmless jokes.

When he came home on a Friday evening in the summer he liked to sit on the front porch with a bottle and a bucket of ice and a glass; he'd call the neighbourhood kids to him, he'd roll around on the grass, laughing and tickling, spilling coins and candies on the lawn, *lookit there, lookit there,* telling the kids there were quarters in his pockets. He let my younger brother wear his conductor's cap.

No one thought there was any evil in this, but everyone understood old man Collins was somehow weak. And there were noises which emerged late in the evening from his house: the weeping of his wife, his own harsh and uncharacteristic bark, and the yelps his sons Jim and Bobby made when they were strapped. This was how men contained their families.

These were familiar sounds.

I lived in terror of the strap and could divine the meaning of what I heard: Bobby's howls were the most fearful; he wept and shrieked and pleaded like a child. Jim bore it sullenly and did not try to wriggle free; there was something twisted inside him, as if the pain nourished him.

When I was eight, we strung a net between two houses and played team badminton in the afternoon, four boys a side. One afternoon a sneer of laughter leaked down upon the game; we looked up to see Jim leaning out the window. He ducked back inside and then re-emerged, shaking a basket of waste paper on our heads; the scraps fluttered

around us like snow. Bobby swore; his brother was a perpetual embarrassment.

I picked up one of the coloured bits of paper. "Jesus,
will you take a look at this." In my hands, a scrap of rouged
cheek and a pair of bright red lips pursed at the tip of a
man's cock.

The picture was no larger than a Communion wafer, and
had been carefully ripped so that there would be no mistak-
ing the image. I looked up, and now it was raining pictures of
tits and cunts and cocks. We fell to our knees instantly,
combing the grass for a patch of hair, a swollen nipple; *Look
what I got, look at this.*

Above our heads, Jim cackled. And then I heard the sharp
sound of a smack on the head; Jim ducked and wailed and his
mother stuck her head out the window: "What in the name
of god are you kids doing down there?" We scattered, our
pockets filled with scraps of sex. We went back later for more.
And found none, a mystery.

When I was ten, Denny Hyde announced that his cousin was
coming to visit. Denny lived a few doors from us, on the
corner. His cousin lived somewhere down east, and her legs
were rumoured to be bowed, and any girl whose legs were
bowed had done it; that was what happened to girls who had
done it, their legs became bowed.

The older boys laughed nervously, they combed their
hair, punched each other in the arm, and talked about what
they'd do to her. Denny shut them up. He said he had plans

of his own; he had dibs. She was, after all, his cousin; she'd be staying in his house. She was coming in a month.

One morning, about a week before she came, Denny sat on his back porch with his cocker spaniel in his lap. He'd come out after his mother had hung out the laundry. I kept an eye on him while I weeded the garden. He was up to something. I couldn't tell what it was.

Risky business, asking; he'd beaten me up once or twice with complete indifference, just to show me he could. He knocked me down, and I got up and I got up again and I got up until he got tired of knocking me down. He didn't like me, but I'd earned a grudging respect.

On the pretext of taking a break to get a pop at Antonelli's store, I walked towards him, cutting across the back yards. Denny cradled his dog in his arms the way he might have held a baby. There was a small jar on the porch. He had one hand between Skipper's hind legs.

He was jerking his dog off.

Skipper didn't seem to mind; apparently, it was something they'd done before; the jar was half full of spunk. I was about to ask a question when Skipper shuddered. Denny held his dog's prick and milked it carefully, and then he let Skipper run away. He screwed the lid back on the jar and dared me, wordlessly, to ask.

But what was the question?

Skipper stopped and peered between his legs. And I kept walking. Denny's cousin came and went. She was pretty. Her legs weren't bowed. He never said a word about her when she left. And no one asked him what he'd done with a jar full of essence of dog.

I avoided him thereafter.

We subscribed to a religious book club, the work of my mother, doing what she could to inflict a little right behaviour on us all. One day a collection of Bible stories arrived, its pages illustrated with black-and-white line drawings. I read about girls who had been raped into sainthood. I opened the book and joined the elders staring at Susannah as she stepped, naked, from her bath; I studied her foot, her thighs, her ample breasts. There was no escape from the message of the drawing.

I learned lessons even when I wasn't looking for them.

A new priest came to the parish when I was in the fourth grade. He had been sent to us from Rome. Father Villa's face was red, his belly was round, his cheap black suit was shiny and ill-fitting; all the children loved him. His hair was steely and closely cropped, he had salt-and-pepper stubble on his cheeks, he smiled easily and often.

He reminded me of Padre Pio, the little priest who had developed wounds on his hands and feet like those of Christ. At Mass, on the rare occasions when Father Villa was allowed to dispense Communion, I stole glances at his hands. I hoped to see the beginnings of wounds. I wanted to see wounds. I wanted wounds of my own.

I was stigmata-crazy then. I thought about the priesthood, and once I scratched and scraped the palm of my hand with the point of a compass every day for a week, hoping the wound might blossom into a miracle of suffering. I healed instead, not even a scar: my miracle.

Father Villa had come to hear confession in Italian. The paisans who lived in the parish were not going to Mass; they mistrusted Irish priests, and Father Corrigan mistrusted the Italians, especially those who were new and spoke very little English.

There was a reason for this mistrust.

You can't fool Italians about the Church. The Vatican is in Rome, and priests, even Oblate priests, have appetites as ravenous as those of other men.

Corrigan tried to peddle intimidation. The Italians would not be intimidated. They would not be hectored into holiness by any Irishman; they simply stayed away from mass, a source of income lost. Father Villa's job was to return the sheep to the fold.

As part of his pastoral duties, he came to school on Fridays to speak to the children of the junior grades. His accent was rich, his tongue was thick, his teeth were yellow stumps, his breath was wretched. He knew just enough English to say, "Be nice, the little children," and "You must love Jesus." It was not easy; he forced himself to speak, as if English were a burning building from which he had to jump; he hesitated, and then leapt into the net of our open hearts. "We love Jesus, Father!"

The nuns were always sour; he was happy to see us. And so it was that one Friday Sister Immaculata stood at the head of the class and said, with bitter satisfaction, that Father Villa was coming to say goodbye.

A silence fell over the room.

"Sister, why does Father Villa have to say goodbye?"

"Child, he is going back to Rome."

"Sister, why does Father Villa have to go to Rome?"

"The Holy Father needs him there." We needed him more than the Holy Father. We wanted him to stay. It was unfair. The Irish priests were hard, unforgiving, cruel; they smelled of whisky and disapproved of us. Father Villa smelled like wine; he was happy in our midst. The nuns seemed to hate us. Father Villa loved us.

Just before lunch, some daydreamer sitting by the window spotted Father Villa's roly-poly figure emerge from the rectory, cross the street, and enter the schoolyard. "Father Villa! He's coming! Here comes Father Villa!"

The nuns lost control of us in an instant. We poured into the schoolyard before the priest had a chance to reach the boys' door. Father Villa stood in the dust and cinders, the yellow grass of the playground; the youngest children ran to him, they called his name, tugged at his clothes. He tilted his head and squinted into the sun, his arms outstretched. Tears rolled down his cheeks.

"You must love Jesus," he sobbed.

"We love Jesus, Father!"

"We love you, Father!"

"Don't go, Father!"

"Goodbye, Father!"

Later, I asked my parents why the little priest had been called to Rome. "He wasn't called, he was sent," my father said. I asked him what he meant. He glanced at my mother;

she smiled as if they shared a secret joke. And then she spoke: the little priest had been using the confessional for purposes other than the relief of sin. Father Villa had been trading penance for the sexual favours of some of the women of the parish, some of whom were married, some of whom were not, but all of whom were lonely. If he had not been summoned back to Rome, and if he had not gone quickly, there would have been a riot.

The following Sunday, we held our breath at mass; almost as an afterthought, Monsignor Corrigan ended his sermon by observing that some priests are unable to make the adjustment to parish life. He did not mention Father Villa's name.

He said we would soon be joined by a new priest, an Oblate from North Bay. Father Desbiens. No more priests from Rome. I watched the Italian men; they scowled. I watched the Italian women; their heads were bowed in submission.

I knew this was a matter of sex and faith and forgiveness; but I was young and did not know who was right or what was wrong, nor did I know who bore responsibility for which sin.

Not right for a priest to take advantage.

Human to succumb to longing.

Wrong to be Italian.

I will not speculate about my father's sex life. I know he was naive. We talked; he told me about some of his adventures. There was an air of haste about his stories. He didn't know much about technique. His sources on the subject had not been sophisticated. There were rumours about his adventures, as well as those of some of my uncles; there was supposed to be a couple of unacknowledged cousins.

Dusty had his share of affairs.

I had two friends in high school, the sons of a woman on his route; they suddenly stopped talking to me. At the same time, my parents entered the darkest period of their marriage; there were many evenings when they talked of divorce long into the night.

For months, Dusty kept to himself when he was at home. And then the affair seemed to be over. He stopped going out at odd times, and there were no more whispered phone calls, and no more notes discovered in the pocket of his jacket.

Eventually my mother thawed.

I didn't care.

I remember bumping into Dusty downtown once, a few months after I'd left home and set myself up in an apartment of my own. He had a full sack of mail around his neck, and there was a spring in his step. "Come on for a walk," he said. He was chipper, all was right in the world, and I couldn't refuse. He whistled as he walked, plucking letters from his bag, tossing greetings everywhere he went.

We stopped for a beer and a burger in the Victoria Hotel. He waved to men he'd played with as a boy, men he knew from the army, men he knew over glasses of beer, and men with whom he'd fought bare-knuckled, black-eyed brawls in the old days. What of that now?

He was famous in a sense. Everyone knew his name, people stopped to say hello, women made eyes at him from across the street. He took a handful of mail into Rikki's Dress Shop, where as a teen I'd once spent an awkward week wrapping tissue around fragile dresses, packaging them in boxes for delivery, my worst summer job.

He swept into the shop with a general "Hello, Gorgeous!" It was intended for any woman within hearing, thrown like a handful of grain before a flock of chickens; it was enough to cause a stir and a flutter and not a little disapproval.

A pretty woman who'd been trying on a skirt in the fitting room heard his voice, and caught sight of the back of him. In her stockinged feet, she followed him out of the store and onto the sidewalk. She threw her arms around his neck and said, "Oh, Dusty, you were wonderful Saturday night."

He'd played a dance at the Polish Legion. Halfway through the evening, when he'd had enough to drink, he'd opened his collar and loosened his tie, set his glass on the edge of the piano, and quietly said, "The St. James Infirmary Blues." He'd taken a drag from his cigarette, squinted as he parked it in the ashtray, and eased the slide on his trombone rapidly back and forth.

Let her go, let her go, God bless her
Wherever she may be.
She can search the whole world over,
Never find a sweet loving man like me.

He'd had just enough whisky that he was beyond care. He was not self-conscious now. He was inside the music; the music carried him. Then the piano dropped a few brittle notes onto the bandstand, the sax pulled them together into a pool of light, and he stepped into "Stardust."

The dance floor was filled with couples.

He was a prism for the music; it shone through him. Men held their women tightly, and women swayed and pushed themselves into the hips of their men, and the smell of perfume rose in the warm air, and a shudder ran through the room. Dusty planted his feet, leaned back from the hip, held the microphone to his lips. When he sang, nothing else existed save the music; there was no bickering over bills, there were no kids arguing. There was only the music, and the sound of his voice.

He was irresistible; ask anyone.

The woman – I never found out who she was – spun him lightly and planted a big red kiss on his cheek; his eyes rolled upwards, helplessly. And then she ran back into the store, tucking in her blouse as she ran. She had wide hips and short legs, she looked as if she were close to bursting out of her skin, like a ripe peach; good to hold.

"Who's that, Pops?"

"Damned if I know."

I didn't believe him. The smooch had not gone unnoticed. Mrs. Hnatiuk, who lived on our block and who was a nasty gossip, had seen all and would be sure to tell my mother. Dusty grinned and shrugged and wiped the lipstick from his cheek.

I was proud of him, in a way.

I once took a date to a bar where he happened to be playing. I didn't know he'd be there; his presence caught me by surprise. I wanted to leave, she wanted to stay. She took me by the hand and led me to a front-row table. She sat with her chin in her hands. She stared at him as he leaned into his bass and plucked the strings, she gasped when he sang. I gave up on her.

Too much, too much.

The Sixteenth Afternoon

*B*efore I go on shift, I take a walk along the lane behind the house. The railroad tracks are still there, but someone has cut the bush where I trapped birds, the ditch of pollywogs has dried up, and the field of twitch grass has been replaced by a public housing development. But the hump of ground where we killed the elephant remains.

The elephant was a giant plush toy, big as a boy, pink and grey. It was second-hand when we got it. Dusty had found it somewhere along his mail route; some rich kid's toy. The sheer size of it had amused him. He brought it home.

I felt embarrassed. The elephant was not new; it hadn't been ours from the beginning. It was not even a hand-me-down. It was simply a second-hand, junk-pile elephant.

It became a kind of joke. I used to beat it. For the amusement of my brothers, I mimicked Dusty: "Where's my strap?

God damn it to hell, I don't know how many times I've told you kids." They giggled.

I hit it with my belt. I hit it with the cord from the electric kettle. And I hit it with the razor strap. Eventually the beatings made it mine. And after a season of amused whippings, I passed responsibility for the elephant to my next-youngest brother. He had it for a season, and he took his turn beating it with glee.

We avenged ourselves by pretending it was a playground bully. We kicked it and twisted its trunk and called it to account with our fists. Sometimes we fell asleep against it; we drooled on it at night and the short grey pile of its skin grew crusty and sour.

When he saw us abandon the elephant, my youngest brother took it as his own. According to our calculations, he was not a baby; he was about to begin Grade One. We let him have the elephant, in the hope that he, too, would learn to beat the thing; but he misunderstood, he was too young for irony. He'd sit with his arm around the elephant's shoulder and watch television. He talked to it, he slept with it, he grew more attached to it as the summer progressed.

With the cruelty of children on whom cruelty has been practised, we decided that the youngest one was too old for a toy elephant. And so, with grave formality, we invited the youngest one to a fraternal council meeting.

We told him this business of the elephant was not right, that the elephant had never really been ours, that it came to us from some other children, that it had been thrown in the garbage — a wrongful bit of strategy, because each of us had inherited Dusty's soft spot for strays.

We told him that the elephant was a joke. He was about to start school, and it was time for him to grow up and leave plush toys behind. He was silent; we were relentless. We gave him two weeks to come to terms with the bedraggled creature. It was old. It was crusty and falling apart.

It would have to die.

Death was nothing new. The old bull in the field behind the house had been carted away. Our first, best cat had grown old, and had died in its sleep; we buried its stiff, cold body in the flower bed in front of the house. One of our dogs had gone crazy, shitting and shivering uncontrollably throughout the neighbourhood; the dog was put down. And we were sent into the garden once a week in the summer to collect cutworms in tin cans, and when the cans were half full, we poured boiling water on them. We caught fish and shot rabbits and partridge with my father, and we helped in the gutting and the skinning. There was blood on our hands. The elephant was old, and sick, and falling apart; it, too, would have to die. It was the natural order of things.

For two weeks, my younger brother and I stopped beating the elephant. We treated it as if it were dying, we stopped mocking the youngest one when he sat next to it. We made no jokes. We let him take it to his bed at night for comfort.

But we were firm.

When the day came, I took the elephant and the longest

of the kitchen knives and the three of us marched into the
field behind the house to a spot in the bush beyond the lane.
We set the elephant in the tall grass. It fell over. We propped
it up on the ash heap and stood back. "It's time," I said. My
brother's eyes widened. "You can't play with stuffed toys any
more. You're too old for that. That's kid's stuff," I said.

My younger brother said, "You have to say goodbye."

My youngest brother nodded.

"It's time to grow up," I said.

He nodded again.

The three of us stood silently paying our respects. If he'd
cried, I think that might have been the end of it. He didn't
cry. I offered him the first cut. He shook his head, but he did
not protest.

And so I took the knife and stuck it to the hilt into the
belly of the elephant. And then again; I did it again. I stabbed
and turned the blade and twisted, and I gave the knife to
next-youngest brother and he, too, struck with the knife.

He gave the blade to me again, and I offered it to the
youngest one. He held it limply in his hand. The elephant's
guts were made of grey stuffing. "Go ahead, you have to stick
it now. You have to let it go. You have to send it off." He
poked at the elephant's belly. There was a deep sadness in my
little brother's eyes, and there were tufts of stuffing rising in
the bright and sunny air. He gave the elephant a poke.

And he gave the knife to me.

"Don't tell anybody," we told him.

"Don't tell Mom."

"Don't tell Dad."

We turned and walked back to the house. My youngest brother was quiet. He wouldn't speak to us but he couldn't avoid us, not in that small house. We'd killed what he'd clung to in his childhood; in return, we vowed to treat him as if he were grown up. His ascension as a brother was, we thought, a proper end to the ritual of the elephant's death.

He told Grace.

She vowed to tell Dusty. My younger brother looked at me. We were sunk; this was going to be real trouble. I whispered in his ear. I had a plan.

He diverted my mother. I took the razor strap from its handle on the bathroom door and hid it in the closet. My father came home and my mother told him the story. He said, "God damn it, that's the last straw. Where's my razor strap? You, Joe, go and get my strap."

If he'd been wearing his belt, it would have come off then and there. But he was wearing suspenders; he needed the strap. Fetching it was an additional punishment, the last mile. I make a pretense of walking slowly to the bathroom, and returned with a downcast face.

"It isn't there. I don't know where it is."

"It's in the god-damned bathroom where I left it."

"No, it's not."

"God damn it to hell, I'll get it myself."

He went to the bathroom; he found no strap. "Jesus wept!" He scanned his bedroom. He went into our bedroom and turned the toy box upside down; still no strap. He was too angry to swear. He took me by the shoulders; his nostrils flared. "If you don't tell me where my strap is, you'll get it with the kettle cord." There was beer on his breath. "You decide. Right now."

It was not much of a decision; the strap was a double tongue of thick brown belting leather with the legend, "Every Dot A Hone," intended for dull razors and not boys' bottoms. But because of its width, there was a cushion of air when it struck; the pain it produced stung, but disappeared. The kettle cord was heavy, and raised painful welts that lasted for days.

I walked to the hall closet. I stood by the door, trembling. I refused to open it. "It's in here." He pushed me aside, pushed coats and blankets aside, moved his bass fiddle, moved the rifles, rummaged in the box of winter scarves. I was frightened, but his fury was funny. And then, under the scarf box, he found his razor strap.

And then it struck him; was this the revolt of the slaves? He laughed; he didn't beat us. Later, he told us the story of the cat in a sack. And made us swear not to pick on the little one again.

The dead elephant.

My dying father.

The Sixteenth Night

_H_e says little now; in fact, he hardly moves. He moans, although his breathing is imperceptible. I begin to think he might die at any time. But he lingers. The cancer scratches and claws at him. He holds it tight, like the boy with the fox in his shirt; as in the fable, he lets it gnaw away.

He courted death when he was young; he flirted with it during the years when he drank hard; as an old man he sat in his armchair and waited for death to come to his door. When it finally came for him he shrank back with a peasant's superstition.

Death was coming for him now.

He slept, and I considered him. He couldn't fix a tap to save his life; with the single exception of the changing of light bulbs, my father made no home repairs without curses and wild blows of a hammer, or whatever blunt instrument was at hand. But if he did not know how things should be done, he made it clear he knew how they should not be done: "Not like that, god damn it!" Followed, as often as not, by a cuff on my ear, and "How many god-damn times do I have to tell you?"

He was cruel when he sensed weakness or incompetence; I suspect it was because he feared weakness in himself. If he was unsure of what he should do, he did nothing, his hedge against failure.

When he retired from the post office – a forced retirement, on a medical discharge because his knees were shot, his spine was crooked, one shoulder was lower than the other, and his pelvis was tipped forward, all the result of hauling sacks of mail – he felt abandoned.

He sat in his chair and moped and nursed his wounded pride until, urged on by a doctor with a profitable interest in treating veterans, he began a paper war. He was not quite of retirement age; his injuries were in part due to his military training; he could still do certain kinds of work. Eventually, they forced the post office to send my father on a retraining program. What could he do? He was a musician, he'd repair musical instruments. He went to Winnipeg, lived in a furnished room for a year, and apprenticed himself to a German craftsman.

He came back to Fort William, rented a tiny red-brick bandbox which had once been the Knights of Columbus Hall, and hung out his shingle. "Dusty Fiorito's Musical Instrument Repairs."

He knew nothing about business; he would have preferred

to do everything on the honour system. He didn't like the idea of sending out bills; the act of sending a bill was an act of mistrust, the equivalent of calling someone a deadbeat.

He started neatly enough, but soon his workbench was littered with spools of solder, stray screws and nuts, packets of matches, envelopes of fine-grit sandpapers, ball-hammers, clarinet reeds, jars of petroleum jelly, oily rags, and overflowing ashtrays. He spent what was left of his rage hammering at rotten brass instruments. He lasted a year and a half, and then he abandoned the shop.

As I grew up, I often met old men who, on hearing my last name and learning I was Dusty's son, would tell me what a swell guy my dad was. My first reaction was to blurt that he wasn't swell: he was damaged, and he damaged his family; he drank, he wept, he raged.

But I didn't want to be disloyal.

He was helpless, but he was likeable. As soon as his rage had blown itself out, he would forgot he'd been angry. If he'd done something sharp or intemperate, the memory of it disappeared as quickly as the deed had been done. He laughed as easily as he cried. I knew he loved me. I forgave him. He was innocent.

He'd told me his brother Tony had wanted to come back to life as a little black dog; a bit cute, but Dusty never failed to stop and greet any little black dog he saw. *Tony? Is that you?*

He'd been bitten often enough when he delivered mail, but never by black dogs. He was a champion of the well-timed kick. He held the theory that if a dog leapt for your throat, you could kill it by grabbing its forelegs in mid-air and twisting them apart like a wishbone; the dog's heart would stop. He had another other theory; you let the dog sink its teeth in your wrist, then you flipped your wrist over, and the dog would break its own neck as it fell backwards. His theories were fine for the beer parlour, and fine for entertaining children, but there were scars on his ankles and his wrists.

Once, a brute of a dog ran up from behind, leapt through the air and sunk its jaws in the seat of his pants. My father kept a pouch of tobacco in his hip pocket; the dog got a mouthful of Prince Albert; it ran away howling, and never bothered him again. From then on, he'd warn all suspicious dogs, "You better not bite me, boy. Haven't you heard? Postmen taste like pipe tobacco."

Trixie picked him up on his mail route.

She was a white pup with a whippet's tail, a black patch over one eye, and a black mark on her back; depending on your point of view, the mark was a *3*, an *M* or a *W*.

Dusty scratched her ear, she followed him home.

She was a happy cur. She ran into the house as if she'd belonged to us all along. She licked my face. Her tail was a blur. I asked if we could keep her and didn't need an answer because I knew then that she was mine; for a moment, all Dusty's faults faded and I thought he was the greatest father in the world.

Trixie wasn't the first dog to adopt him.

Lucky was a German Shepherd who lived in a big house

near the start of his route; every morning, Lucky stood by his master's door waiting for the mail as if it were his job.

Dusty and Lucky grew pally.

One day my father stopped and told Lucky about the trouble he was having with the other dogs on the route; the next day, Lucky slipped out of the house and escorted my father around his route.

Dusty loved his little mysteries and coincidences; I have a hunch Lucky's owner let his dog out on purpose. No matter. Whenever another dog tried to approach my father, Lucky growled a deep-throated warning. He was deep-chested and thick-necked, he reeked of canine gravitas; he rarely had to growl. It was a fair arrangement for all; Lucky's owner was too old to take the dog for its daily walk, and from then on Dusty delivered the mail unmolested.

He brought Lucky home one day. My mother said the dog was as big as a horse. There was a gleeful little squeal; "Horsey," said my baby brother. He wanted to ride on the dog's back.

He grabbed a fistful of hair and swung aboard, kicking his bare heels into the dog's ribs: a horse of a dog and a cowboy in a diaper; giddy-up. And then the cats strolled in for a look.

Lucky endured, but he turned his head and looked at my father, as if to say the kid in the diaper is bad enough, but this business with the cats is pushing it. My father laughed, we all laughed, just like a TV family.

And then one day Dusty was transferred to a route on the other side of town. He and Lucky made the rounds together one last time. Dusty sent the dog on his way with a pat on the head and a word of farewell.

The next morning, at eight o'clock, my father shouldered his mailbag and got off the bus in a strange neighbourhood.

Lucky was waiting for him at the bus stop.

A true story.

These things happened to Dusty.

And he made things happen to us.

Little Trixie was a bitch; she followed him home. We couldn't afford pups, so he took her to the vet to have her spayed. When she came home again, she was so happy to see us she grinned. Lips pulled back, teeth bared, a full-fledged smile.

I was only dimly aware that there were problems. She followed me around the block, she followed me to the park, she followed me into the bush beside the railroad tracks, she fetched sticks and chased balls, she was my pal, but she was a digger; she left neat round holes in lawns all around the neighbourhood.

She'd race across the street in response to a mad urge only she understood; she'd stop and cock an ear, and then dig madly with her front paws; she'd trot home with a long and wriggling dew worm dangling from her grin.

The neighbours were not amused, and neither was my mother. One afternoon Trixie laid a slimy prize on the back steps; my mother slipped and fell, spilled a basket of laundry, and hurt her back. I thought this was proof of how clever the dog was; previously, only the cats had been thoughtful enough to retrieve small creatures, mice and birds, and bring them home. I was alone in this view.

The Shrine Circus came to town that fall, and Dusty's horn was in demand. He was hit-or-miss as a soloist, but he was sweetly unerring as an ensemble player. He was also on the executive of the musician's union, and so he was a natural choice.

One night at rehearsal, he shared a smoke and fell into conversation with Victor Julian, the world-famous dog trainer. Victor Julian's dogs had been on Ed Sullivan, they wore little fireman's hats, climbed little ladders, and jumped through little burning hoops.

To Dusty, this was an agreeable scam: a man could travel the world, wear a tux, have supper every night after the show with his pick of long-legged showgirls, and do nothing more strenuous than throw his dogs a bone. Naturally, Dusty invited him home for supper.

Victor Julian accepted.

LOCAL POOCH JOINS TROUPE

Trixie The Smiler Soon To be Famous
by Jack Snider, Daily Times-Journal Reporter

When Victor Julian of England presented his trained dog show recently at the Shrine circus here he had 19 dogs. When he left he had 20 — including a local pooch.

She is Trixie, a dog that can laugh. She is able to produce a genuine full-toothed smile upon request of her owners and Victor Julian guarantees the 20-months old mongrel will be seen on television screens by September.

That guarantee softened considerably the loss of a playmate for the four children of Mr. and Mrs. Lawrence (Dusty) Fiorito of 317 W. Christina Street, who owned the giggling quadruped.

SMILED UPON RETURN

Some months ago Trixie visited the veterinary where she underwent an operation of an extremely personal nature. Upon return to the family she broke out in a genuine ear-to-ear smile. Mrs. Fiorito says it was because "she was so glad to be home." The family cultivated her new talent until it was produced on request.

Then Victor Julian of the dancing doggies came to town. Mr. Fiorito, a city mail carrier, was hired among 10 other local musicians to fill out the band for the Shrine circus.

On the last night of the show he inquired of Mr. Julian where he obtained the dogs he trained for his act. Said Victor, "I pick them up anywhere. They may be of any breed."

Dusty mentioned Trixie and her smile. "I'll have a look at her," said Mr. Julian.

ON HER WAY

He sent for his trainer. The two specialists were agreed. For an undisclosed sum the deal was made and a Fort William pooch was on its way to stardom.

Previously she had almost gone on another journey.

Trixie liked to dig, particularly in neighbours' lawns and gardens. The Fioritos sadly decided they would have to be rid of her. Mr. Fiorito set out for the SPCA, with the children and Mrs. Fiorito in tears.

But they never arrived at the SPCA. Mr. Fiorito grew softer by the step. He returned home. Trixie was with him.

The children now are comforted and proud in Victor Julian's promise that she will smile on their television screen this fall.

Mr. Fiorito visited the van in which Victor Julian travels his dogs. Each has a clean and comfortable cubicle of its own, air-conditioned and with a heating system thermostatically controlled.

"One need have no fear of any maltreatment of a dog in there," Mr. Fiorito said. "When Julian walks in they simply go crazy over the man." To such a happy family has Fort William's Trixie gone. We wish her well.

As newspaper stories go, this has the whiff of deadline funk. It's a boozy reporter's colour piece, whipped up for a laugh after a short chat and a quick double in a bar.

Jack Snider should have talked to me.

I could have told him how oily I thought Julian was, with his little moustache and his slick hair. I could have told him that I had no appetite for supper that night. I could have told him how suspicious I was when Trixie grinned for the stranger.

It was my first betrayal.

I was sent outside to play. I was never sent outside. If Snider had talked to me, I could have told him how, when I came back in from playing, no one looked at me, everyone looked at the floor. And then my father looked at my mother, and she looked away. And he looked at Victor Julian. And Victor Julian looked at his manicured hands.

My father cleared his throat; he hemmed and hawed and explained that Trixie was going to go and live with some other dogs; she would be happy and she would get to see the world, and there would be no more digging and upsetting the neighbours because she had a talent that she was now going to share with children all around the world. She'd be in show business. She'd be famous. We'd sold her to Mr. Julian.

"How much did you get," I asked.

"A week's pay," said my father.

"She'll be given a good home. She'll be on Ed Sullivan," said Victor Julian. I said nothing. I was trying not to cry. A man with a pencil-thin moustache was taking my dog away, and my father was pocketing the money, and I was being fed a lie about Ed Sullivan.

Snider got one thing right. I wept.

My pals in the neighbourhood asked me about Trixie. I was too embarrassed to say that my father had sold her; thanks to the newspaper story, I didn't have to. It was no secret. Everyone know. We were so poor, we'd had to sell our dog.

What kind of man sells his son's dog?

I knew my parents needed the money; all their arguments

were about money. But I didn't mention the show-biz angle to anyone. I was embarrassed; I had no interest in sounding gullible.

He played with the circus the night after he sold the dog, a Saturday. He came home drunk, and in the morning he refused to look me in the eye. He was supposed to play with the city band in the park in the afternoon. I doubted he'd make it.

My mother was angry, perhaps because she didn't like her part in the affair. The city band gigs paid ten bucks. We needed the money. Dusty straightened up. We went with him, the happy family, all together.

The park was south of the river, south of town, near the reserve on the edge of the lake. There were cabins and row-boats for rent, a carousel with painted horses, and a small zoo, tired animals in rusty cages.

If the weather was bad, the band played under a green-and-white bandshell, an onion dome with gingerbread trim. If the weather was good, they played on a floating platform a hundred feet from shore: scarlet tunics, gleaming brass, the music as light as sparkling water.

The weather was good. There was a Sunday crowd. We stood and watched the bandsmen clutch their instruments and clamber into little rocking rowboats.

My mother never trusted Dusty when he played at night. But on Sundays in the park, she could keep an eye on him and get out of the house at the same time. She had packed a picnic lunch of cold meat, eggs, bread, and pickles; we had pennies for popcorn and bottles of pop. I played reluctant catch with my brothers; they pitched horseshoes and sat on the swings. All I could think of was my dog.

I heard the band; worse, I heard my father's horn, off-key. I'd have explained it away if I could. He'd sold my dog and got drunk because he felt bad; he'd betrayed me, he'd betrayed himself, he hadn't wanted to do it, but he was weak.

When the wind came up, and the clouds rolled in, the band rowed back to shore. They'd finish the second half of the concert on solid ground. I wandered off alone to see the animals.

I didn't do this often; I got lost easily. I still do.

The animals were listless in the summer heat. In a long row of wire pens there were sour-smelling foxes, a pair of wolves, some ratty peacocks, a male lynx, and a couple of martens, which in the heat did not look as if they could move faster than the eye could see. A solitary flightless eagle sat on the limb of a tall dead tree, nothing moving but its eyes, the tree draped in a high net.

In the middle of the grounds there was a small hillock; sunk into it was a dank concrete pen for the polar bear, Snowball. She was the star attraction of the park. Her coat was the colour of urine. Her smell was so rich, the children pinched their nostrils and poured caramel corn on her head.

I peered down at Snowball. She sat, legs splayed, and licked herself. I walked away. And then I saw my father making his way through the crowd. I ran up to him, tugged on his sleeve, tagged after him. I wanted to forgive him. I wanted him to forgive me. I wanted to set aside my hurt, in order to ease his. He was on his way to the pavilion; they served beer in the pavilion.

He gave me a nickel for a bag of peanuts.

"Run along," he said roughly.

I made my way back towards the cages, dropping peanuts like dry tears on the cinder path. I stared at the moose with its tea-coloured eyes, its head bent under the weight of its antlers. The buffalo stood, hooves splayed, nostrils dripping, dazed. The deer were skittish, their sides heaved.

The water in the animal troughs was slimy and sour. I smelled shit and popcorn oil in the air, the sweet perfume of candy floss being spun, and toffee apples rotting in the heat.

I walked towards the monkey cage; the chimps were sitting inside their hutch, out of the sun. One old greybeard remained, perched on his haunches on a swing. Jeering kids aimed french fries at his head. He was listless with contempt; now and then, he let loose a stream of shit. And all the while, he held his hand between his legs, rubbing himself. Men grinned and pointed; boys turned red in the face; women grabbed their daughters and led them across the grass towards the bandstand.

In the distance, filtered through the trees, the sound of instruments tuning up. I listened carefully: a trumpet riff, a vibraphone, and then two flutes chasing each other up and down the scales. I heard a trombone, but only one, and it was not my father's: Dusty always warmed up with a jazzy growl, a snatch of blues, and some slide trickery.

The chimp squinted, hissed through its yellow teeth.

I knew where my father was.

The pavilion was cool, dark and deserted. Dusty was standing alone at the bar. He was the most handsome man in the world: scarlet tunic, gold piping, navy-blue trousers with a scarlet stripe and a knife-edge crease; the boots I'd polished to a mirror shine.

In one hand, he held half a glass of soapy beer; in the other hand, his trombone. A second glass stood empty on the bar in front of him. He was trying to tell a story to the bartender. The bartender turned his back, stacked some glasses, walked to the other end of the bar and wiped the counter, a snub.

My father's horn glowed in the half-light. His lips were pursed, he was shaking his head, he looked as if he wanted to weep. I knew what he was like when he was happy; my heart broke, to see him so.

I was afraid he'd be late, afraid the bandmaster wouldn't let him take his place on stage. He'd be disgraced again, this time for all to see.

I was desperate for appearances; I couldn't possibly explain to everyone that he'd played late at a dance the night before, and he was tired, and he'd had too much to drink, not because he wanted to, but because he couldn't say no. I thought everyone ought to be willing to forgive his weaknesses if I did.

"Come on, Pop, the band is starting to play."

My father looked past me and then looked down at the beer in his glass; he drained it with abrupt gulps, the beer like yellow light through a window. And then he shuddered himself awake.

"Come on," he said. "You want me to go, I'll go."

There was an edge in what he said.

As if I'd been at fault.

And then he stacked his hat on my head, and picked me up and sat me on his shoulder; he carried me like a prize over to the bandstand.

A few months later, when the memory of Trixie was becoming distant, Victor Julian called. He asked for Dusty, and Dusty listened, and then he reported to us.

"I knew it all along. Trixie's a smart little dog. He says she was easy to train, she's the leader of the other dogs. And this is the week, sonny boy. Trixie's going to be on the Ed Sullivan show. I told you so, didn't I?"

I didn't want to believe him. I didn't want to hope, my chest was tight, I couldn't bear the wait.

That Sunday my mother made an early supper so we could eat and do the dishes and be free to watch the show without interruption. We sat in front of the television. I felt as if everyone was watching me.

There were no dogs in the first half of the show.

There must have been some problem, said my father; he said we'd see Trixie during the first half of the show; maybe there were changes to the lineup; oh, we're supposed to see her, make no mistake about that. And then came a commercial. And a comedian. And a singer. I felt sick. I'd been betrayed by my father, by Victor Julian, and now I'd been betrayed by Ed Sullivan.

After a commercial break, Ed Sullivan came back on and introduced some people in the audience. *Get on with it, get on with it.* "And now, all the way from England, ladies and gen-tlemen, let's hear it for Victor Julian and his dancing dogs."

Out came nineteen pups, some in little skirts, all of them wearing hats; they came dancing out in a line. I wasn't sure. Is that . . . ? Could that be . . . ? Not that one, not that one, not that one.

Trixie was the twentieth. She wore a little skirt, a pointy hat, and a doggy tuxedo with a bow tie. She was my little dog. She'd slept at the foot of my bed. She was a Westfort pup, my mongrel, and now the whole world was watching her, and I held my breath. I thought she'd be nervous. I couldn't bear it, I was afraid she'd make a mistake.

The other little dogs stood and formed a conga line, with their paws on the haunches of the dog in front. Then they jumped through a series of hoops, and Trixie stood and pointed a paw to guide them. She was the ringmaster, she watched the other dogs perform, and then she jumped higher and better than the best of them. And then the act was over.

My dog stood and watched the other dogs dance off stage and then, standing on her hind legs, with her little tail whip-ping, Trixie grinned at the audience and clapped her paws.

There's no business like show business.

I went outside when Ed Sullivan was over. I wanted my friends to see me. I simply wanted to be seen. But there was no one around, and all the holes in all the lawns had long since been filled in, and all the worms were safe. Trixie had made it; she was in show business.

My father had sold my dog.

He'd broken my heart; he'd filled it with magic.

Some years later, Victor Julian came to town again. Lots of new dogs in the act, but no Trixie. He and my father shared another smoke. And he gave my father the news: Trixie had gotten too old for the bright lights, so he'd sold her to a man who owned an electrical supply store in Florida. Trixie spent her final days as a greeter. She'd wait by the curb, and she'd escort customers into the store on her little hind legs.

Her little tail whipping.

Grinning all the while.

The Seventeenth Day

_I_ could not bear the thought of going home after my shift was over. I headed for Frederica Street instead. There were two greasy spoons on the block when I was growing up, one at either end of the street, the Coney Island and the Shamrock Grill, a pair of french-fried bookends in a row of small and futile shops: the bowling alley, a hair salon, a bargain clothing store, a radio-repair store, a tailor's, and a bootmaker's. It is a street redolent of hairspray, solder fumes, clouds of steam and starch; and from the restaurants the overpowering aroma of coffee and beef fat, chips and vinegar, raw onions and cigarette smoke.

In the middle of the street is Bando the Bootmaker's, empty now. But I gaze in the window, and suddenly I am fourteen years old, dizzy for an instant from the smell of leather glue.

I've been sent to pick up my father's resoled shoes.

Mimmo Bando sits at his bench, bent over his last, hammer in hand, his shoulders rounded, half a dozen small nails in his mouth. His hair is thin and slick and plastered to his head. His pot belly is draped with a coarse canvas apron. There is a gold ring on the little finger of his right hand; the ring digs into his flesh. His hands are stained, the nails are thick and dirty; he is tacking a sole on an upturned shoe.

In the window of his shop, there are six pairs of handmade oxfords, black and brown and oxblood, never worn, Mimmo's masterworks. Between the shoes are sheets of leather, tins of wax and polish, scattered laces. No one in this neighbourhood wants handmade goods; Mimmo survives by sharpening skates, resoling workboots, repairing purses, reinforcing the seams of baseball gloves, and tacking metal clicks on the heels of dress shoes.

Mimmo keeps a bottle in the back of the shop. I can sometimes smell liquor on his breath when I come to pick up my father's black boots or the shoes my mother wears to work. Mimmo and my father are friends; Dusty is friends with everybody, but this is a friendship which has something to do with Campobasso.

He takes the ticket I give him; he peers over his glasses at me. "You're Dusty's boy," he says. "Fiorito." He knows who I am. He just likes to announce my entry. He pronounces my name with a flourish and a smile. He says it better than I do.

My father delivers Mimmo's mail, mostly bills; now and then an air-mail envelope from the old country, addressed in a spidery European hand, return address, Ripabottoni.

"Fiorito, it's freezing outside. You look cold. Come in, come in, I'll give you something to make you warm."

"Just for a moment, Mimmo."

"I got something for you."

"What's that?"

"I got some coffee. And something nice to put in the coffee. Your boy, I got something for him, too. Come in, come in. What a country, Madonna, you could die. I don't know why I come here."

Mimmo is a single man, not for want of effort.

He attends the dances sponsored by the Principe Piedmonte; he never misses the spaghetti-and-meatball suppers at the Italian Hall. He loves to eat, to drink, and to hear my father play trombone. A little too loudly he cries, "Bravo, Dusty!" He thinks this impresses the women. It doesn't. Everyone knows my old man; nobody around here says "Bravo."

Mimmo asks all the women to dance: the shy and skinny ones, the women on the rebound; women whose girdles are too small, whose lipstick is too red, whose shoes are too tight; women who smoke cigarettes and nurse highballs. But he is light on his feet, he knows how to lead on the dance floor, and sometimes they say yes.

He is courtly, as befits a man from the old country. He is desperate to marry but widely viewed as unmarriageable, he doesn't make much money, and even if he suspects he is being ridiculed, he carries himself well. His hands are creased and stained but they are moist, and softer than a man's hands should be in a mill town. He dresses well, and he holds his dancing partners greedily.

He is not a man who knows how to live alone.

Now Mimmo busies himself with an espresso pot, and greets my father gruffly when he brings the mail. "This is not Campobass'," says Mimmo. He doesn't say Ripabottoni. Ripa is too small. He says Campobasso. Or Campobass'. As Dusty does. As my uncles and my cousins do. "Son of a bitch, it's so cold you need a sheep to keep you warm."

My father considers this; does Mimmo know something about a boy who killed a lamb and fled to America? No, he says sheep; he means a sheepskin coat. Mimmo pours thick coffee in little cups. He hands me a bottle of cream soda; it's warm. For my father, he produces a bottle of grappa, home-made, no label on the bottle, the grappa clear as water.

For a few moments, he and Dusty are two cultured men, the descendants of Dante and Michelangelo, blown adrift and marooned in a frozen land, drinking caffè corretto, staring out the window at the snow.

There have been mornings when my father has taken so much culture with Mimmo that he has to stumble for a mid-morning hot dog and a coffee at the Coney Island in order to sober up.

In my father's mind, getting drunk in the morning is no sin; you can't refuse what another man pours, a refusal is an insult, and who knows what might happen.

He knows what might happen.

It's happened before.

The truth is, he simply loved to drink, and drank every glass as if it were the first; he drank any kind of alcohol as long as you were pouring; and, if it was his bottle, he poured until there was nothing more to drink. He made sense as long as he was sitting.

His troubles started when he stood.

The memories return, unsorted, unbidden. I'd slammed the door on the way out of the house. I'd bounded down the steps, and heard my father calling after me: "Don't slam the door, god damn it!"

I'll slam the god-damned door any time I want, I muttered. I hated running his errands. He could have picked up his boots on the way home in the car; it was as if he thought I needed to do his bidding in order to build my character.

Mimmo was carving a piece of leather with a wicked-looking knife when I walked in. "Hey, Dusty's boy. Joseph Ciufolo. *Va bene?*"

"Yeah, sure. Who's Joseph Ciufolo?"

"Your father, he never told you that story?"

"He tells lots of stories."

"Joseph Ciufolo, the tiller who played the flute."

Mimmo took the stub of a cigar from his mouth. He spat a fleck of tobacco off his tongue, wiped his mouth with the back of his hand, and wiped the back of his hand on his apron. I turned away. I didn't want him to think I'd seen, I didn't want him to think I disapproved of his greasy habits.

I pretended to look at the shoes in the window. I counted the dead flies.

"No, he never told me that one."

Mimmo patted a strand of hair on his head. He'd done it before. I could see shoe polish on his shiny scalp. "I'm going to tell you now. You're not in a hurry, you got plenty of time. There was a boy, Joseph Ciufolo. Nice boy. He play the flute, he dig in the field. One day he find a dead body in the dirt, all covered with flies."

I knew what the dead man was wearing on his feet. Soft black boots, with holes in the soles, in need of Mimmo's attention. I fidgeted and hoped for a short story.

"Joseph, he takes a look at the body, he shoo the flies away, he cut some branches to cover him up. When he go back to work, he find his hoe is working in the field, all by himself; the hoe, all by himself, he's dug up half the field."

I wanted a hoe like that. I could have used it when it was eighty degrees and sunny and without a breath of air and I had to spread the load of horse manure my father said would give us the best garden in the city; it did, too. The only trouble was the back yard smelled like shit for three years.

"Joseph, he was a happy boy, and he liked to do a good job; when he get tired and he want to take a break, he played his flute. He let his magic hoe do the work for him."

Mimmo continued the story:

Joseph wandered the countryside looking for work wherever he could find it. But this master was cruel, and that master accused him of stealing, and the next master beat him.

Hungry and discouraged, Joseph fell in with a beggar on the road who said he would be happy to share alms. And so they begged together, but no one would give any money to Joseph, who was young and strong and able to work for a living.

Finally, one man told Joseph about a king who had many untilled fields. Joseph set out to see if the king would hire him, and he persuaded the beggar to come with him.

The king had many fields. Joseph dug them all, he sowed them all, weeded them carefully, and harvested the crops, and whenever he was tired he'd play his flute and let his hoe do the work. The king's daughter heard Joseph's flute and fell in love, but the king would not consent to give his daughter in marriage to a poor tiller.

So Joseph and the princess ran away.

They travelled by night. When they reached the seashore, they got in a boat. But when they were far from shore, Joseph remembered his friend, the old beggar. He wanted to go back and get him, because the beggar had been kind enough to share alms.

He was about to pull the boat around; he looked behind him towards shore. The old man was walking towards him, walking on the water. The beggar said, "When you had nothing, I gave you half of what I had; now you must give half this princess to me."

He handed Joseph a knife.

Joseph was sore of heart; he was just about to cut his bride in half when the beggar cried, "Stop! I knew you were fair and just. I am the dead man you covered with green boughs.

Go away now, and be happy!" The dead man walked back to shore.

Joseph and his bride rowed to an island.

Mimmo finished up: "And when they get to the other side of the water, the people wait for them on shore, all happy and nice. And they take Joseph and the princess to a palace, and the palace is rich in all good things." He may have been creepy, but Mimmo's voice was deep; his English may have been broken, but it carried me along.

"Here's your father's boots. That's two dollars. A buck a boot. You say hello to Dusty for me. If the soles don't feel right, you tell him to call. I fix for nothing."

Supper was on the table. My father said, "What took you so long?" I asked him if he knew the story of Joseph Ciufolo. He put down his fork, and slanted his eyebrows appraisingly. I helped myself to a pork chop.

"Pops used to tell that story when we worked in the garden. Joseph Ciufolo. I haven't heard that one in years."

After supper, my father went for a quick nap. He called from the bedroom: "Hey, Joseph Ciufolo. How'd you like to shine my dress shoes?"

"Yeah, sure. You seen my magic rag?"

The Seventeenth Night

Although Dusty had no memory of his brother Tony trying to stuff him into the woodstove, he remembered being told, and the memory was as real to him as the broken jug of vinegar, or the stick of firewood his mother had used when she beat his head. He had an inventory of cold cruelties and old horrors which, coupled with the years of drinking, ought to have killed him.

Somehow, he set them aside.

If he got angry, he blew up. His anger blew over quickly. But he harboured a number of lingering grievances and disappointments. All the men in the family were good at grudges.

During the last two years of Dusty's life, he and his brother Frank stopped speaking to each other. They had quarrelled over directions while riding in the car. The quarrel snapped a friendship that had lasted more than seventy years. Frank and Dusty were not inseparable but they were close, I think, because no one else knew how they'd grown up. They drank together, they told the same stories, they'd eaten the same food at the same table. They played cribbage a couple of nights a week, cutthroat games in which there was rarely a need to say anything more than "Fifteen-two, the rest won't do. Fifteen-four, the rest don't score." Every syllable nuanced.

But a stupid quarrel over directions broke them apart.

In spite of all our urging, they never made up. And then Frank died.

As a child, I learned what I knew of friendship from Frank and Dusty, my mother and my auntie Jo. They were easy and adult in each other's company, they met for weekly suppers, they drank rye and gingers and played cards together afterwards.

I used to go over to Frank's to listen to him talk, or to pick up tips about making wine. One day I found him in his back yard, staring at his garden, which was overgrown with weeds. Beyond the garden, an abandoned refrigerator which he had gutted and used as a smoker.

He was sitting under a makeshift pergola; grape leaves cast a net of shadows on his face. He was breathing hard. He'd just laid the bricks for a patio, poured a bag of dry cement over the bricks, swept the cement into the cracks, and then flooded everything with the garden hose. The bricks were still wet.

He was pleased. He never said anything about a patio; he simply thought about doing it until he was ready. And then, in a prolonged spasm of activity, he did it. And now he was having a glass of wine. He smiled to see me, and said the bottle was on the kitchen counter.

I poured myself a glass.

Frank kept a small still in his basement; he had a crab-apple tree in his back yard and made hard cider whenever he felt like it. And that was the purpose of my visit. I'd read that if you slipped a bottle over the branch of a fruit tree at the right time, the fruit would grow inside the bottle, and then, when you pulled the bottle from the branch, and plucked out the leaves and filled the bottle with alcohol, you'd get fruit-flavoured alcohol.

"You think we should do that?"

He gave me his alligator grin, sly and lazy and appraising all at once, which meant he liked the idea; if he hadn't, he'd have wondered, with a hint of a sneer, why the hell anybody would want to waste good liquor.

"Well then, let's give it a try."

He found an empty bottle; there was no shortage. I brought his ladder from the basement, set it against the tree, slipped the bottle over a twig and tied it in place with a rude sling of twine.

"I've got something for you when you climb down," he said.

He put a bottle of white lightning on the table, beside two waterglasses and a spoon. I waited for him to pour. He tapped the edge of his glass with a finger. I poured. "Now you watch this."

He spooned some of the liquor and lit it with a match; a

blue flame wrapped itself thickly around the edges of the spoon. "The bluer the flame, the purer the alcohol."

I raised my glass and took a sip. The liquor was hot, but it did not burn; there was a faint taste of orange on my tongue and the smell of hay at the back of my throat. He watched me swallow.

"How did you make this? What's that taste?"

"Well now, that's my little secret."

Over the course of several weeks, the crab apple grew inside the bottle on the tree in Frank's back yard. And then there was a rainstorm, and by the time I remembered to check, I found that the bottle had slipped, and was half-filled with water, and the water was murky with rotten leaves and the fruit was spoiled.

"Ah, to hell with it," he said.

His alligator grin, again.

Frank had been a first mate on the Great Lakes.

He had an air of authority, a ballplayer's long torso and hard hands, and no tolerance for weakness or fools. It was widely known that he'd taken a ship through the Soo locks, looking behind him, steering by the wake of the boat. The captain of the ship was new, the ship was his first command, and he'd stood in the wheelhouse blocking the view for both Frank and the pilot. Frank asked the captain to move. The captain was too nervous to hear.

So Frank winked at the pilot and turned and looked behind, out the back of the wheelhouse, making sure to keep the wake straight and centred in the lock. Just before they cleared the locks, the captain turned around and found himself staring at his first mate's back. He gasped and asked what the hell was going on.

Frank said, "Well, you wouldn't get out of the god-damn way, so I did the only god-damn thing I could. Next time, get out of the way when a man who knows what he's doing tells you to move. And don't look at me like that. You've got nothing to complain about. I got you through, didn't I?"

Frank was a union man, known and respected up and down the Lakes, from Fort William to the port of Montreal; there was nothing the captain could do except turn red in the face, swallow his pride, and learn to trust his crew.

It is well known by now that Hal Banks was invited by the Canadian government to come north and break the Canadian Seamen's Union. At the time, the CSU was red-run, badly organized, and poorly managed.

Frank had no idea that Banks was corrupt, but the Seafarers' International Union was – at least on the surface – offering a better deal for sailors. So Frank signed on as an organizer.

It was dangerous work: there were threats and broken skulls, and once there was a machine-gun battle on the coal docks of Fort William. Frank was a marked man, briefly. And for a time my cousins were delivered to school in a police cruiser. But Frank stood his ground and, with force of character and SIU muscle, he carried the day for the new union.

Banks hand-picked Frank for higher office. He brought him and my auntie Jo to Montreal for a little celebration *chez*

Banks, a huge house with rich carpets, big cars, cut-glass decanters, and fine food.

Mrs. Banks took Frank and Jo shopping at Ogilvy's one morning; they returned with hats in boxes and shopping bags full of dresses. They found Banks and the maid naked on the couch in the front room. Mrs. Banks screamed. The maid ran off. And Hal Banks casually threw his robe over his shoulders, walked over to where his wife stood, and said, "Are you gonna believe what you see, or what I tell you?" She screamed again.

He slapped his wife in the face.

My aunt was scandalized. Frank, although he was no prude, decided Banks lived a little too high on the hog, and the scene on the couch was a little too sophisticated; better to return to Fort William. He packed his suitcases and brought Josie home.

After that, Banks did what he could to get rid of my uncle. He tried to oust him from the Fort William local, but Frank had men who were loyal to him, and he knew how the game was played.

Banks changed tactics.

Frank ran the Lakehead branch of the SIU with fairness and common sense. He knew that a sailor who'd been without work couldn't possibly keep up his dues; if a man couldn't pay dues, he couldn't get a ship; but if a man couldn't get a ship, he couldn't earn money to feed his family, never mind pay dues. And so Frank was in the habit of marking "Paid" beside certain names in the ledger, with the understanding that, when the men drew their wages, they'd catch up on their dues.

Banks got hold of the books and accused Frank of stealing money. When they heard what was happening, every sailor who owed dues money begged, borrowed, and scraped together what they could and paid up in full. By this time, however, Frank had had enough. He went to Montreal one last time. He elbowed his way past a pair of goons, stood in front of the big desk, and told Hal to go fuck himself.

And then he walked out.

Unharmed.

Frank couldn't get work on the Lakes after that. No one would touch him. He sat around the house for a long time doing nothing, and nursing his wounded pride. When he got tired of sitting around, he looked for work.

Fort William was a small town, and Frank was hot property; nobody would hire him. For a time, he drove a cab. For a man who's used to travelling freely and leading other men, it's a bitch to earn a living delivering drunks to whorehouses, prescription drugs to the elderly, and bottles of bootleg whisky to after-hours card games.

One night, Frank began to drink with Lon Bagnall; Lon was a drunk who didn't work much, but he had a line of patter and a two-bit magic act consisting of a top hat and a wand, a folding table and a deck of cards.

Over several glasses of beer, the two men hatched a scheme: they'd tour the little bushtowns performing magic tricks at Moose Lodge smokers. Lon would do his magic act, Frank would be his assistant. Afterwards, Lon would get drunk and play the big talker from Fort William; Frank would pretend to make excuses, and the two of them would talk their way into a card game. Lon would keep the suckers on edge with his big mouth. Frank was a good poker player.

He'd stay sober. He'd win big.

That was the plan. It was a scandal. A family man leaving his wife and his children to run off with a magic act which was no more than the cover for a con game. The women of the family lined up against the men. My father remained loyal: *God damn it, leave him alone; he's a grown man, he can do what he wants.*

When Frank and Lon packed up and hit the road, it was the talk of the church hall; my aunt had to work hard to keep her head up. My mother took Jo's part and basked in the glow of the grievance.

It was also the talk of the playground.

Lon's son, Lonnie Jr., was the same age as my older brother. They were the school toughs, and they fought an epic and complex battle to silence the chatter about Lon Sr. and Frank — make one remark about the magic act, and this is what we'll do to you also. They beat each other bloody, lips split, knuckles raw and swollen, eyes blackened, clothes torn: a draw.

At St. Martin's School, if your older brother won a fight, you had to give the loser's brother a chance to even the score. And vice versa. It was a matter of playground honour. It is the basis of all blood feuds.

It was decided without discussion: I'd have to fight Lonnie Jr.'s younger brother, Dick. Everyone knew it was the

way things were done. And I was in for a licking. Dick was
ragged, short-haired, black-necked, dirty-knuckled, skinny,
and bone-hard. I was timid and afraid.

On the day we were supposed to fight, I walked to
school with my hands in my pockets, trembling and ready
to cry, which was bad enough; running would have been
worse. My brother made it plain he wasn't going to take my
side; he'd already been up and down a bloody ladder with
Lonnie Jr.

I was on my own.

I wasn't looking for Dick on the appointed day. The
schoolyard was small enough that our paths simply crossed. I
saw him and stopped in my tracks. I was not about to make
anything that might have resembled a first move.

I waited for him to hit me.

A miracle, then: there was a moment's hesitation, a sad
little spark in Dick's eyes that flickered between pity and self-
pity; we both wore hand-me-downs; his father was a drunk
who couldn't hold a job; my father drank. His father had no
job and had shamed his family; my uncle had no job and had
shamed his family; our older brothers had beaten each other
until they bled. Stupid and sad, stupid and sad.

Dick turned away from me.

I never told my uncle Frank; he'd have found a way to
take offence. He'd have said I should have got the first shot in
and taken my lumps.

I never told my older brother; he wouldn't have believed
what I'd seen in Dick's eyes. He'd have thought I was lying

to save my skin. I never told my father; he'd have thought I was a coward. And I never told my mother; she'd have defended me.

But she'd have blamed . . . Fiorito.

After a few months on the road with Lon Bagnall, Frank swept back into town and summoned his family into the living room. He dug into his pockets and threw fat handfuls of money high in the air; it was the first real money he'd had since he was tossed off the Lakes.

Tens and twenties fluttered down from the ceiling; the blue budgie threw itself against the bars of its cage. Afterwards, my cousins found paper money behind the cushions and under the couch for days.

It was not entirely a triumphant return.

In Frank's absence my cousin Matt had quit school and taken a job in order to support the family; he became the man of the house until Frank returned and sat down at the head of the dinner table.

Matt wore his new responsibility like a row of medals; he was not about to remove them from his chest. One night as they ate supper, the baby acted up and Frank slapped his ear. And what had been simmering in Matt boiled over: "Don't you dare do that again. Who the hell do you think you are? You can't just walk into this house and start pushing people around, not with me here!"

Frank had a rebellion on his hands; he moved quickly to crush it. "Who the hell are you talking to? God damn it, this is my house. I'm the one in charge here." Father and son got up from the table.

In what seemed to be a single motion, Frank drew off his belt, doubled it, and lashed his son across the face. Matt did not flinch or a raise a hand in self-defence. Instead, he stepped forward and drove his fist hard into his father's chest, a blow which caught the bigger man off guard and sent him reeling out the kitchen door, through the little hall, past the birdcage, and into the living room. Frank fell against the wall and slumped, wordlessly, to the floor. Auntie Jo screamed, the children cried.

Matt stalked out of the house while his father clutched his chest and struggled for breath. Two days later, Frank had a heart attack.

The father had sinned, and the son had risen up against him. The father had been struck down, and the family had been torn asunder. Matt left home, convinced he'd nearly killed his father. It was years before they spoke again.

They never spoke of this.

For a moment, as we drank the little glasses of hot orange liquor, I considered asking Frank about Lon Bagnall, about what had happened when they were on the road, and about why he and his son Matt had fought. I couldn't find the nerve.

"How do you make this?" I asked instead, pointing to the glass.

"That? Oh, well, now, never mind. I call it Northern

Orange. Help yourself if you feel like more. You want to play some crib?"

"Yeah, I'll play some crib."

There was a complexity which I didn't understand and couldn't explain to myself when I was growing up: my playground pals were English and Irish and Slovak, all-Canadian kids; I was one of the gang, but I wasn't. I didn't know how to belong.

The houses of the other kids smelled of cigars and stale butter. Their cupboards were filled with tins of lunch meat, their fridges with mayonnaise. Their fathers were mild, hardworking men; they had apron-wearing TV mothers.

It was not like that in my house. I had a wild man for a father. I couldn't invite kids home after school for fear my parents would be fighting. I had uncles who disappeared for weeks at a time and came back red-eyed, sick and broke and filled with chagrin. And I had a roving pack of hardboned cousins.

I had to be a good boy because I couldn't fight, I wasn't tough enough for blood on the knuckles, the wild thrill of theft, and the taste of lemon gin in a girl's mouth when you kissed her. I wasn't cold enough to live with the consequences.

But if I was not like my cousins, and not like the neighbourhood toughs, neither was I like the other Italian kids I knew; not like my pal Parente, who came directly from Italy, who spoke Italian at home, and who was Italian at home.

There was a cold cellar in the Parente basement, and in the dust and darkness there were barrels of fresh wine, shelves of tomatoes in jars, and torpedoes of salami strung from the rafters.

Old man Parente worked hard and said little. He had the smell of the old country on his clothes, and the feel of the old country in his hard hands. I didn't know any Italian; all I had was my name and the ghost of a couple of stories – about a murderer, and one who'd been murdered – which I couldn't repeat. I think Parente looked at me and saw *mangia-cake*, the future of his grandchildren.

I was familiar with what my father remembered, but when it came to Italy, I was one more generation removed than he was. Italy was a myth. Real Italians were exotic creatures, feral, and closer to the wolf.

I was not-a-wop in the presence of some, almost-a-wop in the presence of others; mostly I was a small-town kid with a name no one knew how to pronounce. Strangers tripped over my vowels and asked if I was Italian. I answered indirectly: "My father was born here." The fact that my mother was Polish didn't count.

Because of the name, because of the name.

Because of how I looked.

The question of who I was, and how my father's family had came to Canada, was a mystery I might reach for, but could not touch. Ripabottoni was a ghost-word; there were days when my father was unable to point to the map and say with certainty, "This is where your grandfather came from; the family began here."

Ripabottoni, a place too small for maps.

We were the sons and cousins, the grandchildren of a murderer and a man who had been murdered, and we had run from where we were born. There was a shadow of inherited violence in our background; it was rarely talked about, as if naming it would give it form.

It didn't need a name.

The shadow darkened whenever one of my uncles got drunk and spent the mortgage money, or woke in jail with a busted hand, or got caught in the wrong bed, or some cousin had to get married to a girl whose belly was swelling.

I thought this was my Italian shadow.

It was never far away. It was visible everywhere I looked; in the movies, in the pretty-boy weakness of Sal Mineo; in the cleverness and cruelty of all mobsters, real and imagined; in the wide hips of Anna Magnani, the lips of Monica Vitti, the breasts of Sophia Loren. It was there on the radio: Perry Como, Louis Prima, Dean Martin's moon hitting our eye. Tony Bennett didn't sound Italian but all you had to do was look at him to know who he was.

I made Desi Arnaz Italian, even though he was Cuban, because he and my father shared music, shared the same dark looks and flashing teeth; they were instantly happy, or instantly enraged; they looked good, they knew how to wear their clothes; they were generous and suspicious at once; they were always in the moment, and fools for the crowd.

Sinatra was another story.

His presence was a promise and a threat, and if your name ended in a vowel, you had that threat to live up to. Sinatra implied this: I look at you, and I see past you, and when I sing I give what I have, and you may feel as if I give everything I have to you alone, but I keep something to myself.

My old man was the same. He made you want him, that was his magic; if you wanted him too badly, that was your problem. He, too, held something back.

As he got older, Dusty became more Italian.

His beret, the scarf around his neck, the appraising look in his eye; all he needed was a little sunlight, something to drink, a few old friends who were willing to sit and listen to the stories they'd heard yesterday, who would willingly hear them again tomorrow. He looked more and more like a paisan in a black-and-white photo in the family album; age and illness were drawing him back in time, he was becoming what his father had been. I thought he might have a few questions as he drew close to death.

~

When he first became ill, before there was an urgency about his illness, in the days when the notion of a clear and inevitable end seemed somehow indecent, I went to Italy. To my grandfather's village.

To Ripabottoni on the hillside.

I went with a vague notion: I thought it might be possible to see something that would help my father die. I knew he was curious about his father's birthplace; but he'd never had the money to travel. There might be some clue about us in Ripa, some answer to an unposed question.

My wife and I flew to France on a cheap ticket and drove the length of Italy in a little tin can of a rented car, hurtling down the flower-lined Autostrada at 140 kilometres per hour, while black and silent German cars with tinted windows passed us as if we were standing still.

A night in Rapallo; in the morning, we took cups of espresso into the square as the flower merchants and the fruit sellers set up their stalls. The air soft as kisses. And then a long drive again, skirting Rome, heading for Campobasso, where my father said we were from, the way a man from Westfort might say he was from the Lakehead.

Campobasso is an old prison town, new-old, ugly-beautiful, with narrow streets and stone buildings; we made it in the middle of the afternoon. Susan was behind the wheel. She pulled up to a gas pump so we could find our bearings. Filling the car was not the first thing I had in mind. I let her take care of the gas.

There was something I wanted to do.

Attached to the garage was a small bar: a mirror on the wall, a row of polished glasses, a few bottles of liquor, an espresso machine, a single bowl of sugar with a long-handled spoon. And four men watching me. I could hear them thinking: Here is a tourist; soft and underdressed, too much money and not enough sense, obviously not a worker.

Look, he lets his woman drive.

I looked at them, and held their gaze long enough to let them know I was here for reasons which were none of their business. I learned this stare from my father and my uncles: the steady, unblinking gaze which says I don't care who you are, and what you think is no concern of mine. I'm here, I have a right to be here. And if that causes a problem, so be it.

I could have used a cigarette. If there's one thing a smoke is good for, it's a way to signal other men that you are to be taken seriously, the signal contained in the way you handle your smoke, how you use your lighter, the way you take the first drag.

I leaned against the bar as if I belonged and let out a traveller's sigh. The counterman approached. I asked for a grappa; point made. In the middle of a hot and sunny day, a stiff drink has nothing to do with thirst.

Grappa is a man's drink.

I was paying homage to the presence of my grandfather, to his scent in this air, to this dirt, to these trees he would have had to pass when he came along the road to Campobasso for the religious festivals, or for high mass in the cathedral.

Two of the men at the bar watched Susan out the window. Her bare legs. Two of them watched me. Don't react. Give nothing away. I will not provoke, nor will I be provoked.

The counterman set a little glass in front of me and filled it. I raised the glass in the direction of the men: "*Salut'!*" They nodded and smiled and I made a silent toast to the memory of old Matteo and downed the grappa in a single swallow. A long thirst satisfied.

By now, Susan had filled the tank and was paying the attendant. I looked at the four men. They looked at me.

I wished them a good day, and left the bar. They smiled. I drove away.

Supper that night in a trattoria. Afterwards, the owner brought a bottle of homemade grappa to the table: the taste of orange, the scent of hay in the back of my throat; the origin of Northern Orange? Had Frank learned this from his father, had his father learned it here?

The taste of it was proof enough for me.

We set out for Ripabottoni in the morning. There is only one road. I drove slowly. The road was narrow, winding upward; the fields of grain were yellow; bloody poppies in the ditch.

No other road but this one.

This old stone building by the long curve, could this have been a granary a hundred years ago? I stiffened, the hair on my arms prickled, sweat rolled down the back of my neck.

Silvaggio, were you here?

Suddenly behind me, the sound of an air horn, a truck bearing down on us. The driver is waving his hand, he's shaking his fist, he wants to get by. He wants to get by. *Son of a bitch, not again.*

I got out of the car and approached him with a smile. I wasn't going to shoot. The driver was disarmed. I pointed up the road.

"Ripabottoni?"

"Ripabottoni, *si, si!*"

I let him pass by.

If Silvaggio had done that, he'd never have left.

We arrived at noon. The village was deserted, save for an old lady in black carrying a shopping basket. I was polite. She glared at me suspiciously. The conversation went like this, roughly:

"Excuse me, signora, can you tell me where can I park the car?"

"What business do you have here?"

"Can I park the car over there by the church?"

"Who are you? What are you doing here?"

"I think I may have relatives in this village."

"What's your name?"

"Fiorito."

"Ah, Fiorito!"

She smiled broadly; my name was no impediment here, it was a ticket of entry. She hurried around to my side of the car, opened the door, took me by the arm, instructed me to lock the doors and leave the car where it was. She led us up the stone steps of the municipal records office. Before I knew it, a young woman was taking old books down from the shelves and raising a cloud of sneezy dust, and there on the yellow pages were the spidery names of the old Fioritos: Vittorio, Giuseppe, Matteo, Vito, Filomena.

The corners were worn away by generations of record-keepers who, like this clerk, had the habit of licking a finger before turning the page.

Within fifteen minutes, I had copies of birth certificates going back to my grandfather's father. Within an hour, the whole town knew who we were. And everywhere we went, old people – there seemed to be nothing but old people here – waved and called out, "Did you find your relatives yet?"

Not exactly. I learned that it would be impossible to find out how we were related without knowing my grandfather's *sopranome*, the extra name given to the branches of a numerous clan, a way of keeping track of blood relations to avoid inbreeding. Was my grandfather a Seraphina, a Cocciolongo, a Lepore?

That name, if there was one, was lost. Without it, there was simply no way of knowing how we were connected; the name Fiorito, so rare and the source of so many problems at home, was so common here it might as well have been Smith.

The next day we were walking down the main street towards the square. An elderly woman, armed with a string bag and a purse, left her house. Her door was green, and the knocker was a brass hand clutching a ball. I snuck a photo of her door. She marched up to me with a burning glare. "What do you think you're doing?"

I told her I meant no harm, that I was charmed by the little hand.

She was fiercely angry.

I told her that I was in Ripabottoni looking for traces of my family. That stopped her. She examined me, as if my face were a piece of a puzzle.

"What family?"

Fiorito.

Oh, well, she said. I mentioned the names of my grandfather and grandmother, and she nodded; yes, those names

could only come from here. But she was puzzled. She saw the
butcher leaving his store to go sit on the stone wall across
the street. He knows something about Fioritos.

Come here, she waved to him. It's an emergency.

My great-grandfather's name was Giusepp'Antonio; he
was married to Anna DiFabio. And the butcher made a
phone call and I was quickly introduced to an old man
named Giusepp'Antonio Fiorito, who was married to Anna
DiFabio. They were a tiny couple, bent and wrinkled, unsure
of what to say, uncertain about standing next to a tall
stranger who appeared out of nowhere and claimed to be a
relative, who perhaps had a claim on old property, who knows?

I don't care how many branches of the family there might
be, and how much time has passed, you cannot tell me that
we were not, somehow, related. They might have been cautious, but I was so stunned I could not breathe.

On a second visit to the records office, I found the birth
certificate of both the children named Matteo, the one who
died and the one who grew up and left, to become my grandfather. The records clarified an old error: at the start of the
Second World War, my grandfather had to write to Italy to
get a copy of his birth certificate, for the simple reason that he
was Italian, and thus suspect; for some reason, he was sent the
birth certificate of his dead brother, the first Matteo.

But there was no one in Ripabottoni, not even the oldest
person, who could remember anything about the Matteo
Fiorito who left as a young man and went to the wilds of
America, or that America to the north of America.

There was space on the pages of the record books for a date and the notation "emigrato" beside the names of those who had left. The records clerk was curious. Beside the names of Joe Silvaggio, Filomena Fiorito, and Matteo Fiorito, there was nothing. No date. Nothing. Which I interpret to mean one thing: they left in a hurry. They left under a cloud. And at the time of their departure, no one knew or cared where they had gone, nor cared if they came back.

Not exactly answers, but close enough.

I was shown the house where a certain Giusepp'Antonio Fiorito was said to have lived: the name Fiorito was carved above the entrance to the house; perhaps it was my great-grandfather's.

It was typical of the village, and had been abandoned for more than a generation. I think everyone in the village wished it were my great-grandfather's house. For my sake, and for theirs; it's a poor village, in need of a little new money, in need of repair.

The bottom floor of the house had been a stable for the mule, the kitchen was on the second floor, the top floor was split into two bedrooms. The floors were cool, and laid with intricate mosaic tiles that gave the appearance of rich carpets.

All the houses in the village were like this.

The village itself was set on the side of a hill, with the houses falling part of the way off the hill and down into the valley, the way a shawl falls off a woman's shoulder. I took photos of everything, and explained: this was my grandfather's

village, and my father is ill; when I return, the photos will
divert him.

There is a field at the edge of Ripabottoni through which
a road has been cut. Alongside the road there are trees. You
cannot see the graves from town, but the trees hide nothing.
If you see the road, you see the trees; if you see the trees, you
know the graves are there.

The road to the cemetery is long enough for a procession,
long enough to give you time to shape your mourning as
you walk.

The car has raised a plume of dust which hangs in the air
as we pull up near the cemetery gate. Two workmen share a
laugh. One of them is young and lean and brown. The other
is fat, balding, and slow. Both men are powerfully strong.
They are cutting weeds, smoking cigarettes, trimming grass.
The younger man speaks.

"Do you need any help?"

The fat one leans on his rake. There isn't a cloud in the
sky. The air smells of life and death, of fresh earth and rotting
flowers; on a day like this, cigarette smoke and souls rise
straight to heaven.

The two men are cautious. They've never seen us before.
We may be grieving. We may have important reasons for our
visit to the village. We may simply be tourists. They search
my face for clues; they are caught, like all gravediggers, somewhere between irreverence and respect.

"I'm looking for my relatives."

A pair of skinny green *serpenti* escape from the under-
brush. They are the colour of stalks of grass, delicate spring

blades; their skin is as soft. One of the lizards skitters over
Susan's sandal, brushing against her long bare toes. She jumps,
dances on one foot when she lands so as not to squash the
little creature underfoot. I brace her, and she laughs.

Irreverence it is, then.

"There are plenty of relatives here. In fact, everyone here
is a relative. Which ones in particular are you looking for?"

I don't want to mention Silvaggio. A hundred years is not
a long time. These men may have memories similar to mine,
with one vital difference; they might be related to the man
Silvaggio killed. I say, "Fiorito, Delvecchio, DiFabio."

"Plenty of those here. Take your pick."

The graves are neat and garnished with bouquets of
freshly cut flowers, flowers in sconces, flowers in jars and tins.
According to the sentiment of the wreaths, we die but we live
on in eternity. According to the photos of the faces on the
tombstones, we remain in memory the way we were when
we were young and life was a promise. In this cemetery, the
dead are the age they will be in heaven.

If it were not for a murder, this is where I would come to
be buried. This is where I would belong. I saw my name. I
saw the names of my uncles and aunts. I saw faces that looked
vaguely familiar.

I did not look out of place.

On the way back to town, we passed a stone house built
under a tree, close to the edge of the road. An old woman
slept in a chair on the porch. Her skin was papery, her cheeks
hollow, the sockets of her eyes gaunt, her mouth open, her
head thrown back.

Sleep, a rehearsal for death.

In spite of the heat she was dressed in a heavy black sweater. A black shawl lay draped over her shoulders. A woollen blanket, also black, was wrapped around her legs like a shroud.

Although the car raised the dust of the road, and the wind took it in her direction, she took no notice of our passing.

From where she sat, she'd have had a front-row seat for a lifetime of funerals. Her own could not be far away now. I thought of my father, also dying. Would he have been better off here, far from doctors and the cruel mercies of the hospital?

He would have been at home here, temperamentally.

His pride? Ripabottoni, made of stone. His brother Tony, who had second sight? Ripa, looking over the valley. His brother Dave, whose face was sharp as a knife? Ripa, carved into the hillside. His brother Dominic, the fool for love? My uncle Joe, dead before I was born? My uncle Frank, the seaman? Ripa, the one against the many; Ripa, stubborn as an oak tree, pretty as a poppy. They might as well have died here.

"Where are you staying?" asked the policeman.

He was a beautiful man, movie-star handsome, and his uniform was a masterpiece of tailoring. His leather belts and silver buckles were polished to a sparkling finish. His white gloves were spotless.

We had gone to the police station; it seemed to me that it was possible to have your passport stamped at a police station. A Ripabottoni stamp in a Fiorito passport; delicious.

Susan was eager to practise her Italian; she has a good ear, a quick tongue, and she is not self-conscious. She spoke up eagerly. "We are staying at Il Sogno."

A barn of a place, built to be the biggest hotel in the region, suitable for the most lavish weddings, with a grand dining room whose girders are exposed, like a hockey rink at home; the room is so big the waiter could have used a pair of skates, so big we made sure to take a table close to the kitchen to save him work.

The policeman's hand rested on the pistol grip of his machine gun. The grip was smaller than that of the pistol I played with as a boy. He stroked the butt of the weapon reflexively and shook his head.

"No. You could not possibly be staying there."

Il Sogno was not officially open, the owner had yet to obtain the proper permit to allow him to accept paying guests; but we were coming all the way from North America, and so an arrangement had been made.

"I'm sorry, I did not hear you. Where are you staying?"

I understood in a flash.

If the owner of Il Sogno is accepting guests in advance of his permit, that would be against the law; and if a policeman knows a law is being broken, he is required to act. Even if it is a stupid law. And if a policeman knows a law, even a stupid one, is being broken and he does nothing, he could be disciplined, and who knows what could happen? He might be stripped of his uniform, his sleek weapon, his steady salary, or, perhaps worse, removed from his safe post in the provinces.

Assuming, that is, that he couldn't save himself by appealing for the intercession of a benefactor, after which there would be a complex series of negotiations involving the barter of favours and obligations beyond the ones that secured him his job in the first place.

Everyone in town knows Il Sogno is accepting guests and has been doing so for months. But no one is officially aware of this. And so it is simpler for the policeman to pretend he doesn't hear, simpler to ask the question again; it is simpler to keep asking the question until he hears an answer that will satisfy him, his superior, and the owners of Il Sogno.

Susan began to reply, and the policeman shook his head, rolled his eyes, sucked a breath of air through his teeth. He knew she was about to assure him in her clean, precise Italian that we are indeed staying at Il Sogno. But I grabbed her by the elbow and cleared my throat. "We are staying at a small hotel in Campolieto. I forget the name of the hotel; perhaps you know the one I mean."

It didn't come out as clean as that, of course; but what mattered was that I had a firm grip on Susan's arm, and when she tried to correct me I gripped her arm tighter. I raised a shoulder slightly and gestured to the policeman with the open palm of my free hand, as if to say, Excuse me, but women don't understand these things the way men do; we're staying in Campolieto. The policeman smiled; he heard quite clearly now.

"Yes," he said. "A very nice hotel."

My interview with the commander was cordial. He was firm. It is not possible to stamp a passport here; you are mistaken in your impression. I understand that you have a name which some may feel is an important one around here, but you are not from here, and in any case we do not have the authority to stamp a passport, and there is really nothing I can do. This is not exactly what he said.

But it was precisely what he meant.

I thanked him, and he wished us a pleasant stay, and the policeman with the lovely gun offered me a silent warning not to mention any more hotels, and we took our leave.

As we pulled into the courtyard of Il Sogno, I saw a police car chasing us. The policeman was waving his hand furiously out the window. A cloud of dust rose up in a roostertail behind him.

Oh, Christ, we've given the game away. We ought not to have come here directly, we ought to have found a back road to the hotel.

It was the handsome policeman. He did not want to make any trouble. The captain was apologetic. He did not mean to be dismissive. He wanted to give us some police souvenirs, posters and stickers.

"Excuse me, these are for your father."

We were given souvenirs for him everywhere we went. A bottle of herb liquor. A wooden wall plaque from Vanelli's Bar Sport. A stringed instrument used to cut maccheroni alla chitarra, the specialty of the region. And I had taken fourteen rolls of film, photos of every inch of ground, every view of the hills, every stone in the cemetery which might have illustrated the scraps of the stories Dusty knew.

And on the way to Lyons, where we were to take the airplane home, we stopped briefly to see a Roman ruin in

Orange. We left the car locked in a public lot for five minutes. We couldn't find the ruin in the scented woods: it was too hot; we were too tired. And when we returned, the car had been broken into and everything we had, including most of the rolls of film and all the souvenirs, was stolen.

We were too sick at heart to speak on the flight home. When we came to Thunder Bay, I told Dusty what had happened. I felt as if I'd let him down. "Those bastards," he said, instantly. He smiled a hurt smile; not for himself, but for me. And it was better this way, really. I sat with him and began to tell the story-teller my stories of the trip. "In Ripabottoni, the roads are lined with poppies, red as . . .

My father was not an introspective man. There would be no summing up, there was nothing to reconsider, there was no need for forgiveness. He had lived his life, he'd done what he'd done; there was nothing to be undone, and only one more thing left to do.

He had to die.

I owed him this: I had to see him out.

I am sitting in the plastic-and-metal armchair, reading quietly. His eyes are closed. He mutters something, I can't tell what; it is impossible to hear clearly. He's talking in his sleep. He isn't frightened, there's no reason to wake him up. I go back to my book.

His pyjamas are open, his ribs stand out, his arms are sticks. He trembles, although the room is almost unbearably hot.

"Jesus Christ, it's cold in here." I pull the covers up around his throat. He opens his eyes, almost frightened, as if I'd been about to cover his head with a shroud. I pretend not to notice.

Perhaps he will go back to sleep.

When I was a child, I could not possibly measure the truth of the family stories. Instead, I measured the truth of the storyteller; if I caught a grin, or if the facts of the story were too large to fully understand, I suspended truth and heard magic.

He is awake now.

He stares at me. I say nothing. I wait. If he wants to talk tonight, let him. I won't push him; I'm tired. What I most want to know are stories about my grandfather; I am least likely to get them now.

I raise an eyebrow, as if to ask him whether he needs anything. He purses his lips firmly; that means no.

And then, as if he'd been reading my mind, he says, "My old man had another story. The court jester. I just remembered. Remind me in a minute, would you?" He falls asleep. I know the story of the court jester by heart; it was the one story my aunts and uncles told reliably whenever I wanted to hear about my grandfather, as if it was the only story he told. I'd ask what he was like. They'd say, oh well, he was a kind man, he didn't say much, but he had a sense of humour. And I'd ask, what do you mean?

It took a bit of nerve, because my uncles and my aunts didn't like too many questions; it was as if I were doubting them, or trying to embarrass them. But I pushed. And that's how I heard the following:

There once was a king who was very rich. He had a large and powerful army. He had spies. No one was allowed to say anything against the king, on pain of death.

But this king had a court jester who was allowed to poke a little fun from time to time. But nobody could laugh at what the jester said unless the king laughed first.

The jester had to be clever; if he said the wrong thing, if he didn't make the king laugh, it could cost him his life; he was, after all, the most recent in a long line of jesters.

One day, the jester made the king mad. The king said, "I'm sorry but this time you've gone too far. I am going to put you to death. I sentence you to be hanged." The jester asked the king for one last favour. The king said, "You have served me well; I grant your wish."

The jester asked if he might choose the tree from which he would be hanged. The king said, "A reasonable request; so be it."

The king's executioner and his attendants took the jester out into the woods beyond the castle walls. "Here is a mighty oak tree; the branches are strong, it is a very good tree from which to be hanged."

"No, I don't like this tree," said the jester.

The executioner led the jester to an old olive tree. "Look at this olive tree; it is older than the kingdom itself. It is perfectly suitable for a hanging; it will take the rope easily, and you will die a good death."

"No, I do not like this tree," said the jester.

The executioner began to get angry. "You'd better choose a tree, and choose one quickly, because I am getting tired of this game."

"The king made me a promise."

"You are right," said the executioner, "but we haven't got all day."

"Follow me," said the jester. He led the executioner into the deepest part of the forest, examining this tree and that, considering each one's merits with the proper gravity. Suddenly he stopped, and said with a flourish, "Here is the tree from which I would like to be hanged."

The jester pointed to a slender sapling, no more than a foot high. The executioner said, "That's not a tree."

The jester said, "It is an oak; it merely happens to be young. No one said I had to choose an old tree."

The executioner was speechless. It would be more than a lifetime before this tree would be tall enough, and its branches strong enough, to bear a hanged man's weight.

When the king heard the news, he laughed out loud. "What a clever fellow my jester is." And all was forgiven, and the jester lived to a ripe old age.

I tried to imagine my grandfather telling this story. I imagined him sitting at the big table in the kitchen, with the sleeves of his undershirt pushed up to his elbows, his moustache drooping at the ends, and a glass of wine on the table in front of him, and his pipe in his hands, and the long blue ribbons of smoke rising to the ceiling. I imagined a kind of sadness about him, and then that twinkle in his eye.

The jester was a man of quick wit in the face of absolute power, and his was a tale of peasant cleverness. I would imagine myself as the jester, and I'd wonder what I might have done, if there might not have been another solution.

I never found one.

My grandfather was a peasant; he was powerless and good, he was patient and kind, but he lived far from the shadow of a king who might have given him a reward.

My grandfather died in this hospital.

He, too, had cancer.

Dusty used to tell me the old man would sit in the bath-room of the house on Francis Street, moaning and leaking blood into the toilet. They took him to the hospital, and the doctors opened him up. There was nothing to be done. According to my father, the old man's bowels were so badly diseased the doctors couldn't even close him up; my grand-father died with his guts tucked in a bag hung beside his bed.

He died in agony.

Dusty was dying in agony now, in the hospital where he had been born, he was dying where his father had died, he was dying where I and where my son had been born.

I'll be damned if I die there.

The Eighteenth Night

*H*e is sitting up in bed. It is clear to everyone that he does not have much longer to live, but tonight his eyes are clear. He looks alert; he is holding a plastic glass of apple juice and drinking weakly through a straw.

"Hello, Joe, whaddya know?"

"Hey, soldier! What do you say we bust out of this joint? I'll take you fishing in the morning."

"Where to?"

"The Secret Spot."

"Oh, I wish I could."

"Remember the big trout?"

We had gone to bed early. He was on holiday. I was still in my teens. He'd come straight home after his playing job, and we'd taken flashlights and picked dew worms on the lawn. We were going fishing in the morning; there was a creek, practically invisible from the highway, just past the Atikokan cutoff. We'd caught some big ones there, and christened it the Secret Spot. At five in the morning, he was in a chipper mood.

"Time to get up, soldier!"

Reveille.

I pulled the blanket over my head. He shook my shoulder; nothing doing. I hid my head under the pillow. "Wakey, wakey!" He grabbed my foot; I lashed out with my heel and caught him in the belly. "Ooph!" I knew I'd hurt him, but he laughed; he understood.

He was ticklish, too.

"Come on, sleepyhead; no time for fighting, the fish are biting."

I turned over and raised myself on my elbows, grinning and alert. I'd kicked my father in the belly, there was coffee on the stove, we were going to the Secret Spot; perfect.

The Secret Spot was brackish in places, but there were plenty of rocky runs and fat cold pools, and it was full of big trout in the spring. No one knew where it was but us.

There'd been a work camp near the creek during the Depression; my father had helped push the Trans-Canada Highway over the rocks and across the northern bogs. For the privilege of having a job, he'd paid off the local Tory bagman, a dentist: the money in an envelope, the envelope slipped under a door. The job paid five dollars a week.

The payoff was ten dollars.

Dusty said there'd been a week one winter when it was so cold, the horses bled from their nostrils. The teamsters took the horses back to camp; the men worked on.

I was tired of that story.

He drove without talking, hugging the centre line of the highway, over the railway tracks where a truckload of bush-workers had been killed by a train, through Kakabeka Falls, past the truck stops whose signs in the window read, "Try Our Menu Items," or simply, "Food and Gas."

Gradually, the landscape changed from farmland to brief hard hills, hard rock, and swamp spruce. He slowed the car as we neared the creek; sometimes other fishermen followed us from town, trying to find the spot. Not this time. He pulled off the highway, drove down a short stretch of logging road, crossed a small wooden bridge, and parked the car.

We baited up without a word.

He wanted the first pool; I wanted the rapids which fed it. He was not a sophisticated fisherman: he used snelled hooks, split shot, a box of spinners, and a tin of worms. But he could catch fish on a wet lawn.

There was nothing doing at the rapids.

I leapfrogged ahead, left him at the first pool, and went to the next good spot, following the banks of the creek. I heard the dry slither of garter snakes in the hillocks of grass. I made as much noise as I could.

The bush was thick, and without trails, hard work walking. If the fish weren't biting, we could reach the mouth of the creek in a day; if the fish were biting, there was no need to go so far.

Dusty was good in the bush. He always knew where he was. He could leave the creek and take off across country; he'd emerge where he wanted to, every time. I have no sense of direction. I followed the creek.

I was angry at him in those days; we were at each other often: he drank, he stayed out late at nights, he was free with money when we had none, he was friendly with strangers and curt with us; I loved him, but I didn't need to look hard for a reason to dislike him.

"Jesus wept!" His favourite curse. He was crashing through the bush. Aha, I thought, he's cracked his shin, slipped on a rock, taken a twig in the eye; serves him right.

I called, "Any luck?"

"No luck."

"I'll meet you up ahead."

The air was thick and buggy, the morning sun was hot; no fish. We stopped for lunch at a big pool, a mile downstream; we had mugs of black tea, roast beef and onion sandwiches, and we watched our lines in the dark cold water.

His sweat smelled of alcohol, even though he'd come home sober the night before. When he finished eating, he rolled up his pant legs, took off his socks, and warmed his feet in the sun. His legs were pale; there was a fresh red bruise on his shin.

He lit a smoke, wiggled his toes, closed his eyes. I listened to the flow of the stream; the water was high and dark, and dotted with freshwater foam. He cleared his throat. He sat up and checked his line in the water, making sure it wasn't snagged.

He looked at his shin.

Here it comes.

"I hurt my magic leg. I guess I'll have to be more careful. Did I tell you I had my magic leg?"

How many times had he told me? I could recite this one in my sleep; yeah, yeah, yeah. But there was a look which came over my father's face when he wanted to tell a story; he seemed to be a cross between Pliny the Elder and a kid on Christmas morning. I gave up.

"A magic leg?"

"Your uncle Tony came home from the war; he wasn't working, he couldn't work much. His lungs were bad; so were his nerves. I guess I was four years old, maybe five. One afternoon, he called me into the kitchen. He said, 'Dusty, I want to go downtown.'

"I said, 'That's okay, Tony, you can go downtown if you want.' I wondered why he was asking me. I was just a little kid.

"Tony said, 'I don't have any money.'

"I said, 'Gee, Tony, that's too bad. I don't have any money, either.'

"Tony said, 'Yes, you do, Dusty.'

"'I do?'

"Kids didn't have money then. The most I ever had was a copper, maybe a nickel for candy. I got worried. Maybe he thought I'd stolen some money. I was starting to get panicky.

"Tony said, 'You know, Dusty, you've got a magic leg.'

"'A magic leg?'

"He lifted me up and stood me on the kitchen table. He grabbed me by my pantleg and gave my leg a shake; nothing happened. I had no idea what the hell was going on. He said, 'Maybe I'm wrong. Maybe it's this one.' He grabbed my other leg and gave it a shake. He shook it again, and a dozen coins spilled onto the table. I couldn't believe my eyes.

"Tony said, 'I'm not sure that's enough; Dusty, do you mind if I have some more?' I was speechless. I nodded my head. Tony took hold of my leg again, and more coins spilled out."

"He said, 'Gee, Dusty, I think that's enough. Thanks for letting me use your leg. Keep some of this for yourself, and listen carefully; don't tell anybody, and don't let anyone else use your leg, or the magic will go away.' All I could do was gape at him. Tony put the money in his pocket and went downtown."

My father smiled at the memory of this old sleight-of-hand. He lit another smoke. I smiled, I couldn't help myself.

He reeled in his line and checked the hook; something had nibbled away the worm. "We'll get lucky yet," he said. "Is there any more tea?"

"None left; I drank the last of it."

"Have I told you the rest of that story?"

I wasn't sure; his stories never really ended, they roamed

across a landscape peopled with characters who came and went on a whim. The rest of the story could have landed him in England during the war, or in a Chicago bar during Prohibition.

With the least effort I could manage in the heat, I raised an eyebrow; all the encouragement he needed.

"I overheard my mother in the kitchen shortly after that. She was crying because she had to make an insurance payment, and she didn't know where she was going to get the money. I said, 'Don't worry, Mom; I've got a magic leg.'"

He laughed; he could hear himself saying it. He'd been a child, he'd believed in his magic leg and, when he told the story, that belief returned to him. It was the reason he told stories; his capacity to believe.

I lay back on the grass and laughed.

We'd fished here on the opening day of fishing season the year before; I'd been on the north side of the pool, he on the south. It was early in the spring, and the water was running high; it was oily-cold, too dangerous to cross in most places. I couldn't see him. I knew where he was by the sound he made in the bush. I heard him swear. "God damn it! There's a big one here, I just missed him." If there was a big one, there would be two; I began hacking my way to the water's edge when I heard him roar again, "I got you, you bastard!" Then I heard an enormous splash.

And then I heard silence.

He'd caught a monster, or he'd fallen in the water, or both. I looked through a curtain of alder; I couldn't see him. All I saw was water. A thick branch rocked in the current where he should have been; odd to see a branch shake like that. I looked again, carefully, following the line of the branch down to the root.

I saw his fist clenched tight; nothing more. Just his fist. The rest of him was in the creek. He was holding on, but he'd gone under. The water was ice-cold. He was wearing his waders; they'd be flooded, the current would hold him down. I held my breath. I tried to remember how long it had been since I heard him fall; it seemed like forever, and counting.

I looked back to the head of the pool; the bush was thick, it would take too long to fight my way to a spot where I could cross without going in over my hips. It would be too late. He was going to drown. I thought about shucking my boots and trying to swim across.

I couldn't swim.

He'd tried to teach me, once; he'd told me to jump from a dock into a cold lake where he was waiting, treading water and laughing. He urged me to jump, he said I'd float. I splashed into the water and came up sputtering in a panic, scratching hard to haul myself into air; I didn't float. He saved me with a look of resigned contempt. I didn't go near the water at all after that.

A fleeting thought, now: You stupid bastard; if you'd taught me how to swim, I might be able to dive in and save you now.

I knew he was going to die. I had to do something. I started to fight through the bush, sweeping branches away from my face.

And then, another splash.

I looked across the pool in time to see him rise up with a mighty, lung-filling gasp, a spray of water like so many cold diamonds spilling from him in the sun. He was soaking wet, sucking air and coughing, still gripping the branch.

"I got a big one, god damn it!"

He kicked and dragged himself up the bank, crawling on his knees, clawing with his elbows, holding the branch in one hand, his rod bent double in the other. Ten minutes later, he landed a six-pound speckled trout.

I'd reached him by then. He was sitting in the dry grass back from the bank, dripping wet. The big fish flopped between his legs; its sides as red as a sunset, a stream of blood trickling from its dark red gills. Somehow, Dusty's smokes were dry. He lit a cigarette, put the monster on a stringer, and wrung out his clothes.

I told him that I thought he was a goner.

I said there was no way I could have reached him in time. He gave me a look. I never mentioned it again. Neither did he. He baited his hook and threw his line in the water once more. Five minutes later, he had another fish. Same size as the first.

I caught nothing.

He opens his eyes. His eyes are clear and he is, briefly, without pain. There is no morphine confusion; and then there is. His eyes widen, he looks wildly around the room.

"Can I get you a drink of water?"

"No, no!"

Is there anything . . . ?"

"Help me up. I have to go."

"Let me get the nurse."

"No nurse. Give me a hand, god damn it."

I am afraid his bones will break in my hands. I am afraid he'll fall on the way to the toilet. If he hurts himself, he could die here and now. He's dying anyway. He doesn't want help, but he demands mine.

We shuffle forward together in the dark. I could pick him up in my arms. It takes us six minutes to reach the bathroom, six feet from his bed. I try to calculate that in miles per hour. A foot a minute, five thousand two hundred and eighty minutes, divided by sixty minutes is – let's round it off – ninety hours per mile. He cannot pee standing up. He has to turn around, hold the safety bar, and collapse into sitting position onto the seat.

He doesn't have much strength. The walk has exhausted him. He falls asleep before he pees. I wait, I wait, I wake him up. In his eyes, there is a trapped sadness. I am sorry for waking him. He releases a dribble of urine. The effort leaves him helpless with exhaustion.

"Leave me alone a minute."

He cocks his head at me, an old expression: his lips set thin, his left eye in a squint, his right eye taking my measure.

"Did I ever tell you about Nip's pony?"

I know it by heart.

I can recite it myself.

"I was on my way to a dance downtown. I'm walking past the Victoria Hotel when I see a crowd of people backed up into the lobby. I think maybe there's a fight, so I step up and look through the window.

"Nip Montgomery is sitting at a table on the men's side. Nip owned a dray line, he had a Shetland pony, the first one in Fort William. The Shetland pony is sitting next to him. Nip and the pony are drunk.

"Everybody wants to buy the horse a beer. The waiters are wringing their hands; they're afraid the cops are going to come and shut them down. A horse in a bar, you can't have that.

"There was no way I could get in, even if I'd wanted to. I said to hell with it and went to the dance. I met a nice girl and took her back to her place. On my way home, I had to pass the St. Louis Hotel. You know where that is; down the street from the Vic.

"Just as I'm walking by, the front door flies open and something knocks me down. I roll over, I reach out and grab a fistful of hair. At first I think I'm tangled up with some dame. It's no dame. It's the pony.

"Nip comes flying out a second later, hard on the horse's heels; no, its hooves. Anyway, the three of us tangled up together, heels and hooves. I have to laugh. I get up, dust myself off, and leave them lying in the gutter."

My father is sitting on a toilet in the cancer ward. On his face is a parody of a grin, masking all this sad absurdity in the middle of the night. He gives me the usual fillip. "I'll bet I'm the only man you know who got knocked down by a drunken flying horse."

And I give him a parody of a laugh.

"Come on, Pops. Let's get you back to bed."

He stands, but will not budge. "Just a minute. I'm not done." He wants to flush the toilet himself. His fingers are useless. He makes a weak fist, and shoves at the handle with his knuckles. He doesn't have the strength. I take his hand in mine and press down.

When we reach the bed safely, he presses his buzzer for the nurse. She arrives quickly and, without having to be told, gives him an extra dose of morphine. His eyes roll up, his head falls back on his pillow.

Nip and his horse, still in the gutter.

He's angry at me, impatient when he wakes; the effort of his anger leaves him tired. "I feel sorry for you," he says with a trace of contempt. It is an ongoing refrain. I have no idea what he's talking about.

"You feel sorry for me?"

What I do not say is, you're the one who's closer to dying here, not me. He turns his head away, sulking and plucking at the waist of his pyjamas. Perhaps he is angry because his fingers are without feeling. He won't let me help him tie the drawstring; it is his task. He makes slow, blind gestures. He gives up, and leaves the strings untied.

Now he spits up; chalky liquid dribbles from his lips. I give him a tissue, he wipes his mouth, he examines the tissue, he folds it and folds it again; I do not remember him being quite so meticulous. Suddenly he sneers.

"You poor bugger."

Maybe he thinks I won't be able to handle death when my time comes. He is too ill to elaborate. He clasps his hands behind his head. His body is nearly hairless now; under his right arm, I can see a lump the size of a large egg; now and then the egg twitches.

He falls asleep.

He wakes up suddenly. "Where am I? What am I doing here? I'd like to know what I was doing yesterday."

You were here yesterday, Pop.

I tell him that Peter Silvaggio called. He smiles at the name. Peter is his cousin, the son of Joe Silvaggio. Dusty and Peter grew up together on the farm. My father is lucid for a moment, and he reaches for another story.

"Pete's dad had a mule named Queen. It was the damnedest thing; Queen refused to set foot in a puddle. If she saw water on the road, she'd stop. She wouldn't move; you had to cover her eyes with a sack and lead her by the halter. But by God, she could pull a mountain down a dry road.

"Peter was scaling timber up north of Nipigon; one night he got talking with the dray man, Nip Montgomery. I told you about his pony. Nip was telling Peter about a man who'd tried to bring a load of Missouri mules across the lake from the United States. Two dozen mules on a barge; a bargeful of stubborn.

"A storm blew up. All the mules drowned except for one; she swam thirty miles and washed up on shore near Fort

William. She was too stubborn to drown. Yeah, she swam ashore. It was in the paper.

"Nip bought that mule and kept her with his horses for a while. Showed her off; the swimming mule. Peter always claimed that was the mule his father bought. It would sure as hell explain why she wouldn't step in a puddle; she'd had enough water for one lifetime."

My father smiles and sleeps again.

The closer he gets to death, the smaller and more concentrated he becomes. He is approaching pure spirit; it seems to me that he floats an inch above his bed. I fall asleep in the chair. My back hurts. It seems absurd to notice that it does.

I have no nightmares, and I am not especially sad, because underneath the smell of illness I can sense my father's smell. He wakes again. Asks for a drink. Whisky-flavoured water with ice chips.

He continues to talk.

I hear weakness, resignation in his voice.

I think he senses time is running out.

"Peter's mother and mine, they had certain powers; they knew how to ward off the evil eye. My mother used to put olive oil and water on a plate. She'd say a prayer of some kind. I don't know any more. The oil would gather up. Or maybe it wouldn't. I was too small to be able to see. I remember one of the neighbours got sick, and my mother put the olive oil on a plate, she said something, and the woman coughed up a long hair.

"One time Pete's little brother had a fever; his lungs were filling up. Pleurisy. None of their usual tricks worked. The baby was dying. They sent for the doctor.

"The doctor came from town in a buckboard. He wanted to operate right there on the kitchen table, open him up, take out a rib, and drain the baby's lungs. But the fever was too high. He couldn't cut him. Those two old girls, they weren't going to stand there and let the baby die. So my mother went out into the farmyard, got a rooster, and brought it into the kitchen."

And?

"Filomena held the baby. My mother took hold of the rooster by the neck, tucked its wings under her arms, and split it open with a knife. And then she clapped the rooster on the baby's head. That rooster died right there. On the baby's head."

Dusty takes a sip of his drink, the cords in his neck tugging as he swallows. He pauses to let me savour the thought of it: a baby with a bloody rooster on its little head, the rooster's wings flapping, blood and feathers flying, the doctor with his sleeves rolled up, specks of rooster blood on the doctor's shirtfront, Angela holding the rooster, Filomena holding the baby.

"I'll be damned if it didn't take the fever down. The doctor operated on the kitchen table, took out the rib and drained the lung. The kid was no worse for wear after that. I think that was Mike. It must have been Mike. When he was growing up, we teased him; we called him Adam."

One rib missing.

"You saw them do that?"

"I heard it."

"You believe it?"

"God damn it, I'm telling you what I heard. Who the hell would lie about a thing like that?"

The story, and the defence of the story, drains him. His heart races, his chest heaves, he shivers as the pain outruns the morphine. He clicks the pump for another shot of juice. I watch the rising of his swollen chest.

He drops off suddenly.

I am half-asleep when I sense movement in the room. He is trying to rise from his bed. There is a wild look in his eyes. My tongue is too thick, my mind too sluggish; all I can do is watch him. He falls back in bed again, and tries once more to rise. I ask him what he's doing. He shakes his head, he won't take my help; and he shits himself.

He has been taking laxatives because of the morphine, but I hadn't thought there was anything in his bowels to void. He makes a sobbing noise. He is filled with shame. He doesn't want anyone to see him like this. But cleaning him is not a task I can bear. I ring for help.

A nurse's assistant rolls him over; he groans at the rankness of his smell, and the invasion of her hands. His eyes are shut tight in humiliation. She means well; she says, "Now I'll just give your anius a wash." His anius? If it were happening to someone else, he might have laughed. She changes his bed.

She dresses him in a diaper. He holds the blankets tight to his chest and moans.

The time spent with him is a constant, gruesome, and orderly comfort: nurses with loud or gentle voices persuade this old man to eat, that old man to get back into bed, this one to turn over, that one to swallow his pills. Someone sobs, a cart squeaks, an orderly scuffs his heels down the hall.

Gradually, after the final round of meds, there is silence; the nurses work quietly in the half-light of their station, making notes on charts. Now and then, a body is carried out on a stretcher. Now and then, someone curses. I watch my father breathe.

He does not breathe often now; the interval between each breath is punctuated by the silent throbbing in his neck. His heart marks time, half again as fast as the second hand of my watch. He holds his breath for forty-six seconds; takes five long gasping breaths and three fast shallow ones. He stops breathing again.

Forty-six seconds.

Last week, it was thirty seconds. Next week, it will be fifty seconds. I have to fight to hold my breath that long. The capacity of his lungs is extraordinary, the result of years of blowing into the trombone.

A nurse comes into the room and watches him, wordlessly. Her arms are folded across her chest, her head is cocked to the side. She chews her gum slowly, almost sadly. It is instantly ridiculous, but I can tell she is chewing spearmint, a fresh stick.

Without waiting to be asked, and without looking at me, she whispers, "The intervals are going to get longer." I understand: she means that soon there will be one more breath. And then nothing. I am overcome with fatigue, and weakened by her kindness. I want her to comfort me in the dark. Instead, I return to my book.

Yellow lamplight, a warm room, no sound save the long plume of Dusty's sigh. I turn a page. My father lifts his head and looks at me; another moment of rising panic. He's not sure who I am.

He says, "Who brought the charges?"

I am suddenly alert.

In the ether of a dream, he thinks he is in some long-ago jail. If he can just find out what the charges are, he can beat the rap and go home. It occurs to me that he may have suddenly remembered a story he hasn't told before, one I haven't heard.

"What do you mean, who brought the charges?"

His eyes widen. His voice is timorous, as if he thinks a cruel trick is being played. "There had to have been charges."

If only it were so.

It is my duty to tell him where he is. I don't want to tell him; I don't want to remind him that he is dying. But he doesn't have much time now, and he ought to be aware of where he is.

"Dusty, you're in the hospital. There are no charges."

He wakes up. "Oh, Joe. There you are."

"How are you feeling, Pops?"

"You know. Shitty."

A small joke; he is forcing himself into the present tense, such as it is. There are no charges. There is only cancer, and he is in the hospital, and he will not get out of this bed alive. He falls back against his pillow, closes his eyes, and floats above sleep.

One night after a dance job, he made the mistake of taking a couple of drinks on top of some medication. On the way home, he fell asleep at the wheel and drove his car gently into a snow-filled ditch. He woke up, startled, in the drunk tank. There were charges, then. Dangerous driving, driving under the influence. Ironic, because he hadn't exactly been drunk; no matter. He lost his licence for a year.

I return to my book. He wakes again. There is no more sleep tonight. He stares at the ceiling. "It isn't worth a thing."

"What isn't worth a thing?"

"A scrap of paper."

"You want a scrap of paper?"

"No."

"You had a scrap of paper?"

"It was in my pocket."

"What was on the scrap of paper?"

"It doesn't matter; it wasn't worth a thing."

The Nineteenth Night

I enter the room and take my place in the chair by his bed. I arrange my books. I do not say a word. I simply sit and look at him. I want to see what will happen. He and my uncle Dave used to do that often. Dave would enter the house without knocking on the door, no matter the time of day. He wouldn't say a word to my father. He'd nod. He'd take a chair. If it was after supper, my mother would offer him a cup of tea. He and Dusty would glance at each other.

Not a word between them.

Dusty would stare at his newspaper. Dave would sit still with his tea. Maybe they'd smoke. It used to drive me crazy. I was afraid to speak; I thought Dave's face was sharp as a knife and I was unwilling to turn my back on him. I sat silently, too. I watched them. After half an hour or so, Dave would seem to wake up. He'd appraise Dusty and say, "I gotta go."

Dusty would look at him.

"I'll see you."

When I was a boy, all I could do was look for clues and try to understand. When I was older, and asked Dusty what the hell that was all about, he'd get huffy and say, "None of your god-damned business," or "What's it to you?" They were brothers. There was a loyalty between them. And this thing, never explained.

I have no way of knowing now, but I have read the veiled references in the letters from the war; they may have been trying to speak without words, the way Tony had spoken to them.

And so I enter without a word and sit in the same room with him as he is dying, and I send him thoughts. It doesn't seem to work. I am not in the game. And he is very nearly out of the game, whatever it is.

An old man prowls the corridor by himself tonight, shuffling from room to room. He has sloped shoulders, long arms, huge hands. There isn't much of him left, but it's clear he was once muscular, that he was a massive man, and that he too is being eaten by some form of cancer. Everyone here has cancer. The old man's wide and bony chest fills the doorway. He is looking for something, someone. He looks at me: will I help?

And then he sees that I am healthy. I am wearing street clothes and not pyjamas, and I am one of them. I am in on the conspiracy. He shakes his head and looks to my father, who lies helpless in his bed.

The old man mutters. It sounds as if he's saying, "I have to find a way out, I'm going to get us out of here." He wants to escape and lead a shuffling parade of cancerous old prisoners onto the streets of his derangement; he'll find a way or die trying. He turns. His thin grey ass is visible through the hospital gown.

An hour later, a nurse breaks the silence of the floor, she speaks over the intercom. Her voice disguises urgency; she is whispering in code. Missing patient, sixth floor. Two hard young men in white come on the run and begin a room-to-room search. Half an hour later they find the old man in a stairwell, lost and sobbing, huddled with his arms around himself, unable to find his way up or down. He has forgotten where he is, who he is. He has failed to escape. He has left one hell and found another.

The orderlies cannot lift him. The dead weight of his despair is too great; he cannot, will not stand. Finally they make a soft stretcher with a blanket and carry the old man up the stairs and back to his room. The nurse, her loud voice cloaked in a whisper, says, "All right, now. There, there, you just swallow this."

The old man has endured the Depression and fought a war; he built a house and raised a family; he was a leader of men; he worked at his job until he was too old to work any more. He is out of his mind; he will be dead within a month.

And I hope he tries to escape again.

Dusty stirs. I fill a pale-blue hospital cup with ice chips, top it with whisky and water. How many times have I poured him a drink? It's clear there will not be many more drinks. I bend the straw and hold it to his lips. He sips once, and swallows as if it hurts; he closes his eyes and sips again. Our conversation is now in its simplest form. A word from me, a nod from him. "Good?"

He nods. There was never a drink that didn't give him pleasure. He moans now. Weakness washes over him, his eyes roll upward.

"I'm down, and I'm out."

I have brought a Walkman and a set of earphones. I don't know why it took me so long to think of it. Now is as good a time as any. He is not beyond hearing, and not so stoned he won't recognize the voice.

I cue the tape and slip the earphones over his head. An annoyance; he doesn't know what I'm doing, his eyes are closed, it's too much an effort to open them, he can't raise his hands to brush the earphones away. And then the music starts; it is Ella.

. . . there's no one in the place except you and me.
So set 'em up, Joe; I've got a little story you oughta know.
We're drinking, my friend, to the end of a brief episode.
Make it one for my baby, and one more for the road.

He smiles and purses his lips, working them in and out as if preparing his embouchure. His bare foot begins to keep time under the sheet and somewhere he is on stage, and he is wearing his good suit, the dark-blue one with the narrow lapels, and his shoes are shined; somewhere, a woman smiles;

he eases the slide of his trombone back and forth with a flick of his wrist, and she knows what he means.

He is waiting to take his solo.

He falls asleep. I take off the earphones. The memory of the music doesn't last long. He begins to breathe rapidly. He talks to himself. "I don't know what kind of school you're sending me to."

I answer silently: *It is the school of death.*

"I don't know where I am. I don't know why I let you talk me into this twice. I don't know what's going to happen. I don't know where it will lead." *It leads to the grave.*

"How long will I have to hide out?" *You will hide in death forever.*

"I'm cutting our throats here."

If I had a knife . . .

I lay a hand on his forehead. I tell him everything is all right. I tell him that whatever is happening is what's supposed to happen, that it's normal, that his work is done, that he has no reason to fight unless he wants to fight.

His hands are well-formed; the nails remind me of almonds. In spite of the years of pounding a mail route, his feet are without blemish. I imagine how his feet would look with crucifixion nails.

He makes a fist.

The Twentieth Night

*H*e pushes the earphones away with his hand.

He doesn't want to listen. Not any more.

I have none of his music, except for the album he made with a pickup band of spaghetti-job musicians. I don't care to listen to it, and I don't like to look at the cover photo.

The session was important and expensive. The boys were reaching for a little local posterity; they'd rehearsed for weeks, a sacrifice because it meant giving up time they didn't have. Most of them had families, they held down steady day jobs, and they played on weekends; it took a long time to get the group in shape.

"Georgia" was one of the tunes; it had been chosen to showcase Dusty's voice. The night before the taping, he played a dance job. He got drunk and stayed out almost all night. He woke in such sour shape, and his head hurt so bad, he had a ready excuse not to do well.

When it didn't matter, if there was nothing at stake, he could break your heart with his horn, with his voice, with his stance, his nonchalance. But when the pressure was on, when he was expected to bring the house down, he had a tendency to fold. He wouldn't compete. He didn't think he was good enough. and he did what he could to prove it.

To hell with you if you thought it mattered.

None of your god-damned business.

I don't like to look at the photo on the cover of the album. His face is puffy, his eyes are sad, his smile regretful. I don't think he played the album, either. It was a reminder. He'd let the boys down.

He hurt himself.

He has slept all day; he has been sleeping since I have arrived for my shift, although perhaps it is better to say he is hovering somewhere above sleep and below death. And now he is startled by yet another fantasy; he lifts his head as high as he can manage, and looks at me. He has a question. He isn't sure how to frame it. He sighs helplessly. His head falls back.

"They can't keep my shoes from me, can they?"

It's three in the morning. I understand the construction of this terror. Yes, they can keep your shoes. Without shoes, you can't go anywhere; therefore, there is no escape. You're stuck in bed, Poppy, until they carry you away. Morphine is a miserable drug: too little and he cannot bear the pain; too much and he hallucinates.

The first week, he told each of his stories in full, and if the one did not lead to the other, it didn't matter; the telling of the stories was a comfort. The second week, he'd begin a story and fall asleep halfway through. As he shrank, so did what he had to say.

Now is the beginning of the end.

Now he can hardly speak.

Now he no longer recognizes my son; I tell my son to pay it no mind, that this is nothing more than the progression of disease, that his grandfather is no longer always capable of his own thoughts, that the disease is thinking for him now.

I tell my son that he should continue to take his turn at the bedside if he wishes to, and if Dusty looks at him in terror, he should speak softly and smooth the old man's brow. He agrees. He continues to take his turn.

There will not be many more days or nights.

Dusty is failing quickly now. He can no longer tell me that his brother Tony had once persuaded his cousin Mike to shoot himself in the leg; but in his sleep, he whispers, "Dutchman's rubbers."

He speaks in code.

Slaughter the lamb. The horsewhip at his neck. He had a magic leg. Shot him with his pistol. Tony, are you here? Sore tooth, sonny?

These are not the ravings of a deranged old man on his deathbed, they are the chapter headings of a life, the instinctive twitches of a story-teller. He is dying to talk; he is dying.

I lean back in the chair, put my feet up on another chair, and drift off. I wake, and he is watching me. An odd sensation, to wake under someone's gaze, odder when it is the gaze of a dying man, oddest of all when the dying man is your father.

I give him the look: one eye narrowed, one eye open wide, head cocked, small tight smile. The mirror of his expression. A man's appraisal of a man. He is studying me.

Or has he forgotten who I am, and is he trying to remember?

The room smells of leakage now.

It is the smell of piss; he can no longer get up in the middle of the night and dribble. He leaks into a diaper; he is so stoned he can't give voice to the humiliation.

He is no longer eating, he is drinking no more than a single glass of juice, his nourishment is whisky with water, intravenous fluids, and morphine.

And now the whole floor begins to smell of fluids dripping in and out of bags, of open wounds in other rooms; I can smell old men dying all around me.

Dusty had always smelled good.

His sweat, his breath, his skin had a spiciness; I was always glad to breathe him in. It was one of the mysteries of his attractiveness, apparent at all times: the saltiness of the nicotine on his fingers, the sweetness of his hair, the Yardley for Men on his cheeks, the rye and ginger on his breath.

But now there was something stale in the air he expelled from his lungs, an unfamiliar scent rising from the pores of his skin. His smell was no longer vital; the air of death was on him.

I tried not to let him see the wrinkling of my nose.

My mother arrives for the start of her shift. She smiles, and I shrug, and that's how we acknowledge that the end is near, the vigil almost over.

I drive into Westfort, park the car, and walk down the street to the Coney Island. Through a curtain of the morning's cigarette smoke, I order breakfast: I'm alive, I'll eat if Dusty can't. God damn it. Eggs over easy, sausages, home fries, brown toast, coffee. While I wait, an old man approaches the counter and sits down next to another old man; their voices are thick with breakfast tobacco.

"How's she goin'?"

"She's goin' good. You?"

"Not so good. I can't get my pension."

"Why not? You look old enough, ha, ha."

I want to shut them up. I want to explain to them that, not a mile away from this greasy little restaurant, my father is dying. He drank, and at times he may have been a drunk, but he was never as bad as these old sots. I want them to shut up and let me be alone with my thoughts.

Dusty would have known both of them: he'd have been in the army with one, gone to school with the other's sister, played at the weddings of their children. He could have charted each man's ruin from some particular moment. He could have heard their voices and, as if it were a game of pin the tail on the donkey, he'd have stuck each old man with an anecdote. Not any more.

My eggs come. The waitress asks if there is anything else. I shake my head. She wouldn't understand. I can't make myself clear. There is too much else.

Under the low hum of the greasy spoon, I hear the little sounds of death – the ping of the short-order cook's bell is the sound of the elevator opening onto the cancer ward; the splash of the soda fountain, the gurgle in a dying man's throat; the dripping of a tap, the hot tears of all the old men dying here, dying now, dying all around.

I leave my breakfast uneaten.

I want a cigarette. I want the old feeling again, the first lungful of smoke, that brief swimming sensation just behind the eyes; I want to taste the sweetness of a double whisky; I want to drink again until helplessness sets in and carries me to sleep.

The Twenty-First Night

*H*e lies with his whole body clenched, his lips drawn in a firm line. He refuses to push his morphine pump to the maximum. I have a hunch he thinks that, by bearing as much pain as he can, he is doing penance for as many of his old sins as he can.

During the day, the doctor ordered a catheter pushed up through his penis and into his bladder. He can no longer urinate by himself. He will drip slowly into a bag. He arches his neck against the pillow and pushes the breath from his nostrils as if he doesn't want to breathe any more.

The bag is secured to the side of the bed. It contains a scant ounce of urine, another measurement of his nearness to the end: an ounce because he has not eaten anything, nor has he had much to drink. He is starving, he is dehydrated.

I place a hand on his brow, and I whisper into his ear. I tell him I have arrived. He says my name. He whimpers and makes an almost imperceptible movement; his hand inches slowly down his chest and comes to rest between his legs. At first, I'm not sure what he's doing. He clutches blindly at his prick, he moans. He wants to pull out the tube. His hand is a useless, unfeeling claw. I take his hand in mine. He tries to push me away but I hold him fast. He struggles weakly for a few seconds, and then collapses into himself. His heart pounds rapidly.

Now he begins to move his left hand slowly downward, slowly, as if he thinks I will not notice. I am holding both his hands. He tries to push me away. He begs me to rip out the catheter. He moans, he doubles up, he stiffens against the pain which runs deep inside his prick. He wants to rise, he cannot open his eyes, he wants more than anything to reach down and rip the tube away. I push him back gently, I pin him against the mattress with my forearm and press the buzzer for the nurse.

I urge him to die while he sleeps.

I stroke his forehead now and whisper. I tell him it's okay to die, it's time to let go, everything will be all right, there's nothing left to do. I do not sleep. It is a long night.

In the morning, I hear my brother's voice. He is speaking to my mother; they are here, and my shift is over. I pack up my books and papers and walk to the edge of Dusty's bed. I kiss him on the forehead.

He winces; there is pain. He is here, but far from here.

"Hang tough, Poppy. I'll see you later."

He can't open his eyes.

He raises his fist and shakes it.

He died that afternoon.

After the funeral, the top drawer of his dresser no longer seemed forbidden or forbidding, which caught me off guard and saddened me more than it should have. It meant he could not possibly object; it was proof he no longer existed in the flesh.

I pulled the drawer out of the dresser and laid it on his bed. There was the service revolver which had weighed so heavily in my memory. I took it from its scuffed brown holster. The revolver was tiny and cheap, an Enfield .38 with a six-shot chamber. It was light and mass-produced, almost a toy. It did not appear to be the kind of gun a man would use to kill himself. The barrel was too small, it was not the kind of thing you could stick in your mouth with any confidence; somehow, you'd want a weapon with a bit more heft. Not what I'd have chosen. I shivered nonetheless.

It would have done the trick.

There were other familiar, more comforting objects. A brown glass bottle in the shape of a pipe which had once held aftershave, a Christmas present. A scattering of tortoiseshell guitar picks. An old Toronto streetcar token, dating from the war years, presumably from the time he went to see Tony at the Veteran's Hospital.

The brittle newspaper clippings about the murder in Spokane.

Three plastic-handled pocket knives; the sailor's knife he'd used for splicing rope. Several buttons cut from his paratrooper's jumpsuit. A compass. A string level. A bottle opener. Three cigarette lighters. A small cardboard box of English coins. A drawstring bag of shirt buttons. Various badges and insignia of the Lake Superior Regiment.

A fancy porcelain pipe with an alder stem and a painting on the bowl of the pipe: a dead deer lying in a field; a hunter lying next to the deer, clutching a red wound at his chest; the wounded hunter's partner, clutching a rifle and staring into the woods. And two evil poacher hunters lurking in the bushes. Not exactly an unfamiliar tableau.

There was a Tensor bandage; he always had a rolled-up Tensor bandage, although I don't remember him using one. A box of cufflinks; I pocketed the amber ones.

A little white plastic coffin, in which lay seven slivers of pale purple amethyst and two tiny plastic dinosaurs, one red and one green. A blue porcelain snuff bottle, with snuff still inside. His old hairbrush; it no longer held his smell.

The handwritten lyrics to "Gloomy Sunday," one of the songs he'd sing when limbering up his voice in the basement. I think he'd like to have tried it on stage. I think he was afraid of the song. He flirted with it, but it must have been too close to death for him. His antidote to "Gloomy Sunday": a book of naughty cartoons, and a book of bawdy songs.

She wept, she cried, she damn near died.
She said, "What shall I do?"

"Jump into my bed, my pretty girl," I said.
"I'll keep you from the foggy, foggy dew."

Half a dozen brier pipes, still smelling of tobacco. A little ivory donkey on a cord. His army service medals, three of them. A box containing some more old coins and a couple of old, soft dollar bills. A sleeve garter. A couple of machine-gun rounds.

A photo of the Lake Superior Regimental Band taken at Camp Borden in 1940; he was the little soldier, ramrod straight, holding the trombone. And a packet of letters, including one from a girl named Allie MacMillan dated April 30, 1944:

Dusty Darling – I'm sitting out here in the back yard writing this. It's a beautiful day – yes, I wish you were here. It's a bit windy, and my skirt keeps blowing up – you don't mind much, do you?

A letter from his brother Dave, dated November 7, 1944:

Hi, Jocko:
I hear Tony's got you in on our little experiment. More about that later. Am healing fine now, and should be back in action soon. Wait till I get my uniform on again. What was that crack about draping crepe around a raped shape? Look out, girls!
Say hello to the gang for me.

Dusty had copies of his own military file, because forty years after the fact he'd tried to get compensation for the injuries he incurred while riding his motorcycle. He'd been riding drunk.

The documents clarified why he'd been reluctant to discuss his time in the army. When he was overseas, both Matteo and Angela became seriously ill, and Tony's condition grew critical. Tony died on February 19, 1944. Dusty was refused leave to attend the funeral. He was disconsolate.

When it became apparent that his mother was going to die, he applied for leave and was again turned down. She died.

And Dusty went around the bend.

Ward 22   INDOOR CONSULTATION   20 CGH
          DEPARTMENT OF NEUROPSYCHIATRY   23 June 44

No: 5871 Rank: Pte. Name FIO RITO Lawrence Unit: First Cdn. Para.

Report: Enlistment 25 June 1940. Overseas 1 Sept 42.

Age: 25 Cat. "A"

PROBLEM: This man with knee cartilage that requires operation does not want to serve in the army.

HISTORY EXAM & RECORDS:

1) We have only this man's story. He denies previous frank neurotic or psychopathic traits but it is clear that he is a temperamental Italian-Canadian with strong home attachments, a selfish code of values and capable of aggressive stubborn refusal to comply when frustrated.

2) His story is that he had an invalid father and mother and an invalid brother, Anthony FioRito, who was gassed in the last war and has been unable to care for himself since. This group were cared for by his older brother until he was called up in June 43 by army. Since then patient states his own morale, previously good, collapsed. He tried to get home on compassionate grounds and failed. His mother dies in Feb 44 and his urge to get home increased. He describes anger, frustration, anxiety, tension, loss of appetite and sleep constantly for last 6 months. He says he has absolutely no interest in the army, is unwilling to serve longer and that he will simply go from bad to worse if kept over here.

3) He appears as a hostile tense angry soldier, bitter about the army keeping him here and thoroughly unwilling to subordinate his personal wishes to the military necessities. No psychosis, no neurosis, except acute conflict and anxiety.

OPINION:

1) History too unreliable to identify the basis for this collapse of morale. The present reaction is almost purely volitional and yet I do not feel that he has flexibility and stamina enough to adapt and be of further use to the army. This inflexibility is the expression of his inadequate personality when faced with a present challenge. His usefulness in future will be even less – with a pathological knee which will give him grounds for complaint and symptoms both before and after operation as long as he is in the army.

2) Advise MI S-5 – unfit for military service as Psychopathic Personality Inadequate. (0611).

(J.A. Walters, Major)

Neuropsychiatrist RCAMC

This letter, and the incidents it describes, was a source of some conflict between my parents. It is not hard to imagine Dusty losing his mind when he was overseas. Put in a different light, however, it is also possible that the major got him out of the army the best way he knew how. We'll ship him home as a mental case; he's just another temperamental bloody Italian-Canadian, don't you know.

We're better off without him.

One way or the other, not wanted again.

My mother, who suffered Dusty's rages and torments and who picked up after his demons, made reference to these records during one of their endless wrangles; she taunted him about his sanity. She told him he was nuts; she turned to us and said she'd seen the papers.

He became instantly calm, his nostrils flared and he began to breathe the air around him slowly. I could see his peripheral vision widen as he scanned the living room. My mother knew she'd gone too far. She backed off without a word.

Other bits of paper in his drawer: Tony's obituary; the obituaries of his mother and father; some military pamphlets, including *Precautions to Be Taken by Canadian Military Personnel in the Event of Capture*; *Field Service Pocket Book of Conventional Military Symbols*; *Standing Orders for Drivers of M. T. Vehicles and*

Motorcycles; the second and third editions of a pamphlet called *Back to Civil Life*; a pamphlet entitled *The Mounting and Wearing of Decorations, Campaign Stars and Medals*.

Bits of detritus: amateur-theatre playbills; a Liquor Control Board of Ontario passbook; a Soldiers and Sailors Prayer Book; a couple of military paybooks; old furlough tickets; a packet of negatives of some anonymous young soldiers; and a passport issued in 1937, unstamped, used when he was working on the Lake boats. He looked like a young villain.

Next to the passport was a manila envelope containing the three short stories he'd tried to write about his sailing days: one set in a steak house in Chicago; one set in a bar in Detroit; and a third one about the time he almost jumped ship to play the banjo for some gangsters. The stories were painfully typed; he'd had to hunt for every single letter of every single word, he'd stabbed each key with his forefinger. The stories were awkward; the language was formal.

He couldn't write.

He could talk.

Epilogue

I talk to him more often now than when he was alive.

I test myself against what he might have thought, what he might have seen, how he might have felt. He no longer exists, but he has as much immortality as any of us gets; he exists in memory.

Even if memory is counterfeit.

I can remember sitting on the couch eating the last of the apple pie when I was three years old; the world was sunny and tasted of cinnamon. I can summon the taste; the sensation of light caught in my open mouth.

But perhaps I am simply remembering whatever came to mind the last time I looked at the photo of that moment; perhaps I remember the image of an image. If so, after nearly fifty years, it's possible that I have made so many copies of this memory, of all these other memories, that what I have in mind bears no relation to the original.

But I have the photos. They do not change. I see how my changing face fits in among these others. I have some of Dusty's letters; they remain the same no matter how many times I read them. His pistol is still in his drawer. And I have Tony's pocketwatch; Dusty left it to me in his will. It is a small elegant Waltham, with a twenty-four-hour dial, in a gold case, with a gold chain and gunmetal-blue hands. The hands are stopped at 7:28.

I have no intention of winding it.

I keep it in my drawer.

Every effort has been made to secure permission from the copyright holders of excerpts and lyrics quoted in this book.

Excerpt from *Dreamtigers* by Jorge Luis Borges, translated by Mildred Boyer and Harold Morland, Copyright © 1964, renewed 1992. By permission of the University of Texas.

Excerpt from "Less than One" from *Less Than One: Selected Essays* by Joseph Brodsky. Copyright © 1986 by Joseph Brodsky. Reprinted by permission of Farrar, Straus, and Giroux, LLC.

Lyrics from "Georgia on My Mind," Words and Music by Hoagy Carmichael and Stuart Gorrell, Copyright © 1930 by Peer International Corp., Copyright Renewed, International Copyright Secured. All rights reserved. Used by permission.

Lyrics from "St. James Infirmary," by Joe Primrose. © 1929 (Renewed) EMI Mills, Inc. All rights reserved. Used by permission. Warner Bros. Publications U.S. Inc., Miami, FL. 33014